Goblet d'Alviella

Lectures on the Origin and Growth of the Conception of God

As Illustrated by Anthropology and History

Goblet d'Alviella

Lectures on the Origin and Growth of the Conception of God
As Illustrated by Anthropology and History

ISBN/EAN: 9783744747035

Printed in Europe, USA, Canada, Australia, Japan

Cover: Foto ©Lupo / pixelio.de

More available books at **www.hansebooks.com**

THE HIBBERT LECTURES, 1891.

LECTURES

ON THE

ORIGIN AND GROWTH

OF THE

CONCEPTION OF GOD

AS ILLUSTRATED BY

ANTHROPOLOGY AND HISTORY.

BY

COUNT GOBLET D'ALVIELLA,

PROFESSOR OF THE HISTORY OF RELIGIONS AT THE UNIVERSITY OF BRUSSELS.

WILLIAMS AND NORGATE,
14, HENRIETTA STREET, COVENT GARDEN, LONDON;
AND 20, SOUTH FREDERICK STREET, EDINBURGH.

1892.

LONDON:
PRINTED BY C. GREEN AND SON,
178, STRAND.

TO

THE UNIVERSITY OF BRUSSELS,

FOUNDED BY PRIVATE INITIATIVE

ON THE PRINCIPLE OF FREE INQUIRY.

PREFACE.

MANY attempts have been made to trace the development of the conception of God; and, apart from the work of the theologians, the anthropologists and historians have often been led by their respective methods to widely different solutions of the problem. It has appeared to me, however, that these methods do not exclude each other; nay, that each finds in the other its necessary supplement.

I may be reproached for associating such different methods together, and I have already been told that as soon as we apply what is known as the comparative method to the investigation of the origins of Religion, or endeavour to trace its pre-historic development, or even to elucidate the evolution of Religion in general, by reference to the fortunes of the several creeds, we have already left the domain of history, and entered upon that of pure philosophy.

I should myself prefer to give a wider signification to the word history, and make it include all attempts to recover the past of mankind; but if we are to restrict its application to facts of the "historic age" of civilized communities, then history must assuredly be supplemented by other studies which can throw light upon a remoter horizon. It is true that these studies cannot give us certainty—nor, indeed, can history itself always do that;—but at least they can give us information concerning the origin and early stages of human culture, the details of which may lend each other mutual support, and may find confirmation in historical facts. And what, after all, do the names we give our methods signify, provided they bring us nearer to the truth?

While my premises wake the suspicion of those who shrink from applying the ordinary canons of investigation to religious phenomena, my conclusions, in their turn, may prove unacceptable to those who see in the spirit of free inquiry the standing foe and the destined destroyer of the religious sentiment itself. Yet I cannot tax myself with want of logic or with partiality, if my attempt to deduce the laws of religious evolution from the admitted facts has brought me to the conclusion that the scientific treatment of Religion does not affect the religious sentiment in the revolutionary manner feared by some and hoped for by others. Rather does the study of comparative theology seem to reveal a growing tendency towards the admission of the principle laid down by Herbert Spencer, as a bond of union between religion and science,—that "the power manifested throughout the universe distinguished as material, is the same power which in ourselves wells up under the form of consciousness," both modes of force being regarded as phenomenal manifestations of one absolute Reality by which they are immediately produced.

I trust that in this treatment of my subject I have remained faithful to the spirit which inspired the founder of the Hibbert Trust and the promoters of the Hibbert Lectures.

I have only to add that I regard this work as a continuation of my previous studies on "The Contemporary Evolution of Religious Thought in England, America, and India."[1] Having described the most advanced forms of Religion amongst the enlightened minds of our age, I felt a special interest in investigating the gradual development of these forms and the relation in which they stand to the lowest manifestations of religious culture. Enormous as the distance appears, it does not prove impossible to trace the road that leads from the one extreme to the other; and here again we find an illustration of that adage which is now coming to dominate every branch of knowledge, *Natura non facit saltus*.

I ought to express my gratitude to the Hibbert Trustees for having offered me this unique opportunity of developing my views before an English public whose hospitable welcome I shall always remember. But what adequate terms can I find, when M. Ernest Renan himself described a similar invitation as "one of the rewards of his life"?

I have also to offer my special thanks to Mr. Wicksteed for the patience and accuracy with which he has executed the translation of these Lectures.

GOBLET D'ALVIELLA.

COURT ST. ETIENNE, *Dec. 1891*.

[1] English Translation by the Rev. J. Moden. London: Williams and Norgate, 1885.

ERRATUM.

P. 5, line 10, for "Boechoven" read "Bachofen."

TRANSLATOR'S NOTE.

The references to Tylor's "Primitive Culture" have, through inadvertence, been made to the first edition (1871), except in a few cases.

The following table will enable possessors of any edition to find the passages referred to.

On p. 56 the passage referred to is ii. 285 of the editions of 1873 and 1891.
" 83 " " ii. 300 " "
" 112 " " ii. 178 sq. " "
" 114 " " ii. 177 sq. " "
" 115 " " ii. 174 " "
" 117 " " ii. 216 " "
" 140 " " ii. 349 " "
" 189 " " ii. 69 of the edition of 1871.
" 190 " " ii. 73 " "

TABLE OF CONTENTS.

	PAGE
PREFACE ...	vii

LECTURE I.

ON METHODS OF RESEARCH INTO THE PRE-HISTORIC MANIFESTATIONS OF RELIGION.

Religious beliefs and institutions discovered at the dawn of history.—Inability of the historic method to reconstruct their origins.—Recourse to the comparative method necessary ... ... 1—5

Reasons for believing that the general evolution of humanity has been progressive; and inferences as to our humble origins.—Refutation of the theory that man began at a high level of culture.—Point of departure of the religious development.—Estimate of the value of the ancient traditions and Sacred Books of the several peoples ... ... 5—12

Conclusions drawn from philology.—Essence and form of the conceptions formulated at the dawn of languages.—Inability of their framers to formulate abstract ideas ... 12—14

Data of pre-historic archæology.—Funeral rites in the mammoth age; in the reindeer age; in the neolithic period.—The megaliths.—Scull-trepanning.—Traces of idolatry; the worship of the axe.—The method of pre-historic archæology ... ... 15—30

Folk-lore.—Religious survivals in popular customs; in social usages; in ecclesiastical liturgies ... ... 30—38

Comparative ethnography : its legitimacy and its importance.—How far is the contemporary savage the counterpart of primitive man? ... ... 38—41

Applicability of the general law of continuity and progress to the religious sentiment.—Present position of the problem ... ... 41—46

Lecture II.

THE GENESIS OF THE IDEA OF GOD.

(i.) THE WORSHIP OF NATURE, AND THE WORSHIP OF THE DEAD.

Definition of religion.—Did religion spring from the emotions or from the reason?—Have animals religion? ... 47—51

Unwarranted extension of the idea of personality.—Attribution of all movement to personal agents.—Metaphorical language fosters but does not create the illusion.—To what extent do children and savages confound the personal and the impersonal? ... ... 51—63

Deity implies superiority and mystery.—Original distinction between the natural and the abnormal.—Deification of phenomena which man cannot understand or control.—Nature-worship.—The emotion of fear and the sense of the Infinite as religious motives.—Worship addressed to an active power with which it is possible to enter into relations ... ... 63—71

Confusion of concomitance and causality ... ... 71—73

Assimilation of dreams to reality.—Effect of dreams in multiplying the superhuman beings and extending their attributes ... ... 73—76

The idea of the "double."—Future life.—Sources of the worship of the dead ... ... 77—82

(ii.) PRIMITIVE RITES.

Prayer.—Primitive theory of sacrifice.—Intimidation of the gods.—Sorcery.—Sources of symbolism.—Did conjuration precede propitiation? ... ... 82—96

Lecture III.
POLYDEMONISM AND POLYTHEISM.

(i.) Spiritism, Fetishism and Idolatry.

PAGE

When natural objects are adored, it is the personality with which they are supposed to be endowed to which the worship is addressed.—This personality is conceived, by analogy with that of man, in the form of a "double" that can be separated from its envelope.—The distinction between body and soul extended to all personified objects.—What becomes of the crowd of souls released by the disappearance of their visible envelopes.—Spiritism.—The belief in spirits not necessarily the result of necrolatry ... 97—106

Religious phenomena connected with spiritism.—Obsession, possession, talismans, fetishes.—Belief that the appropriation of an object secures the services of the spirit lodged within it.—Sources of fetishism.—The idol an elaborated fetish.—Sundry springs of idolatry.—Criticism of the theory that idols were at first symbolic representations.— Is idolatry a step in advance? ... ... 106—122

(ii.) The Divine Hierarchy.

Arrested development and indications of degeneration in the beliefs of certain peoples.—The progressive evolution of the conception of God starts from the differentiation of the superhuman powers.—Preponderance granted to the regents of the great phenomena of nature, to the souls of the illustrious dead, to the genii of species, of social groups and of moral abstractions ... ... 122—138

Subordination of spirits to gods.—The divine societies modelled upon those of earth.—The divine societies of the Indo-Europeans; of the Egyptians; of the Mesopotamians; of the Western Semites; of the aboriginal Americans; of the Chinese ... ... 138—152

Lecture IV.

DUALISM.

(i.) The Struggle for Order.

PAGE

Selfishness of the first gods.—Alliance between the gods and man.—Relations of mythology and religion.—How the gods became interested in securing order in the universe   153—158

Dualism of the superhuman personalities representing the hostile and the beneficent forces of nature respectively.—Accentuation of dualism as religion advances.—Confidence in the final triumph of the beneficent deities.—The idea of the cosmic order generated by the spectacle of the regular recurrence of phenomena   ...   .   158—167

Gradual restriction of the field abandoned to divine caprice.—Personifications of the natural order exalted above the ancient gods.—The supreme god the author and sustainer of the cosmic order   ...   .   168—174

(ii.) The Struggle for Good.

The absurd and immoral actions attributed to the gods sometimes to be explained as metaphorical descriptions of natural phenomena, sometimes as survivals from the barbarism of earlier generations.—Original independence of morals and religion.—Influence of the religious sentiment in consolidating the social relations   ...   ...   175—179

The divine sanction of the oath.—Intervention of the gods in the ordeal.—The gods punish attacks on the community.—Conception of a moral order on the model of the cosmic order   ...   .   179—186

Unpunished violations of the moral order argue either the feebleness or the injustice of the gods.—Solution offered by a future life.—Conception of the future life as similar to the present, as better, or as worse.—Assignment of the souls to different abodes according to their conduct in this world.—The theory of continuation and the theory of retribution.—Recompense after death and recompense on earth   ...   .   186—200

Purification of the character of the gods by the assimilation of the moral order to the divine order.—The attributes of Deity reduced solely to justice and love ... ... 200—203

Lecture V.

MONOTHEISM.

Monolatry.—National pantheons.—Gods attached to the land or the people.—Monolatry founded on the belief in the superiority of the national god.—Conception of a supreme god, sovereign of gods and men.—Formation of divine genealogies in the national pantheons.—The supreme god conceived as the universal father ... ... 204—211

The place of metaphysical speculation in the development of monotheisn.—Monotheism implies superiority not only in power, but in nature, on the part of the Supreme Deity as conceived by his worshippers.—Simplification of the pantheons by the assimilation of the gods representing analogous phenomena.—Conception of a single god of whom all other deities are the several members, forms or names.—The triune God of Egypt.—The Semitic monotheism.—God as distinct from matter.—Indo-European pantheism.—God evolving the universe out of his own substance.—God as the soul of the universe.—The One without a second 211—226

The ancient gods before the face of the Only God.—Their transformation into hypostases, demiurges and mediators.—The religious syncretism of the declining Greco-Roman paganism.—The Christian theodicy.—God reduced to the absolute unity by modern philosophy.—Opposition of science, not to the belief in God, but to the supposition of interventions by secondary deities.—The divine intermediaries transformed into abstractions or ideal types.—The eternal and infinite energy whence all things proceed.—The eternal power that makes for righteousness.—Corollaries ... ... 226—244

Lecture VI.

THE FUTURE OF WORSHIP AS DEDUCED FROM ITS PAST.

PAGE

Transformation of the motives of worship.—What fear and admiration tend to become.—Love takes its bearings afresh.—Disappearance of the lower elements of worship.—Divination and sorcery in our day ... ... 245—250

Transformation of the expressions of worship.—What prayer tends to become.—Evolution of sacrifice; its spiritualization and attenuation; offerings pass into acts of homage; the moral transformation of sacrifice.—Evolution of symbolism.—Applications of imitative symbolism.—Services rendered by symbolism to free inquiry and religious progress.—Evolution of the priesthood.—Growth and dissolution of theocracies.—Place of the ministry in modern society .. .. 250—277

Is worship destined to disappear?—Societies for ethical culture.—Satisfaction demanded by our æsthetic and spiritual faculties.—Religious progress in the churches and mutual relations of the religions.—Religion and the masses.—Religion and contemporary Socialism.—Need of a stronger altruistic motive than is supplied by the teachings of science or even the love of humanity.—Causes of pessimism.—Danger of a religious reaction ... ... 277—288

Brighter prospects for religion.—Importance of the question, Has life a goal?—Conclusion: the conception of God in the future ... ... 288—296

LECTURE I.
ON THE METHODS OF RESEARCH INTO THE PRE-HISTORIC MANIFESTATIONS OF RELIGION.

WHEN the first volume of the *Hibbert Lectures* appeared, in 1878, the general history of religions was but just beginning to take its place in the courses of advanced study on the Continent; and I can well remember the delight and admiration with which—devoted as I had long been to this branch of historical study—I devoured the pages on which Prof. Max Müller had lavished the wealth of his knowledge and the charm of his style in drawing out the lessons to be derived from the study of the Religions of India.

I little imagined that in thirteen years I was myself to have the honour of succeeding that illustrious master in this Chair. And may be I owe so flattering a distinction in no small degree to the efforts I have made, from the very beginnings of my work as a writer, to dissipate a prejudice concerning England, and the Anglo-Saxon race in general, that still lurks amongst us west of the Channel. It is the idea, based on very one-sided observations, that in matters of religion you are at once the most formal and the most superficial of all the nations upon the earth; or, in other words, that you divide your lives into two sharply-defined sections, in the first of which (embracing one day out of the seven) you passively accept all the ceremony, discipline, and even doctrine, to which tradition has attached the label of respectability, whereas in the other (including all the rest of the week) you are completely absorbed by your material interests, and never give a thought to the great Beyond. This view can only be held by those who do not know or do not appreciate the strength of the movement which has never been lacking amongst you towards gaining a rational satisfaction for the religious needs of the mind and heart of man.

The institution of the Hibbert Lectures in particular has helped to show how this progressive spirit may find support in the comparative history of religions; and perhaps still more to point out how the impartial study of the very subject that has so long divided men into hostile camps may now serve to bring them together. I would add that these Lectures, after bearing fruit in England itself, where it would not be difficult to trace their influence upon the temper and the method of religious discussion, have re-acted most happily upon Continental thought itself, in helping to enlarge its horizon; and this even apart from the specific services they have rendered to purely historical research. Indeed, all this is so true, that in coming here to expound my views on the evolution of the religious idea, I am in danger, on more points than one, of simply returning to you the echo of your own thoughts, in place of the original, not to say revolutionary, ideas which, for anything I know, may in some quarters be expected of me. For this you have only to blame your own ethnographers, your own sociologists, and your own historians, upon whom it is impossible for any one to help drawing, in whatever part of the world he may undertake to treat of the history of religions, and still more of the history of Religion.

<small>Pre-historic development of Religions.</small> The scholars who have devoted themselves to the study of ancient religions, and specifically my illustrious precursors in this Chair, have laid before you the methods by which the developments of the religious systems underlying the worship of the most important civilizations have been respectively traced. We are in a position to say that, in spite of some divergences in detail, the main lines of this work of reconstruction are now definitively laid down. This result is chiefly due to the application of the historical method; that is to say, the collection, classification, and interpretation of written evidence, together with the monumental inscriptions which have been discovered in such vast numbers during the last half-century.

Nevertheless, the historical method can give us no information at all concerning the origins of the most important ancient worships. A glance at the genealogical tree of the higher religions will at once convince us that they all depend upon each other in an unbroken line of filiation, or are derived from a small number of systems that rose up independently in the bosoms of sundry groups of distinct and unrelated peoples. But we cannot trace them beyond this point by direct observation.

In every instance we find that, as we go back through the ages, written documents become ever scarcer, till they cease altogether, and the ground seems to fall away beneath the investigator's feet. And yet at this remotest point we already find beliefs and institutions fully recognizable, which have maintained themselves right on, across the whole series of intermediate systems, into the heart of the religions of the present day.

These elements, common to all organized religions, may be classed as follows:

1. The belief in the existence of superhuman beings who intervene in a mysterious manner in the destinies of man and the course of nature.

2. Attempts to draw near to these beings or to escape them, to forecast the object of their intervention and the form it will take, or to modify their action by conciliation or compulsion.

3. Recourse to the mediation of certain individuals supposed to have special qualifications for success in such attempts.

4. The placing of certain customs under the sanction of the superhuman powers.

Unless we are to suppose that these factors of the early religions were suddenly formed at a given moment, we are compelled to admit that they must have had a rudimentary development before their first appearance in history. To re-discover this development, we must appeal to psychology, philology, pre-historic archæology, folk-lore, and ethnography. Every one of these sciences has some contribution to make, and nothing short of the combination of them all will suffice to solve the problem. But amongst these, it is comparative or descriptive ethnography which supplies us with the richest material to make good the deficiencies of historical data.

And, after all, this is but an application of the comparative method so justly glorified by Freeman as one of the most precious acquisitions of our century—an application already accepted without question in researches into the origins of language, of art, of the family, of property, of law, and even of morals, as is obvious from the classical works of such authors as Boechoven, Freeman, De Laveleye, Giraud-Teulon, Sumner Maine, McLennan, Max Müller, Lubbock and Starcke; not to mention the numerous sociological works which, especially in England and France, have employed the comparative method in attempting to retrace the general course of human evolution. Religious phenomena, in their turn, have been subjected to the same treatment by enlightened theologians such as Professors Tiele and Réville, who can join hands on this field of research with ethnographers like Mr. E. B. Tylor, sociologists like Mr. Herbert Spencer, and students of folk-lore like Mr. Andrew Lang. I shall endeavour to tread in the footsteps of these eminent writers in my attempts to reconstruct, so far as possible, the first manifestations of the belief in the Divine; with a view to tracing subsequently, in the facts recorded by history, the sequel of a development which, if we may judge of the future by the past, has not yet reached its goal.

Theories of progress and of retrogression. By separately examining the chief factors of contemporary civilization, or the chief races who now share the dominion of the globe, we may establish historically that the march of civilization has been progressive; that is to say, that there is a constant and growing tendency to secure the same results at the expense of smaller efforts, and to utilize the surplus of forces thus left disposable for the satisfaction of more and more exalted wants. It must, indeed, be admitted that this movement is not continuous; it is sometimes arrested, sometimes even reversed; but taken as a whole, its direction cannot be mistaken. From the other side, palæontology shows us that before the appearance of man upon the earth, life had always been progressive; that is to say, that studied in its great successive periods, it reveals a tendency to produce a succession of creatures of growing complexity, the crown of all being found in man, whether we consider the range of his intellect and moral faculties, or his power of re-acting upon the forces of external nature. This in itself raises a strong presumption that humanity in its pre-historic period was not exempt from the general law of development of living beings, and therefore that its origins must be sought in a state inferior to anything that the oldest evidence of primitive civilization reveals to us.

Pre-historic archæology turns this presumption almost into a certainty. We now know beyond the possibility of doubt that wherever the super-position of several industrial strata has been established, the age of iron was preceded by an age of bronze or copper, the age of metals by an age of stone, and the age of polished stone by one of cut or chipped stone. We discover a period at which man, though he had not yet arrived at the relative civilization of which the earliest inscriptions preserve the memory, already practised agriculture, possessed domestic animals, raised rough monuments of stone, and gathered into little groups on fortified heights or in lake cities. Another period reveals itself in a yet remoter antiquity (for it corresponds to the deposits of the quaternary rocks), in which men lived exclusively by hunting, clothed themselves in the skins of beasts, and dwelt in narrow caves or were scattered in nomadic hordes on steppes desolated by the rigour of the glacial epoch. Finally, we can trace a period yet further withdrawn into the twilight, in which, under a gentle and moist climate, man, the contemporary of the *elephas antiquus*, perhaps still ignorant of the use of fire, clothing, and earthenware, but already in possession of a cut flint mallet or hatchet, realized the state of nature vaguely conceived by certain poets of antiquity:

> "Vita feræ similis, nullos agitata per usus:
> Artis adhuc expers et rude vulgus erant.
> Pro domibus frondes norant, pro frugibus herbas:
> Nectar erat palmis hausta duabus aqua."[1]

It is true that because the wielder of flint implements preceded us on the soil of Europe, it does not absolutely follow that he was our ancestor. At the time when the hunters of the reindeer and the mammoth, and perhaps the erectors of the megaliths, occupied this part of the world, is it not possible that the ancestors of the Aryans, the Semites, the Egyptians, the Chinese, not to mention the Aztecs and the Incas, may already have been in possession elsewhere of a semi-civilization far more advanced in type? Yes; but we are justified in asking for

[1] Ovid, *Fasti*, ii. 291—294.

the traces of this supposed civilization. It is true that we have not yet explored and ransacked the whole planet, but it must be admitted that the chances of any such discovery are diminishing day by day. More than twenty years ago, Mr. E. B. Tylor could already write, "There is scarcely a known province of the world of which we cannot say certainly, savages once dwelt here;" and I would add, there is hardly one of which we cannot say with equal right, "Man has been progressive here." Pre-historic archæology thus unites with palæontology to assure us that, if the golden age exists in the possible nature of things at all, it is not in the past that we must look for it.

It has been asserted that savages have never been able to rise into civilization except through the instrumentality of a people already civilized. It is very true that the transition from savagery to civilization, or even to the demi-civilization from which we ourselves are admitted gradually to have risen to our present level, has never been actually observed; but there are excellent reasons why this link should be missing. In the first place, until they have reached a certain level of culture, nations have no history, and therefore cannot themselves enlighten us as to their own past; and as for external observation, as soon as savages come into contact with a superior civilization, the latter deflects and absorbs their spontaneous development, unless indeed it paralyzes it. This much, of course, is obvious—that there are some peoples worse equipped than others for the struggle for life and progress; nay, perhaps there may be some permanently incapable of rising above a low level of civilization. But because, in running a race, the most agile are the only ones that reach the goal, it does not follow that all the competitors did not start from the same post, or that the victor has not had to pass the very points at which his less fortunate competitors have stopped.

In the second place, we may well ask where savagery ends and civilization begins. We can of course lay down a more or less complicated criterion depending on evidence collected from industrial processes, ways of living, religious and social institutions, and all the current manifestations of the moral and intellectual life. But we shall not be able to force all the populations of mankind into one or the other of the two categories, unless we are prepared to ignore transitional cases. In truth, the different groups of mankind may be arranged on a scale the bottom of which is lost in the extreme savagery of the Bushmen, the Tierra-del-Fuegians, the Samoyeds, the Akkas and the Australians, while the most advanced peoples of the Indo-European race stand at the summit; and between these extreme limits the gulf seems impossible to cross. And yet the space between the successive populations which occupy neighbouring positions on the scale is almost insensible, and the slightest progress in a given tribe would suffice to raise it to the level of those immediately above it. There is, therefore, no reason why we should not believe that the same nation may have gradually scaled all the steps which separated it from the culminating-point; and perhaps, even so, the steps it has already passed may be as nothing compared with those which will yet permit the most favoured nations of the future to continue their ascent; for civilization too is a Jacob's ladder, the top of which we cannot see because it reaches to the heavens.

<small>Point of departure in the development of religion.</small> One often meets with men, free enough from prejudices in other matters, who readily admit the extreme barbarism of primitive society, but are nevertheless disposed to make an exception in the case of religion. They would have us believe that the ancestors of the Semites, the Aryans, the Egyptians, and the Chinese, or at any rate the ancestors of some one or other of these races, started with a very simple and elementary industrial and social life, but with pure morals and exalted beliefs, and even in full possession of a monotheistic belief.

In support of this hypothesis, they allege, in the first place, that these peoples retain reminiscences of far more elevated beliefs than those they afterwards held. But to begin with, the assertion in this form is far too sweeping. For the fact is that there are other traditions, quite as worthy of attention, which relegate the past to a state of religious ignorance from which the teachings of some heroic or even superhuman founder of civilization first drew mankind. And, in the second place, little reliance can be placed on these legends, either in the one sense or the other. Peoples have asked themselves in every age whence their knowledge of the gods came; and since they were unable to trace it back to any other origin, they naturally concluded that it had been instilled into them by the gods themselves at an epoch, as Alfred de Musset puts it,

"où le ciel sur la terre
Marchait et respirait dans un peuple de dieux."

Moreover, parallel questions have in every age presented themselves with reference to arts, letters, sciences, customs, and what-not; and the answer has always been found in similar mythical attempts to explain the secrets of the past.

The theory of primitive purity has sought to entrench itself behind a second line of defence constructed from the pictures of certain primitive peoples, such as the Germans and the Pelasgians, given by the classical authors. But now that we are better acquainted with uncivilized races, we can see that the state of moral innocence attributed to the infant populations of ancient Europe, reduces itself to simplicity of manners and such virtues as commonly prevail amongst the savages of our own day where they have not been corrupted by premature contact with civilization. As for the absence of idols, or even of any more definite deities than the vague *numina* of the Italiots, it simply means that the peoples in question had not yet reached the stage of polytheism and idolatry, and were still dominated by the savage conceptions of nature-worship and fetishism.

Finally, our theorists have not forgotten to appeal to the lofty sentiments and even the theological reasonings which occur in the sacred books of the Persians, Hindus, Jews, and Chinese, to say nothing of some of the Egyptian and Chaldæan hymns. But recent researches tend more and more to dissipate the illusions that were natural enough in the first enthusiasm awakened by the discovery of these marvellous literatures. The aureole that surrounded them is gone, and we have come to a more sober appreciation alike of their significance and of their antiquity, though they have not lost their value or even their charm in becoming less anomalous and more human— that is to say, in taking their place in the general history of human evolution.

However this may be, we are forced to recognize the fact that not one of these venerable documents carries us back to the first period of religion in general, or even of the special systems into which they respectively enter. What they represent is, not the naïve aspiration of primitive humanity, but the result of a sacerdotal elaboration that has already made its selections and rejections amongst the beliefs of the past. The further we ascend towards the origins of the various races, the more completely do we see the beliefs of the Semites assuming the appearance of a veritable polydemonism; those of the Egyptians, of a systematized sorcery; and those of the Indo-Europeans, of a kind of universal physiolatry in the course of a polytheistic transformation. All this amounts to saying that, as we ascend towards the origins of these peoples, we trace, in every instance, a growing predominance of the forms of thought and the expressions of feeling which characterize the religions of savages in every age and in all parts of the world.

<small>Evidence of Language.</small> Philology enables us to mount a little higher towards the sources of all civilization. But its conclusions are still less calculated than those of history to encourage the belief in an early religion high above the level now observed amongst savages; for they tend to show that, in all cases, the abstract significations of the words employed to render general ideas have been preceded by concrete and even material senses.

Language is now a marvellous mechanism which not only enables us to register the mutual relations of things down to the subtlest shades, but even guides our minds, from abstraction to abstraction, up to the very threshold of that inaccessible region, beyond the world of forms and of ideas, where we verge upon the mysterious Reality that is above all definition. Yet modern philological analysis takes us back to a time at which language reduces itself—with the exception possibly of a few onomatopoetic words—to a closely restricted number of sounds and cries, each expressive of a physical action, and that action performed by man. I need not here explain how the monosyllabic accompaniments of human actions came at last to convey the idea of those actions to others, nor the part played by the progress of language in leading thought into conscious possession of itself. It is enough to note that the phenomena in question fully justify the conclusions, first, that the primitive creators of our languages freely ascribed faculties like their own to all the things they saw around them, if their manifestations could in any way be likened to human actions; and secondly, that their equipment of conscious ideas was confined to a small number of essentially concrete notions embracing actions and physical events of daily occurrence.

This being so, not only must these men have been incapable of rising spontaneously to such abstract ideas as are suggested to our minds by the words, God, soul, infinite, absolute, self-existence, and the like, but they could not even have been in a position to comprehend them had they been suddenly communicated to them from without.[1] Such is still the case with modern savages, whom the preponderating evidence of travellers represents as absolutely inaccessible to abstract ideas.[2] Every missionary knows at the cost of what effort, and, I may add, of what distortion, he succeeds in introducing some gleams of the Christian metaphysic into the minds of the really inferior races. Professor Max Müller has told you of the Benedictine who attempted in vain, during a three-years' stay amongst the natives of Australia, to discover the deity to whom they rendered homage. But at last, one day, he discovered that they believed in a god who used to be omnipotent, and had created the world by his breath, but was now so old and decrepit that folk took but little count of him.[3] No doubt this was really an echo of his own teaching coming back to him in the form of a belief in an omnipotent deity who had created the earth with his breath. Only the natives could not help thinking of him as reduced to complete decrepitude, since he was old enough to have helped in the formation of the world and been present at the birth of their ancestors.

[1] Pfleiderer points out that if we require whole years to develope abstract ideas in the minds of our children, though they have the benefit of all their inheritance from the past "which thought for them," it must have needed centuries, and even millenniums, for primitive man to arrive at the same results.—*The Philosophy of Religion*, London, 1888, vol. iii. pp. 4, 5.

[2] See Sir John Lubbock, *The Origin of Civilization*, London, 1870: chap. viii. "On Language."

[3] *Hibbert Lectures*, 1878, p. 17.

PRE-HISTORIC MANIFESTATIONS OF RELIGION. 15

Pre-historic archæology. Pre-historic archæology, in its turn, takes us yet another step, inasmuch as the material remains with which it deals indicate the existence of certain beliefs prior to all civilization. It is true that no such traces have yet been found amongst the deposits of the very earliest period in which the existence of man has been established; that is to say, in what is known as the Drift period, which seems to have preceded the great glacial age in Europe. But we must be on our guard against basing any definitive conclusion on this fact. Remember what happened, in this respect, with regard to the rest of the palæolithic age. There, too, scholars whose names carried authority maintained that man in the quaternary period had no religious beliefs, and did not even pay attention to the dead; but the discoveries of the last five-and-twenty years, especially in the caves of France and Belgium, have established conclusively that as early as the mammoth age man practised funeral rites, believed in a future life, and possessed fetishes and perhaps even idols. A glance at the discoveries that authorize these conclusions will perhaps not be out of place.

Man in the mammoth age and his funeral rites. In the cave of Spy we can trace through thousands upon thousands of years savage inhabitants whose bones exhibit such an ape-like character that they have supplied a new link in the descending scale from man to the animals. Armed only with flints to defend themselves against the terrible beasts that wandered round their retreat, exposed to the rigours of such a climate as the present inhabitants of the Polar regions can scarcely endure, though supported by resources which in comparison with those of the primitive inhabitants of Moustiers almost represent civilization, these contemporaries of the mammoth and the cave-bear, whose energies one would have thought would have been wholly absorbed in the struggle for existence, still found time to attend to their dead, to prepare them for their future life, and to offer them objects which they might have used for themselves, but which they preferred to bestow on the dead for their use in another life.[1] The custom of placing arms, implements, and ornaments in the tombs, may be regarded as general amongst the ancient cave-dwellers, as it still is amongst all savages who bury their dead. It implies the belief in the survival of the personality after death, and the idea that the future life will be a repetition of the present, or at any rate that the same wants will be experienced, the same dangers incurred, and the same enjoyments tasted there as here. All this was well explained by the ancient Peruvians when, in answer to the question why they sacrificed animate and inanimate objects, and even human beings, to the dead, they answered that in dreams they had seen men who had long been dead walking about with the creatures and the objects that had been buried in their tombs. Certain natives of Borneo go so far as to say, that if they throw objects that have belonged to the deceased upon the waves, he will at once come and reclaim them. Amongst the Patagonians, the Comanches, and the Bagos of Africa, the custom of sacrificing all his belongings to the deceased is actually pushed so far, that

[1] De Puydt et Lohest, *L'homme contemporain du mammouth à Spy*: Namur, 1887.

travellers have declared it interferes with the maintenance of the family and the accumulation of even the smallest capital.¹

Traces of funeral feasts have also been found in the caves of the mammoth age. We must remember that amongst all uncivilized peoples these feasts redound, not only to the honour, but to the welfare of the dead, just as the feasts in honour of the gods are supposed to be of actual service to them. The natives of the Red River expressly declare "that while they partake of the visible material, the departed spirit partakes at the same time of the spirit that dwells in the food."² The observance of this custom by pre-historic man carries with it, therefore, the fact that he had already drawn a distinction between the material object and the spirit to which it served as a body; and further, that he believed in the possibility of that spirit quitting its case and surviving it. But still more incontestable proof of this belief occurs a little later, when the objects deposited in the tombs are broken or burned, with the idea that they must be destroyed or killed in order to enable their souls to follow the soul of the deceased.

In certain caves, the earliest of which go back to the reindeer age (those of Mentone, for example), the bones of the dead are painted red with oligist or cinnabar; and

¹ De Lucy-Fossarieu, *Ethnographie de l'Amérique antartique*, Paris, 1884, p. 151. Capt. Grossman, *Report of the Bureau of Ethnography, 1879-80*: "Smithsonian Institute," Washington, 1881, p. 99. René Caillié, *Voyage à Temboctou*, Paris, 1830, vol. i. pp. 245, 246.

² Dr. S. G. Wright, cited by H. C. Yarrow in *Mortuary Customs of the North-American Indians*, in the *Report of the Bureau of Ethnology, 1879-80*: "Smithsonian Institute," Washington, 1881, p. 191.

in our own day some of the North-American tribes, who expose their dead on trees, collect the naked bones and paint them red before finally burying them. An analogous custom has been observed amongst the Mincopies of the Andaman Islands, and the Niams of Central Africa.[1] The explanation of this custom has sometimes been sought in the fact that red is the colour of spirits. Thus in Polynesia, painting an object red suffices to make it *tabu*, that is to say, the property of the superhuman powers, and as such inviolable and unapproachable. But it may well be asked whether, in the funeral rites I have just described, the red paint was not rather intended to imitate the infusion of blood—that is to say, the restitution of life—in conformity with the idea so widespread amongst uncivilized peoples that blood and life are equivalent essences. To paint the bones of the deceased red would in this case be to assure, or at least to facilitate, the renewal of his existence.[2]

Another custom to be traced in the caves of Central France from the age of the reindeer downwards, and

[1] Cartailhac, *La France préhistorique*, Paris, 1889, p. 292. Du Pouget de Nadaillac, *Les decouvertes préhistoriques et les croyances chrétiennes*, Paris, 1889, p. 13. Letourneau, *Sociologie*, Paris, 1880, pp. 211, 220; Eng. trans. by H. M. Trollope, London, 1881, pp. 224, 233.

[2] Thus the ancient Peruvians smeared the doors and the idols with blood while sacrifice was being performed in the temples. A. Réville, *Hibbert Lectures*, 1884, p. 220. The Arabs of pre-historic times used to sprinkle the walls of the Kaabah with the blood of victims; and the Bedouins of the Sinaitic district still throw blood, drawn from their camels' ears, upon the door of the tomb of one of their most famous saints. Ignace Goldziher, *Le culte des saints chez les Musulmans* in the *Revue de l'histoire des religions*, 1880, vol. ii. p. 311. Cf. Exodus xii. 7.

gradually spreading as the age of polished stone advances, consists in burying the body, folded up upon itself, so that the knees touch the chin. It has been maintained that the idea was to give the corpse the position taken by the living man as he slept by the fire at night after a day's hunting or war.[1] But no peoples really sleep in this posture: and I incline to the belief that they meant to put the deceased in the position of the infant in his mother's womb. Many peoples believe that life is a re-birth, from the Algonkins, who by a touching attention bury little children on the paths most frequented by the women of the tribe, down to the peoples on both continents who explain family likenesses or cases of atavism on this principle. For the rest, this custom—re-discovered by Dr. Schliemann in the tombs of Mycenæ—still exists in the Andaman Islands, in New Zealand, in Melanesia, in South America, amongst the African Bongos, and amongst the Hottentots. Almost all travellers explain the custom as I have done above.[2] Mr. T. L. Hutchinson, in describing the mummies of ancient Peru, says that "the bodies were generally placed in the same position as they are known to exist [in] during the progress of uterine life."[3] The idea that the earth is the common mother of mankind reappears in all the mythologies that have made any considerable

[1] Letourneau, *Sociologie*, pp. 207, 208; Eng. trans. pp. 220, 221.

[2] On the Hottentots, see Peschel, *Völkerkunde*, Leipzig, 1874, p. 494, Eng. trans.; *The Races of Man*, &c., second edition, London, 1876, p. 460. On the Andamans, E. H. Man, *Journal of the Anthropological Institute*, 1883, vol. xii. p. 144. On the Araucans, d' Orbigny, *L'homme américain*, Paris, 1839, vol. i. p. 92.

[3] *Journal of the Anthropological Institute*, vol. iv. p. 447.

progress. The Aryans of the Vedic epoch, when they buried their dead without reducing them to ashes, implored the earth to receive the body as a mother her son.[1]

Idolatry in the palæolithic age. Did man, in this remote age, worship the dead alone? I would remark that this is almost the only form of worship capable of leaving material traces. We may easily find the articles deposited in a tomb; but where are we to look for traces of sacrifices offered to the celestial bodies, or of symbolic dances performed in their honour? As for written records, we might as well expect the phonograph to transmit us the text of the prayers or the charms which bore to heaven the first manifestations of the religious ideas of man! We do possess a certain number of carved or scratched representations, however, which ascend to the reindeer age; and it is difficult not to admit that this primitive art had a religious bearing. The objects represented are generally animals, such as mammoths, reindeer, horses, serpents, and fish, often drawn upon fragments of bone or ivory, with a fidelity of expression, and even a feeling of life, which are equally surprising and noteworthy. Amongst the Negroes similar representations are always fetishes, or at any rate are used as charms, and I confess that I have not much faith in any purely æsthetic impulses of savages. With them, everything has a practical purpose, even art and religion. Moreover, it is a common idea amongst uncivilized peoples that a likeness provides the means by which we can act upon the original. Finally, as Mr. Andrew Lang very appositely remarks,[2] "If one

[1] *Rig Veda*, x. 18, 11.
[2] Andrew Lang, *Custom and Myth*, London, 1884, p. 294.

adores a lizard or a bear, one is likely to think that prayer and acts of worship addressed to an image of the animal will please the animal himself, and make him propitious."

The human figure appears to have been less frequently and less successfully attempted. Several examples of it are known, however; and M. Edouard Dupont found a rude attempt at a human figure cut in reindeer-horn in the cave of Pont-à-Lesse. This figure was perhaps an idol. The same discoverer also found the tibia of a mammoth on a slab of sandstone near a hearth belonging to the reindeer age, in a cave of Chaleux. It is impossible to deny the character of a fetish to this tibia, for the mammoth was already extinct in that locality at the period in question, and M. Dupont points out that the bones of gigantic extinct species still play an important part in the popular beliefs everywhere.[1] The Dacotahs and other Redskins, for instance, carefully collect the bones of the mastodon and place them in their huts for the sake of the magic virtues which they attribute to them.[2] We should also note the perforated snail-shells, fossils, crystals, quartz-stones, and reindeer-horns, deposited in the tombs, and sometimes even in the hand of the deceased. These objects, none of which are of any practical use, may sometimes have served as ornaments, but must surely in some cases have been talismans or amulets.

No doubt all these remains indicate infantile and

---

[1] E. Dupont, *L'homme pendant les âges de la pierre aux environs de Dinant sur Meuse*, second edition, Brussels, 1872, pp. 92 and 205 sqq.

[2] Ed. B. Tylor, *Researches into the Early History of Mankind*, third edition, London, 1878, p. 322.

gross conceptions; but nevertheless they show that man was already aware of something mysterious and mighty beyond his limited horizon; that he attempted to contract relations with the superhuman beings by which he believed himself to be surrounded, on the basis of an exchange of services; and finally, that he was already capable of the idea of abstinence, that is to say, of relinquishing a tangible and immediate advantage in view of a more considerable but more distant and uncertain one.

Passing to the age of polished stone, we see the religious manifestations which I have just defined taking a more developed and general form; nor are there wanting such new elements as the worship of megaliths, trepanning the skull, and special veneration of the mallet.

<small>Megaliths of the neolithic age.</small> I shall not enter upon the question, still hotly disputed, of the use of the stones, erected in lines, found almost all over the two worlds. It has been maintained that they were simply commemorative monuments, like the twelve stones from the bed of Jordan which Joshua erected at the first camp of the Israelites after their passage of the river, to serve, as the Bible supposes, "as a memorial for ever."[1] I will not deny that some of these monuments played the part of mementos, or even of international boundary-marks; but when I see how widespread the worship of stones still is amongst uncivilized peoples,

[1] Josh. iv. 5—8. It appears that within recent times it was customary amongst the Kabyls for the representatives of confederated tribes each to set up a great stone when they had arrived at an important decision. If one of the tribes subsequently broke the engagement, its stone was cast down.—Cartailhac, *France préhistorique*, pp. 314, 315.

especially the worship of stones set up on one end, I am far more disposed to conclude that megaliths in general are the legacy and the evidence of a veritable litholatry, whether they were worshipped in and for themselves, as amongst the natives of India, Malaysia, Polynesia, North Africa, and the two Americas,[1] or whether they were regarded as the abode or the image of some superhuman power, like the Bethels of the whole Semitic race, or the shapeless masses which, as Pausanias testifies, the earlier Greeks worshipped instead of images.[2] We shall presently see that worship of stones set up on end was the first step towards idolatry everywhere.

Man in the age of polished stone, like his palæolithic predecessor, disposed of his dead in caves; but when natural caves were wanting, he made artificial ones, either by hollowing an excavation in the rock, or by arranging four stones, in a sort of rectangle surmounted by a large slab, and covered with a mound of earth. This is the origin of the dolmens, which are now universally admitted to be connected with funeral rites. The only question is, whether they were tombs of the first or the second instance; that is to say, whether the dead were placed in them at once, or whether decomposition was first allowed to do its work. On the latter hypothesis, which is the more probable, the dolmens

[1] *Mythologie du monde minéral;* leçon professée a l'école d'anthropologie, par André Lefèvre : in the *Revue des traditions populaires* for November, 1889. Paris.

[2] Pausanias, vii. 22, 4; cf. *infra.*

were only ossuaries, like those still met with in some cemeteries in European countries. But the very desire to secure a kind of perpetual abode to the incorruptible elements of the body, is itself only another proof of the importance attached to funeral rites.

There is a certain detail, frequently observed in these dolmens, which has not failed to exercise the minds of the archæologists, especially when the dolmens were supposed to be the work of one particular people. It is the presence in one of the walls—generally the one that closes the entrance—of a hole not more than large enough for the passage of a human head. In the Caucasus and on the coast of Malabar, these holes have given the dolmens the popular name of "dwarf-houses."

The hole is too small to serve as a passage for living men, or for the introduction of the skeleton; or even for inserting the sacrifices, which moreover would be found piled up against the interior wall. The most probable explanation seems to be that it was intended for the soul to pass through. Numbers of savage peoples suppose that the soul continues to inhabit the body after death, though from time to time it makes excursions into the world of the living. Now we shall see presently that amongst these peoples the soul is generally regarded as a reduced and semi-material copy of the body. It therefore requires a hole if it is to escape from the enclosure. It is for this reason that, at the death of a relative, the Hottentots, the Samoyeds, the Siamese, the Fijians, and the Redskins, make a hole in the hut to allow the passage of the deceased, but close it again immediately afterwards to prevent its coming back.[1] The Iroquois make a small hole in every tomb, and expressly declare that it is to enable the soul to go out or come in at its pleasure.[2] At Koulfa, in North Africa, the same idea was combined with a desire to clear a passage for sacrifices. They buried the body, in a sitting posture, in a round, well-like shaft, into which they left an open hole, and then put cloths and other things close to the mouth, so that the dead man himself could come and fetch them, and take them to others who had died before him.[3]

Trepanned skulls. It is the same desire to secure a way for the spirit to pass, which best explains the curious phenomenon of trepanning the skull, first observed, in 1872, by Dr. Prunières, in the neolithic caves of Central France; and subsequently in tombs of the same period, in Denmark, Bohemia, Italy, Portugal, North Africa, and the two Americas.[4] Some of these skulls have been trepanned after death; others during life, as appeared from the reparative efforts of nature which had followed. As for the circles of bone extracted,

[1] Compare Frazer, *On certain Burial Customs:* in the *Journal of the Anthropological Institute*, vol. xv. p. 70; see also Herbert Spencer, *Principles of Sociology*, vol. i. § 94.

[2] A. Reville, *Religions des peuples non-civilisés*, Paris, 1883, vol. i. p. 252.

[3] Clapperton, *Second Expedition into the Interior of Africa*, London, 1829, pp. 141, 142. Note that the Greeks, too, pierced the soil near the tomb to pour libations into it, under the impression that this would enable them to reach the dead more easily. J. Girard, *Le sentiment religieuse en Grèce d'Homère à Eschyle*, 1879, p. 182.

[4] Broca, *Sur la trépanation du crâne et les amulettes crâniennes à l'époque néolithique:* Paris, 1877.

they had sometimes been pierced and hung upon a necklace, a custom which survived down to the Gaulish period.

It would appear that trepanning is still practised by the Kabyls. M. de Nadaillac believes that the object is religious, but M. Broca takes it to be therapeutic. If we follow the former, we may suppose it intended to allow the soul free communication with the superhuman powers; or it might be an offering to the gods of a substitute or representative in place of the whole person, on the principle which rules religious mutilations, from the sacrifice of a finger-joint to the offering of the hair or a nail-paring. If we follow M. Broca, it must have been intended to facilitate the expulsion of the spirit that had gained entrance into the body, and was causing disorders in it; conformably to the theory of uncivilized peoples that every malady is caused by diabolic or divine possession. It is evidently with this view that savages in the Old and the New Worlds apply the processes of massage and suction to their sick, give them purgatives and emetics, and even bleed and cauterize them. The efficacity of such treatment is often real though always empirical, and it is invariably attributed to the departure of the disturbing spirit.

The trepanning of the dead is perhaps more difficult to explain, especially as we can find no similar practice amongst known peoples. M. Cartailhac, on the strength of a species of embalming still practised by the Dyaks, thinks its object was to allow of the extraction of the brain.[1] But one would suppose that such a procedure

[1] *France préhistorique*, p. 286.

must have left some further traces; and, in any case, it would not explain the value attached to the severed fragments of the cranium, as amulets. Perhaps the very object of the operation was no other than to procure these precious talismans; or it may have been to provide the soul with a special passage through which to leave the body. It deserves notice that the trepanning has not been applied indiscriminately to all the bodies in the same tomb; that on some of the skulls it must have been performed both during life and after death; and, finally, that in some cases the holes thus formed have been closed by means of disks evidently borrowed from other skulls. All these facts are in full harmony with the hypothesis that trepanning was reserved—as certain funeral rites and even certain privileged methods of burial certainly were—to particular individuals, who, in virtue of their rank, their knowledge, or their character, were regarded as superior in nature to their fellows, or even as holding direct communication with the super-human world.

Worship of the mallet. We have incontestable proof that idolatry was practised in the age of the lake dwellings and artificial crypts. In the caves of Marne, Oise, Eure, and Du Gard, an attempt at a female figure has been found, always on the left wall of the ante-cave, which implies a deliberate arrangement. The eyes, nose, mouth, breasts, and even the representation of a necklace, are distinctly recognizable.[1] This rough representation, which is always the same, is generally accompanied by the picture of a flint hatchet, or double-headed mallet, sometimes with

[1] Baron de Baye, *Mémoires sur les grottes de la Marne:* Paris, 1872.

the handle. It is not surprising that the man of the stone age venerated the instrument which characterized his civilization, the arm which assured him his rule over nature, and which represented the foundation of his power. Do not we still find the Redskins, the Polynesians, and even the Hindus, offering homage to their arms and their tools? This worship of dressed flints and *a fortiori* of the stone hatchet, has been almost universal to the human race. And even after the discovery of the metals, these primitive implements have been connected with the lightning and supposed to be stones fallen from heaven. But the representations we are now speaking of force us to ask whether we ought not to attach the hatchet to the worship of some feminine divinity, whose arm or symbol it was, just as in the tombs of a later age it becomes that of Thor and Taran, the Germanic and Gaulish divinities of thunder.[1] This, however, does not at all imply that it was likewise the thunder which the men of the age of polished stone worshipped under the features of a woman; and perhaps the wisest course in the present state of our knowledge would be to renounce all attempts to penetrate the mystery further. And yet if, without transgressing my limits, I might suggest an hypothesis, I should ask whether we might not recognize in this naïve and fragmentary idol the personification of nature, or rather of the earth. As a matter of fact, we find the earth worshipped in feminine form by all peoples

---

[1] It is interesting to note that the axe reappears in the hand of the thunder-god amongst the Chaldæans, the Greeks (Zeus Labrandeus), and the Hindus (Çiva).

who have attained a sufficient faculty of generalization to be able to conceive the idea of such a power. Going a step further, I would even suggest that the association of the hatchet with the goddess may well have been drawn from some myth of the union of heaven and earth, in which the fructifying powers of the storm were symbolized by the flint axe. The presence of such conceptions amongst almost all the peoples who have attained a certain level of mythological development, is my only excuse for hazarding this explanation, which is in perfect agreement with all that we know of the religious ideas of the occupants of France, at the moment when they come into contact with more advanced civilizations.

We frequently find on the Gallo-Roman altars a god grasping a long mallet, associated with a goddess bearing a cornucopia. Archæologists agree in taking the former to be Taran, or Taranis, the Celtic thunder-god (corresponding to the Germanic Thor), who is sometimes Latinized into Dis Pater or Sylvanus. In the latter they recognize a goddess of the earth or of nature.[1] The mallet is the emblem of the storm, with its life-giving streams, and was also the symbol of fertility, amongst the Germanic populations. In Scandinavia, when the bride entered the conjugal abode it was customary to throw a mallet into her lap;[2] and the German minnesinger Frauenlob naïvely makes the Virgin Mary explain the conception of the infant Jesus by saying

[1] *Le dieu gaulois au maillet*, by Ed. Flouest and H. Gaidoz, in the *Reveu archéologique* for March—April, 1890.

[2] *Reveu des traditions populaires*, Jan. 1889, vol. iv. p. 23.

that "the smith from the upper land threw his hammer into her lap."[1]

Most of the rites which I have just explained have also left their stamp on the age of bronze or copper, and we can even follow them into the first iron age, in which we enter almost everywhere upon the field of history.

It will be thought, perhaps, that this harvest of information is meagre enough, and that hypotheses form a great part even of what there is. But the facts we have been able to establish suffice, if not to re-constitute the whole religion of pre-historic man, at any rate to show that he stood on a religious plane hardly superior to that of the peoples of our own day, who stand midway between absolute savagery and the beginnings of civilization. You will observe that, to recover the beliefs implied in our data, we have had recourse to the similar usages we can trace amongst uncivilized peoples in the present day, and to the recognized explanations they receive. In like manner, to recover the use of certain pre-historic implements, we turn to populations amongst whom their like may still be found; and indeed the scholars who have attempted to re-construct the industry, the occupations, and the manners of pre-historic savages, have not hesitated to generalize the conclusions drawn from such analogies with considerable freedom. All I ask is to be allowed to do the same with respect to religious beliefs and institutions.

Folk-lore. There is yet another branch of study

[1] Karl Bliud, in *The Antiquary* for 1884, vol. ix. p. 200.

which leads us to the same results. It is Folk-lore, that is to say, the study of the traditions which previous civilizations, as they disappeared, left like so many sedimentary deposits in the lower classes. It cannot be denied that these classes, specially in the country districts, have been much less sensitive than the rest of the nation to the modifying influence of progress, and have therefore preserved much more of the intellectual and social habits once common to all strata of the population. Hence beliefs and customs prevail amongst them which appear absolutely inexplicable if judged by the scientific or even the religious ideas generally accepted in our day. To understand the significance and the genesis of these survivals, we must replace them among the surroundings from which they respectively issued. Some of them may be explained by the beliefs and rites of the historic religions immediately anterior to Christianity. Others point back to a more rudimentary and gross religious state. If these last were incorporated in the ancient religions, they were veritable survivals even here, and were recognized as such by more than one writer of the period. Now if we search for their equivalents amongst the materials supplied by modern ethnography, not only is it nine chances to one that we shall find them amongst one or another of the uncivilized groups, perhaps amongst almost all, but further, when we study them amid their actual present surroundings, they will acquire a rational meaning,—that is to say, a meaning in conformity with the general ways of thought current amongst savages.

In certain departments of France, when the peasants

enter upon a newly-built house, they cut a chicken's neck and sprinkle the blood in all the rooms. In Poitou, the explanation given is, that if the living are to dwell in the house, the dead must first pass through it.[1] Thus presented, the custom is without meaning; but it is no longer so if we bring it into connection with the belief, almost universal amongst peoples who possess the art of masonry, that the soul of a victim buried under the foundations protects the solidity or guards the approaches of the edifice. And if we combine this belief with the principle, no less widely spread, that in the matter of sacrifice (as we shall presently see) the inferior may be substituted for the superior, an animal for a man, the whole meaning of the ceremony becomes clear. In Germany, it is often an empty coffin that is built into the foundations; whilst the Bulgarians confine themselves to the pantomime of throwing in the shadow of some passer-by. To find the explanation of this last trait, we have only to transport ourselves into the ideas of the numerous peoples who regard a man's shadow as the spiritual part of him—that is to say, as his soul. Our own languages bear witness that our ancestors were of the same opinion. The belief that the dead have no shadows is found amongst the Negroes of Central Africa, as well as in Dante's *Purgatory*. And the Zulus imagine that there is a crocodile or some other beast in the water that can draw in a passer-by if it can get hold of his shadow.[2]

[1] Cf. *Les rites de la construction:* in "Mélusine" for Jan. 5th, 1888.

[2] See Arbousset et Daumas, *Voyage d'exploration au nord-est de la colonie du Cap*, Paris, 1842, p. 12. Compare *Journal of the Anthropological Institute*, vol. x. p. 313; vol. xvi. p. 344.

Two years ago, I was present at the Crematorium in Milan, at the cremation of the remains of a young teacher. When the cremation was over and they were about to seal the urn, the mother and sisters of the deceased asked leave to put their photographs in, with the still warm ashes of the deceased. Surely we can all feel a touching appropriateness in placing the likeness of the beings he most loved during life on the tomb or even at the side of the dead; but is it not strangely significant to see a family, sufficiently emancipated to break with the traditional routine of interment, still subject to the traditions of the most distant past, and offering a form of homage to the deceased which, in spite of the intervention of the photographic art, carries us to the funeral sacrifices of the Negroes and the New Zealanders? To this very day, throughout the whole of pagan Africa, they surround the dead, especially if he is a distinguished personage, with his wives and attendants and even his favourite animals. But here the process of attenuation has not yet set in, and they actually slaughter the miserable victims whom they send to follow their husband and master in his life beyond the tomb. In China, in Marco Polo's time, they had already begun to replace the sacrifice of actual victims by parchment figures, which they burnt with the body.[1] The Chinese of our own day, with a still keener eye to economy, confine themselves to writing out the schedule of their sacrifices on a piece of paper, which they then burn upon the tomb.

[1] *Marco Polo*, bk. i. chap. xl., in Yule's *Book of Ser Marco Polo*, London, 1875, vol. i. pp. 207, 208.

The populace, however, has not a monopoly of survivals. Try the experiment, as I myself have done, of asking the mourners at a military funeral why they make the deceased officer's horse follow the coffin; and especially why they make the poor beast limp during the funeral procession. Some of them will tell you they cannot say, and they suppose it has always been so. Others will tell you that it is a tribute to the deceased, and perhaps a way of compelling the horse to take part in the mourning. Only one here and there, who has read a little ethnography, will remember that the sacrifice of the horse at the funeral is almost universal amongst uncivilized peoples who practise riding. And indeed we know, from the direct evidence of historians, that it was once practised on a large scale by the Celts, the Germans, the Slavs, and the Mongols. Amongst the Caucasian Ossets it appears in a transition stage, analogous to that with which we are acquainted ourselves. They content themselves with making the horse and the widow circle the tomb three times; only the woman may not marry again, nor may the horse serve another member of the tribe. In Europe, we confine ourselves to imitating the effect of hamstringing the horse; and at the funeral of Prince Baudouin at Brussels, I noticed that even this piece of useless cruelty was suppressed. Thus the old customs disappear; but now and then the original feeling which still survives in the popular consciousness rises to the surface again, and throws an unexpected light upon the past, like a flame leaping up from the embers of a dying fire. Mr. Andrew Lang reports the case of a peasant woman some years ago in

Kerry, who killed her husband's horse when he died, and when reproached with her folly, exclaimed, "Would ye have my man go about on foot in the next world?"[1]

Liturgical survivals. Religions—at any rate such as are organized into orthodoxies—generally declare war on the superstitions of preceding ages; but they are themselves compelled to take under their patronage the survivals which they cannot uproot. This is the explanation of traditions and practices, imbedded in relatively high religions, entirely foreign to the intellectual and moral atmosphere of their professors. You know with what zeal and, I must add, with what success Mr. Andrew Lang has applied this principle in explaining the shocking and grotesque stories of the Greek mythology. He has shown how these myths were formed at a period when the ancestors of the classical Greeks had the manners and ideas of savages. The same observation may be applied to more than one rite in the worships of the present and the past.

The saying has often been repeated, that dogma, inasmuch as it represents the fixation of beliefs dominant at a given moment, soon comes to represent the religion, or rather the theology, of *yesterday* rather than *to-day;* and in the same sense one might say that the cultus generally represents the theology of the *day before yesterday*, for nowhere does the conservative spirit maintain itself so toughly as in religious rites. Here the dominion of custom is fortified by the fear of displeasing the Deity by altering the practices which he is himself supposed to have inspired, or the efficacy of which has been

[1] *Custom and Myth*, pp. 11, 12.

established by long and repeated experience; and thus there is no religion which does not embrace in its cultus ceremonies and symbols borrowed from the whole series of previous religions.

The lamented Edwin Hatch, in his Hibbert Lectures of 1888—one of the most lucid, conscientious, and complete treatises ever published on the part played by Greece in the development of Christian dogmas and rites—has shown how the pagan mysteries gained admission, with a new significance, into the bosom of nascent Christianity. Now amongst those ceremonies there were certainly some which classical antiquity itself had borrowed from more ancient forms of worship; and it follows that we may still see certain Christian churches performing ceremonies that we may safely say have traversed at least three religions, and the equivalent of which—perhaps even down to the explanation officially given—may still be found on all hands amongst barbarous peoples. I must content myself with citing, as one of the most characteristic examples, the renovation of fire in the office of Holy Saturday. The priest, after extinguishing all the lights, re-kindles the Paschal taper by means of a spark struck by the old method of the flint and steel. Does not this ceremony carry us straight back to the solar or fire rites, which were already more or less touched with metaphysical conceptions in almost all the ancient polytheisms, but which reveal their purely naturalistic origin in the customs of certain savage peoples, and, for the matter of that, in the traditions of our folk-lore also? Formerly the renovation of the fire took place in the church on the dawn of Easter Sunday (the day of the

Resurrection), and the fire which the clergy had struck from the flint and steel served to re-kindle the fires of private individuals which had all been previously extinguished. This is the very ceremony which took place annually at Lemnos in the temple of Hephaistos, at Rome in that of Vesta, at Cuzco in that of the Sun, in Mexico in honour of Xiuhtecutli, "the Lord of the year." It is the same which is still observed in kindling the sacrificial fire amongst the Brahmans;[1] in conducting one of the principal religious ceremonies of the Chippeways;[2] in celebrating the renewal of the year on the Zanzibar coast;[3] in securing rain amongst the Kaffirs;[4] on every solemn occasion amongst the Australians;[5] in putting a stop to epidemics in certain remote districts of Europe; or simply in celebrating the summer solstice. On the banks of the Moselle, and in other localities of Western Europe, it was the custom, on St. Jean d'Été (Midsummer-day), to kindle a wheel and then roll it across the fields or the vineyards to secure a good harvest.[6] It was the custom in certain provinces of the Slavonic and Germanic countries to extinguish all the fires at this same season of the year; then to fix a wheel upon a pivot and whirl it round till

[1] J. C. Nesfield, *Primitive Philosophy of Fire*, in the *Calcutta Review* of April, 1884, p. 335.

[2] A. Réville, *Religions des peuples non-civilisés*, vol. i. p. 222.

[3] J. Becker, *La vie en Afrique*, Bruxelles, 1887, vol. i. p. 36.

[4] Capt. Conder, *On the Bechuanas*, in the *Journal of the Anthropological Institute*, vol. xvi. p. 84.

[5] E. Tregegar, *The Maoris*, in the *Journal of the Anthropological Institute* of Nov. 1889, vol. xix. p. 107.

[6] H. Gaidoz, *Le dieu Gaulois du soleil et le symbolisme de la roue*, Paris, 1886, pp. 17—21.

the wood caught fire, whereupon every one present took a light to re-kindle his own fire.

I have selected this rite as an excellent example of the parallel development of one and the same usage on the three-fold track of organized religions, popular traditions, and savage rites; and, further, because we can trace it back to its original source without wounding any one's feelings, or creating too harsh a sense of discord between the meaning now put into a religious ceremony and the ideas that first gave it birth. But the same process might be followed with reference to far other rites, performed every day before our eyes. And if such loans are found even in the Christian Church, one may imagine how they must abound in rituals which can have no reason for disguising their naturalistic origin. We soon come to accept M. James Darmesteter's assertion, that one need not search very long amongst the historical religions to find, often under forms of striking identity, most of the essential elements of the non-historical religions.[1]

Right of comparative ethnography to be taken in evidence. Here, perhaps, I shall be arrested by the question: "What right have you thus to credit savage populations with the preservation intact of the heritage of primitive religion? Is not the savage, whom we wrongly call primitive, as old as the civilized man? Has he not as long an ancestral line behind him? Has he not traversed, in the course of ages, an endless series of fluctuations, alternating between progress and decadence, which must have very greatly modified his original conceptions?

---

[1] James Darmesteter, *Revue critique d'histoire et de littérature*, Paris, 1884, 1er trimestre, p. 42.

And, moreover, the superstitions and the rites of savages differ to some extent from one people to another. To which special group, then, shall we address ourselves by preference in order to re-discover the primitive beliefs? Amongst some peoples the dominating system is Shamanism—that is to say, belief in the power of sorcerers. Amongst others it is Totemism, the worship of animals; or Fetishism, the belief in the supernatural influences emanating from certain concrete objects. There are populations which assign a single soul to man; others which give him two, three, or even four. Sometimes it is the sun that occupies the first place in the worship; sometimes it is the moon, the heavens, the mythical ancestor, or some casually selected spirit."

All very true. But I do not for a moment maintain that the savages of to-day reproduce, trait by trait, the beliefs of our pre-historic ancestors. No doubt we may reasonably suppose that between races so far separated in time, there must be differences analogous to those which part the chief sections of savages now existing one from another in matters of religion. But these latter divergences are themselves largely counterbalanced by the far more numerous and significant resemblances which fill the narratives of travellers and the treatises of ethnographers. Moreover, a really attentive examination soon shows us that if the detail of the beliefs, and even of the rites, varies from people to people, the mental and religious state of which these ideas and customs are the manifestation is identical throughout. What does it matter, for example, whether the fire lighted on the tomb is intended to warm the dead man in the other world, as with the Redskins, or to hinder him from returning to this world, as with the Kaffirs? The two ideas bear impartial witness to the belief that the soul is a semi-material being capable of feeling heat and cold. Or, again, what does it matter that the magic operations for healing maladies or securing rain now and then vary on the two continents, since they all alike imply that the malady is attributed to the presence of a spirit in the body, and that certain individuals are recognized as having power over the genii of the elements? Of what consequence is the nature of the superhuman beings placed in the first rank, or even the infinite diversity of the stories told about them, if they are everywhere represented after the guise of chiefs or sorcerers, with faculties more or less magnified, but subject to all the limitations and weaknesses of human nature at its lowest level of culture?

The real interest for us is found in the underlying analogy of reasoning and of motive; and under this aspect I affirm that the savage of every age represents primitive man—not because he is his authentic likeness, that has defied the ravages of time, but because he has remained in, or has re-entered, the same stage of civilization; and at that lower level, the same conditions beget the same ideas, and even the same applications of those ideas. It is only at a higher stage of development that man can even begin to free himself from a close dependence upon external nature. Liberty is not the point of departure, but the goal of human evolution. This explains at once the diversity of historical religions and the uniformity of savage beliefs. The latter represent the common foundation, hardly yet organic, out of

PRE-HISTORIC MANIFESTATIONS OF RELIGION. 41

which all the great religious systems have respectively issued by a process of differentiation and organization.

Thus history, pre-historic archæology, folk-lore, and comparative ethnography, combine with philology and psychology to tell us, that if we would re-construct the early forms and primitive developments of religion, we must of necessity address ourselves to the beliefs of the uncivilized peoples, while collecting for comparison the corresponding elements still to be detected in the historic forms of worship and in the popular survivals. Where these three sources of information yield identical results, especially when gathered from divers regions and races, we may presume that we have before us no accidental or transient facts, special to this or that people or climate, but general facts of humanity, characterizing all peoples placed under similar conditions of social development, and therefore common to our own ancestors at a certain period of their evolution.

Continuity and progress in the religious evolution. To complete the demonstration, however, we must see whether it is really true that even the most exalted religious ideas and institutions of our own times can be connected, without breach of continuity and without recourse to the hypothesis of an intervention from without, with the natural development of beliefs still observed amongst populations at the lowest stage of human culture. This is the question with which I propose to deal in the present course of Lectures, at least as far as concerns the idea of Deity and of its nature and function in the universe.

I do not disguise from myself the difficult and delicate nature of the task, in spite of the positions made good by those who have preceded me in the attempt. I shall have to contend against the repugnance not only of orthodox minds, which find the origin of religious ideas in a supernatural revelation, but also of all who, while regarding the different religions as the spontaneous product of a sentiment inherent in human nature, nevertheless shrink from admitting the lowly character of their origins and antecedents. Yet those independent minds who love to insist on the perfectible and progressive character of religion, and who have formed too lofty a conception of it to be content to confine it within the limits of a particular revelation, ought to perceive clearly enough the confirmation and support which their views must find in the thesis which I am defending. If, so far, religion has always been exalting and purifying itself—and this implies its humble origin—then there is all the more certain prospect that it will continue to do so in the future. The important thing is, not what our ancestors believed concerning the Deity, but what our own ideas on the subject are. And will our conception of God be less sublime when we have found a place for its development in the divine plan of creation?

Do what we may, we can no longer escape the necessity of submitting the religious sentiment to the general law of evolution, which affirms the concurrent principles of continuity and progress, whether in the cosmography of the sidereal world, the geology of the terrestrial sphere, the palæontology of living beings, or the archæology and history of the human race. The only position which will thereby suffer will be the old metaphysical argument which made the reality of God rest upon the impossibility of our ever having conceived of Him, had He not in some fashion written His signature on the consciousness of the first man. But this is simply a more refined form of the argument which undertakes to found upon miracles—that is to say, on the reversal of natural laws— the existence of the Author of nature.

How much more satisfying, both to the reason and the conscience, is the hypothesis of gradual development, explaining, with Lessing, that the succession of religions represents the religious education of the human race. If man has long suffered from ignorance or misconception of the Deity, it is simply because his education has long been incomplete. Who shall dare to say that it is yet completed?

Present position of the question. I have not the least intention of discussing the dogmas of the positive religions. I shall remain on the field of what may be called Natural Religion; though not using the term in the old sense of a system of doctrine embracing the beliefs common to every worship, but rather as including all manifestations due to the spontaneous development of the religious sentiment. I cannot, however, abstain from expressing my regret that the belief in the progressive evolution of religions should find its chief opponents amongst the exponents of a theology founded, like the Christian creed, on an application of that very principle. Special interest attaches, in this connection, to the following declaration by a Catholic writer, who represents, *par excellence*, Roman Catholic orthodoxy on the subject of the history of religions, to wit, M. l'Abbé de Broglie, Professor of Apologetics at the University of Paris:

"The Judaism of the later period shows progress from the religion of Moses, and the latter from that of the Patriarchs. Christianity . . . . is an immense step in advance; and in the Church itself, as the great Doctors maintain, there is progress in the knowledge of truth."[1]

Since the learned Professor admits that Christianity is a progressive outcome of Judaism, Judaism of the religion of Moses, and the latter in its turn of the religion of the Patriarchs, he has only to make one step more, and admit that the religion of the Patriarchs is a progressive outcome of the beliefs common to a lower level of humanity, and we shall then be completely at one with him in method, if not in results.

There are orthodox scholars who seem to have taken this last step, at any rate as far as the pagan religions are concerned. One of the most eminent Professors of the Catholic University of Louvain wrote not long ago: "The belief in a primitive monotheism only concerns a period too remote for historical researches ever to reach. . . . . This original monotheism does not affect any of the religious transformations and vicissitudes which history can trace, and which may become the subject of our studies. The worship of material objects and the corresponding state of intelligence may perfectly well be admitted by us all, as existing in an age which is lost in the night of time, and from which man successively raised himself, at several centres, to loftier conceptions."[2]

[1] *Problèmes et conclusions de l'histoire des religions*, p. 319.

[2] *De la methode dans l'étude historique des religions:* in the *Muséon* of Jan. 1887, p. 58.

And one of the most enlightened and sympathetic defenders of Protestant orthodoxy, M. de Pressensé, admits, on his side, that in consequence of a moral fall, humanity must have lapsed from its primitive culture into a state of absolute savagery, and that from that point onwards the study of savages is the best means "of re-constructing, with some degree of precision, the social and religious condition of the rude infancy of humanity, of which they are themselves survivals."[1] Hierographic science can ask no more.

These declarations are a significant sign of what is going on even in the minds most attached to orthodox beliefs. Consider, moreover, what has come to pass within the last third of a century as to other once burning questions, in which the future of Christianity and even of Religion was said to be involved. What has become of the polemics which lashed the last generation into fury over the explanation of the days in Genesis? What has become of the pleadings and the anathemas which a few years ago filled the Reviews, and the Professorial Chairs, apropos of historical researches into the age and authenticity of the sacred books? These controversies, it seems, have sunk into deep peace because men have come to see that their solution is not a question of religion, but one of scholarship—which is a way of saying that the scholars were quite right, but that religion has taken no harm! It is true that from time to time some brilliant essay still appears which gives itself the airs of a challenge to battle; but in truth these efforts may more properly be

[1] Pressensé, *L'ancien monde et le christianisme*, Paris, 1887, pp. 5, 6.

compared to the last cartridges fired by a retiring rearguard, or to charges of cavalry protecting a retreat. The actual seat of war seems to be transferred to problems concerning the origin of man and of religion itself. It is easy to foresee the result. Here, too, Religion will benefit by the victory of Science, not only because that victory will eliminate a source of conflict between two necessary factors of human culture, but also because it will give us a sublimer and more harmonious conception of the ways of God's revelation of Himself to man, or, to employ Hegel's expression, "of the way in which the finite spirit has come to a consciousness of its essence as absolute Being."

LECTURE II.

THE GENESIS OF THE IDEA OF GOD.

(i.) THE WORSHIP OF NATURE, AND THE WORSHIP OF THE DEAD.

Definition of Religion. BEFORE formulating a theory on the origin of Religion, we must seek an adequate definition of the word.

The definitions of religion are innumerable, and I have no intention of discussing them here. To do so would be to pass the whole history of the philosophy of religions in review. I shall confine myself to explaining the sense in which I mean to use the word in these Lectures. By religion, then, I mean *the conception man forms of his relations with the superhuman and mysterious powers on which he believes himself to depend.*

This definition does not touch the question whether the end pursued by religion is based on a reality or not. On the other hand, I think it sharply defines the sphere of religious phenomena, and at the same time indicates the common and essential character of all religious manifestations.

Did Religion spring from the emotions or from the reason? Most writers on religion, as distinct from its particular forms, recognize that it embraces two factors pertaining respectively to the reason and the feelings, but they differ as to which of these two came first; in other words, whether the conception of the divinity engendered the religious sentiment, or whether the presence of that sentiment brought man to believe in the existence of the gods and to reason as to their nature.

According to the one view, man instinctively attempted to put himself into relations with the superhuman influences by which he felt himself surrounded, and it was only subsequently that he thought of defining them. No one in our day has formulated this thesis with more eloquence than M. Renan, who compares man's religious impulses to the instinct that makes the hen-bird "sit," which instinct spontaneously declares itself as soon as the appropriate stage is reached.[1]

Others, on the contrary, maintain that before worshipping his gods, man must have had some conception of their nature, and that the sentiments he entertains towards them must of necessity flow from the ideas he has formed of their character and workings.

At first sight, this latter theory seems to have logic on its side. Clearly, one can neither love nor fear a being before having conceived the idea of its existence. Nevertheless, inevitable as it seems to place a purely intellectual operation at the source of religion, we must recollect that the sentiments that sprang from it must have long preceded even the most ancient formulæ of primitive theology.

The infant in the cradle, when he stretches his arms towards his mother or his nurse, is conscious of an agreeable sensation which he instinctively associates with the approach of certain persons, and he will manifest this

[1] *Dialogues philosophiques*, Paris, 1876, pp. 38, 39.

sentiment, or in the opposite case sentiments of repulsion and fear, long before he has taken to reasoning on his relations with the beings around him. In like manner, primitive man must from the first have experienced more or less vague and unreflecting feelings of sympathy or repulsion, of joy or terror, not only with regard to his fellow-men, but with respect to the other beings and even phenomena which he supposed to influence his destiny favourably or the reverse; and the day on which he deified these beings and phenomena—that is to say, attributed to them a personality analogous to his own, but more mysterious and exalted—was the day on which the sentiments he experienced towards them became religious.

Religion in animals. It has been asked, in this connection, whether animals can experience the religious sentiment. A century ago such a question would only have provoked a smile; but now that we have accustomed ourselves to search in the lowest strata of animal life for the antecedents of physiological and intellectual characteristics which only receive their full expression in the best-endowed representatives of human culture, it is no longer possible to dismiss the question of the religion of animals in this summary style. Animals share the philosophic fate of savages. They are alternately exalted and humbled, according to the exigencies of the current theory as to the position of man in nature. Under the influence of Descartes, they were regarded simply as machines, and their absolute automatism served to throw the liberty of the lord of creation into relief. Under the influence of Darwinism, we tend to regard them not only as the precursors and the elder brothers of man, but even as his equals, not to say his superiors; and to represent the ant-hill or the bee-hive as the ideal of a well-organized society.

Not so long ago the opponents of religious ideas used to reply to those who would make religion a natural characteristic of the human mind, "Religion is nothing but an accident, a parasitical excrescence. It is so far from being natural to humanity that most savages are without it." Now that this position can no longer be maintained, they have reversed their batteries, and it is not uncommon to hear them maintain with equal fervour, "Religion, so far from being a distinctive sign of humanity, is found in the animals themselves."

We need take no notice of these partizan attacks, for the position we have taken up is entirely unaffected by them; but we must not forget that serious and impartial authors have maintained that religion exists among the animals. Four years ago, a talented writer, M. Van Ende, published a thick volume of 320 pages filled with ingenious and suggestive observations to show that animals attribute the grand phenomena of nature to the action of powers superior to all the beings they know, and that those powers inspire them with most of the characteristic sentiments of religion.[1] I think the author has sometimes let his imagination run away with him, and has taken advantage of the fact that we cannot check him by getting into the animal's hide and learning what it thinks and how it thinks it. I am quite

[1] *Histoire naturelle de la croyance:* première partie, *L'animal:* Paris, 1887.

II. THE GENESIS OF THE IDEA OF GOD.

willing to admit that animals apparently experience more or less spontaneous feelings of joy or terror in the presence of certain natural phenomena; but I very much doubt whether their powers of analysis can take them the length of reasoning upon the character and dispositions of the beings they imagine they find behind the manifestations of nature. Still less can I believe that they endeavour to enter into relations with those mysterious beings, based on their conception of their nature. Undoubtedly, if the word religion be made to imply a simple feeling of dependence, as Schleiermacher has it, we may answer with Fichte that the dog must be the most religious of beings. But (with M. de Pressensé) we shall decline to believe that it is so until the dog has combined with his fellows to found a religion implying the desire to establish ideal relations with the mysterious higher powers.[1] This would require a capacity for abstraction and generalization and a perception of analogies which we could hardly expect from an animal, even were it Haeckel's Anthropopithecus.

Unwarranted extension of the idea of personality. But a day came for nascent humanity when our ancestors were no longer content, like animals, to look for the sun to warm them; to greet the return of the dark-dispelling moon with cries of joy; to howl in terror at the rumbling of the thunder; to demand of the rock a shelter from the wind and rain; and to spy out the beasts of the forest so as to capture or escape them. The savage began to ask what were his own relations to the beings who

[1] E. de Pressensé, *Les Origines*, Paris, 1883, p. 471 [omitted in the English Translation, p. 158].

thus affected his destiny; and the mental process which gave him his answer differed in nothing save in complexity from that which contemporary thought accepts to explain the course of phenomena in the last analysis.

The philosophy which, resting on the most recent discoveries, has established the constancy of the same energy under all the varied manifestations of nature, can only conceive of that ultimate force by relating it to our own sense of effort springing from the consciousness of the resistance of our surroundings to the action of our will. The savage, on his side, wherever he finds life and movement, refers them to the only source of activity of which he has any direct knowledge, namely the will. He therefore sees in all phenomena the action of wills analogous to his own,—wills which he locates sometimes in the moving beings themselves, the celestial bodies, clouds, fire, running waters, plants, and animals; sometimes in invisible beings of which he can only perceive the manifestations, such as thunder and wind.

Personification of phenomena. Not only the beliefs of uncivilized peoples, but the traditions of our own folk-lore, abundantly establish the fact that uncultivated minds ascribe the attributes of life to stones and waters; the faculties of animals to plants; and the feelings and even the arguments of man to animals.[1] The savage believes that animals understand his language. If the dog does not answer, it is because he is proud, says the Kamchadal.

---

[1] See especially E. B. Tylor, *Primitive Culture*, 2 vols.: London, 1871. Albert Réville, *Les religions des peuples non-civilisés*, 2 vols.: Paris, 1883. Th. Waitz, *Anthropologie der Naturvölker:* Leipzig, 1876. Sir John Lubbock, *Origin of Civilization:* London, 1870.

II. THE GENESIS OF THE IDEA OF GOD. 53

If the ape remains dumb, it is because he is lazy, according to the Negroes, and knows that if he spoke they would make him work. The Redskin talks to his horse as to one of his companions; and the Arab believes that certain horses can read the Koran. The natives of the Philippine Islands, when they meet an alligator, beg it to do them no harm; and when the Malagassy catch a whale-calf, they beg its mother to go away.

They also believe that animals have the same relations with each other that men have. The inhabitants of Borneo maintain that the tigers have a Sultan and a court. According to the traveller Crevaux, the Redskins believe that animals have sorcerers of their own. Perrault's fairy-tales, La Fontaine's fables, and the popular traditions of our country districts, are no more than the echo, in this respect, of the actual beliefs of our ancestors of yore, and of the Polynesians, the Redskins, and Negroes of our own day.

Even trees are put upon the footing of equality with man amongst comparatively advanced peoples. There are numerous legends attributing to certain men the power of understanding the language of plants, and *vice versa*. Ibn-al-Awam's agricultural treatise recommends the intimidation of trees that refuse to produce fruit. You are to flog them mildly, and threaten to cut them down if they go on bearing no fruit.[1] So, too, the Bohemian Slavs used to cry to the garden trees at even, "Bud, ye trees! bud! or I will strip you of your

[1] E. Chevreul on J. J. Clément-Mullet's translation of *Le livre de l'Agriculture d'Ibn-al-Awam* in *Journal des Savants*, Paris, 1870, pp. 633, 634.

bark."[1] Water, again, suggests the idea of movement and so of life to the primitive imagination, and is therefore invested with conscious faculties everywhere. When the brothers Lander were descending the Niger by boat and a thick cloud rose on the horizon, their boatmen begged them to hide themselves at once in the bottom of the boat, because the river had never seen whites before, and that was why it was raising a cloud. Cameron tells us of a spring in Unyamuesi which the natives declare stops flowing if, instead of calling it marwa (palm-wine), they call it maji (the ordinary word for water), or if they fire guns in its neighbourhood, or, finally, if they go near it with their boots on.[2] At Whydah they offer presents to the sea to induce it to allow the merchandize of the whites to be discharged. Natives of Sumatra from the inland, on first seeing the ocean, are said to sacrifice cakes and sweetmeats to it in deprecation of its power of injuring them.[3]

The savage has no difficulty in ascribing, not only the powers of movement, but life and personality, even to stones. Caillé saw a big stone in an African village which they said circled the place three times whenever it was threatened by danger. This recalls the stones of the Celtic countries which dance and turn on certain occasions, and the Breton rock which, according to a legend cited by M. Cartailhac, goes down every year on Christmas-eve to drink at the neighbouring river.[4]

[1] Girard de Rialle, *Mythologie comparée*, Paris, 1878, p. 57.
[2] Cameron, *Across Africa*, London, 1877, vol. i. p. 144.
[3] W. Marsden, *Sumatra*, London, 1783, p. 256.
[4] *La France préhistorique*, pp. 164, 165.

II. THE GENESIS OF THE IDEA OF GOD.

The Lapps, the ancient Peruvians, the Fijians, and the dwellers on the shores of Tanganyika, believe that rocks marry and have children. The myth of Deukalion, which attributes the origin of our race to stones, transformed into men, has its counterpart amongst the ancient inhabitants of Central America, who say that the ancestors of man were stones.

The same delusion recurs with respect to the atmospheric phenomena and the celestial bodies. Not so long ago the celestial bodies were universally personified, and almost all the mythologies contain stories of people who have talked with the sun and moon. The Karens of Burmah, the Zulus, and the Redskins of the Washington district, make the rainbow a monster which drinks the water out of rivers and ponds. The same belief is found in the folk-lore of the Slavs, the Greeks, the Germans, and Central France. The Karens, according to Mason, cry to their children, " The rainbow has come down to drink. Play no more, lest some accident should happen to you."[1] By a strange coincidence, the rainbow is called "the Sucker" in Volhynia; and when the little Ukranian children see him, they run away and shout, "Run! run! or he'll eat you up."[2]

The Egyptians, according to Herodotus, believed that fire was a living creature; and Cicero himself calls it "ignis animal." The Aryans of India personified it under the name of Agni, the Agile; "the blessed one," as a Vedic hymn has it, "who is born white and becomes

[1] *Journal of the Asiatic Society of Bengal*, 1865 (vol. xxxiv.), part ii. p. 217.

[2] *Melusine*, deuxième année, 1884-5, p. 42.

red as he grows." And to this very day, in Dahomey, they offer sacrifices to the hearth to prevent the fire eating up the house. In Europe itself, the Bohemians keep the crumbs of their repast for the fire; if any food falls into the fire-place while they are cooking it, it is because the fire has demanded the offering; and old people still exist who attribute the frequency of destructive fires to the neglect of these usages.[1]

Our own languages, especially those which have no neuter gender or which make but little use of it, take us back to a period which knew no scruple in indefinitely extending the categories of life, of personality, and even of sex. Sometimes it is the sun, sometimes the moon, which is of the masculine gender; but in almost every known language these two heavenly bodies differ in gender, and can therefore be regarded as husband and wife. The same observation applies to the ancient cosmogonic couple of heaven and earth. When the Frenchman says, "Il pleut; il vente; il tonne," is it not as much as to declare "Some one is sprinkling, blowing, growling"? This "some one" may mean a hidden being who only reveals himself through his manifestations, or may indicate a visible being, the Sky or the Cloud, invested with the chief meteorological powers, and at the same time with faculties modelled on those of man.

Such examples might be multiplied indefinitely. I

---

[1] Tylor, *Primitive Culture*, vol. ii. p. 259. Compare, for what may be called the "theology of fire" in the ancient beliefs, Prof. Max Müller's beautiful studies in his *Gifford Lectures* for 1890, delivered at Glasgow, on *Physical Religion*: London, 1891.

II. THE GENESIS OF THE IDEA OF GOD.

have been content with drawing upon the standard treatises of ethnography for a few characteristic facts which establish the tendency of man, at a certain stage of his mental development, to anthropomorphize everything. The difficulty is not to say what kind of beings and phenomena he personifies, but rather to say in what category of objects he does not seek arbitrary personifications.

Nomina numina. Scholars, who have carried linguistic preconceptions into the study of mythology, have maintained that it was the forms of language, at an epoch when every verb implied a concrete act, so that every subject must necessarily be an animated being, which led to the attribution of life and personality to inanimate and material objects, *nomina numina*. M. Michel Bréal, one of the greatest linguists of the French school, declares: "However vivid and poetical may have been the first flights of imagination in the infancy of the human race, they could never have risen to representing the rain which waters the earth as coming from heavenly cows, or the cloud which conceals the lightning in its flanks as a monster vomiting flame, or the sun with his darting rays as a divine warrior discharging his arrows upon his foes. . . . . Whence, then, come these images? . . . From language, which spontaneously created them without man himself being aware of it."[1]

To refute this thesis, it is enough to recall the naïve dialogue, apropos of an eclipse, between the Algonkin and a missionary of the sixteenth century, Père Lejeune, who certainly will not be suspected of being under the influence of our present theories on the subject of mytho-

[1] M. Bréal, *Mélanges de littérature et de linguistique*, Paris, 1878, p. 8.

logy. "I asked them what caused eclipses of the moon and the sun. They answered that the moon was eclipsed and appeared dark because she held her son in her arms, and that concealed her brightness. 'If the moon has a son,' I replied, 'she is married or was married once.' 'Yes, certainly,' said they. 'The sun is her husband. He is out all day and she all night; and if he is eclipsed or darkened, it is because he, too, sometimes takes the son that he has had by the moon in his arms.' 'Yes; but neither the moon nor the sun has any arms at all,' I said. 'You've no sense; they always have their bows strung in front of them. That's why you can't see their arms.' 'And what do they want to shoot at?' 'Oh! how should we know?'"[1]

Do you say that the Algonkins had already been led to personify the celestial bodies by the metaphors of language? Well, then, here is a page of mythological autobiography in which we catch these personifications in the act of birth. De Gubernatis relates in his "Zoological Mythology" that when he was four years old, as he was walking one evening with a brother, the latter pointed to a fantastical cloud on the horizon and cried, "Look down there; that is a hungry wolf running after the sheep." "I well recollect," continues the author, "that he convinced me so entirely of that cloud being really a hungry wolf running upon the mountains, that fearing it might, in default of sheep, overtake me, I instantly took to my heels, and escaped precipitately into the house."[2]

---

[1] *Relation de ce qui s'est passé dans la nouvelle France en l'année* 1634, Paris, 1635, pp. 96, 97.

[2] *Zoological Mythology*, London, 1872, vol. i. p. xxiv.

II. THE GENESIS OF THE IDEA OF GOD. 59

You will perhaps maintain that this is simply another proof of the influence of words on the imagination. But in such a case the words are but the vehicle of a thought; and that thought, though suggested to the mind of our young mythologist from outside, might just as well have sprung up spontaneously in his own imagination as in that of another. In any case, we see that it is not necessary, as a certain school of philologists maintains, that before a conscious personality can be ascribed to inanimate things, the primitive sense of the concrete terms applied to them must have been lost. The unwarranted extension of personality which forms the basis of mythology is due, not to a "disease of language," but to a "disease of thought," if, indeed, one may apply such a term to an illusion which enters into the normal development of man.

The testimony of De Gubernatis in this anecdote is the less open to suspicion, inasmuch as it seems to contradict his favourite thesis on the formation of meteorological mythology; for he maintains that the myths in which animals appear as personal and conscious agents were originally histories attributed to clouds to which the names of animals were given, and were afterwards transferred to the terrestrial animals which bore the same name;[1] whereas in this case we have the story of a ferocious beast of earth transferred to the cloud.

Distinction between the personal and the impersonal. According to another hypothesis very commonly received, which I myself long advocated, but which I can hardly defend now in the same unqualified fashion, man

[1] *Op. cit.* pp. xvi sqq.

used to regard everything as living that appealed to his senses with a sufficiently pronounced character of individuality to wake a distinct image in his mind; and it was only after a long series of accumulated experiences that he came to conceive the notion of inanimate things; from which moment his progress consisted in restricting more and more the category of living and personal beings, and increasing that of lifeless things.

In confirmation of this thesis it is urged, first, that the savage personifies everything around him; second, that children look upon the articles of furniture and their playthings as living and reasonable beings; third, that civilized men under the impulse of passion are capable of treating material objects as if they were sensible and responsible agents.

In answer to this last argument, it has been urged that even in our explosions of anger and grief, we never so far lose sight of the distinction between animate and inanimate things, as really to suppose that the reproaches or blows we lavish upon material objects fall upon beings capable of receiving any moral impression. As regards children, it has been observed—and personal observations have inclined me more and more to believe it—that if they talk to their dolls, or strike the table or chair that they have knocked against, it is generally under the influence of ideas first suggested to them by some one else; unless, indeed, it is simply a conscious piece of acting in which their youthful imagination indulges for its own entertainment.

There remains the argument that savages have no conception of the inanimate or the impersonal. The

II. THE GENESIS OF THE IDEA OF GOD. 61

Jesuit missionaries to Canada, in their accounts published in 1635, note that to the Redskin "not only men and animals, but everything else is alive."[1] The facts that we have already dwelt upon seem at first sight to confirm this generalization. But does it really follow that because savages extend the idea of personality in so wild a fashion, that they have no sense at all of the distinction between animate and inanimate? Or does it only follow that they make the distinction in the wrong place?

If we look more closely into the travellers' stories, we shall soon perceive that the savages do not really personify everything without distinction, but only such objects as they select in virtue of their form, their origin, their behaviour, or their association with particular events. To the savage, as to the animal, it is movement which is the sign of life. "The zi (supernatural power)," observes Professor Sayce, in his Lectures on the beliefs of the ancient Babylonians, "was simply that which manifested life, and the test of the manifestation of life was movement."[2] Only we must note, in the first place, that objects may be credited with movement in virtue of highly complex and indirect deductions, as we see from the phenomena of rock and stone worship; and, in the second place, that if any object is supposed to be capable of acting at a distance, even though no spontaneous movement takes place, this is quite enough to carry with it all that is essentially implied in the power

---

[1] Père Lejeune, *Relation de ce qui s'est passé dans la nouvelle France en l'année* 1634, p. 58.

[2] Sayce, *Hibbert Lectures. Religion of Ancient Assyria and Babylonia*, London, 1888, p. 328.

of locomotion.¹ Thus man comes to personify not only everything that he supposes to move, but everything which seems to exercise an influence upon him implying the existence of an active will. "The Indian [in British Guiana]," says Mr. E. F. im Thurn, "is occasionally hurt either by falling on a rock or by the rock falling on him; and in either case he attributes the blame to the rock."² Even so advanced a people as the Athenians present us with the spectacle of the tribunal of the Prytanies condemning to death inanimate objects which had accidentally caused the death of a man.³ An analogous custom is still found amongst certain tribes of Indo-China, where a tree which has caused any one's death must be completely hacked to pieces.⁴

We must not suppose that the savage's investigations into the nature of the creatures about him is inspired by simple curiosity. However exuberant his imagination may be, nothing is less in his line than speculation. With him, everything has a practical end; and in the present instance the end is to form connections, advantageous to himself, with the extra-human beings by which he believes himself to be surrounded. And since he has assigned to these beings motives and

---

[1] "The king of the Koussa Kaffirs having broken off a piece of a stranded anchor, died soon afterwards, upon which all the Kaffirs looked upon the anchor as alive, and saluted it respectfully whenever they passed near it."—Lubbock, *Origin of Civilization*, p. 188.

[2] E. F. im Thurn, *Indians of British Guiana*, in *Journal of the Anthropological Institute*, vol. xi. 1882, p. 370.

[3] Pausanias, i. 28, 10.

[4] Ch. Ploix, *La nature des dieux, étude de mythologie comparée*, Paris, 1888, p. 4.

II. THE GENESIS OF THE IDEA OF GOD.

reasonings analogous to his own, he naturally thinks that he can act upon them by just such measures (hereafter to be enumerated) as would be effective with himself. And, from the other side, he cannot but feel gratitude for their benefits, terror in the face of their wrath, even a certain confidence in their protection, and depression or indignation when deserted by them.

Deity implies superiority and mystery. Now, are all these elements, even when united and combined, enough to constitute religion? The idea that certain beings, whatever their nature, may be of service to us, and that we can secure their help by the same means as are current in human society, even when we add the feelings of hope, fear, gratitude, and anger, provoked by such relations, is no more than what springs out of the mutual relations of men themselves, without its constituting a religion.

Religion, at any rate as I have defined it, implies, in addition to this, something exalted and mysterious in the character of the being adored. Note that the superiority and mystery may be only partial. The being deified may have the advantage over his worshipper only in some one important faculty, or may escape his comprehension under some one aspect only. It has often been said that the savage can have no idea of the supernatural, for the excellent reason that in his eyes everything is natural, even the impossible. The assertion is justified if it means that, having no idea whatever of a regular course of things, he cannot distinguish between what contradicts and what does not contradict such a course; but although he has no notion of the supernatural, he cannot be without an idea of the extraordinary and the unforeseen, or without the power of distinguishing between the facts he understands, or thinks he understands, and those which he considers incomprehensible. Experience has taught him that he increases his power by arming himself with a knotted branch or a chipped flint; that he increases his chances of success in securing game by setting certain traps for animals; that he can cross the river by getting upon the trunk of a tree; and can provide against thirst by keeping water in a clay vessel, baked in the sun. But neither the way in which he gets his implements, nor the result upon which he can rely, has anything extraordinary or mysterious about it. He is dealing with foreseen and forseeable effects, which are dependent on his own will, which he can reproduce indefinitely by means of simple methods of which he knows the secret and feels himself to be the master.

But side by side with all this, which may be considered normal, he comes across phenomena produced by methods which he cannot explain, and by beings which he can neither control nor even understand. Jarvis tells us that when the North American Indian cannot understand a thing, he says it is a spirit.[1] Garcilasso de la Vega informs us that the ancient Peruvians applied the name of *huacas* to "all those things which, from their beauty and excellence, were superior to other things of a like kind;" further, "things that were ugly and monstrous, or that caused horror and fright;" and lastly, "things which

[1] Appendix to J. Buchanan's *History, Manners, and Customs, of the North American Indians*, London, 1824, p. 228.

were out of the usual course of nature."[1] Amongst the Chinese, according to the *Yuen-kien lui-han*, as cited by M. Léon de Rosny, the name of *Chin* is given generally to the producers of clouds and the provokers of wind and rain, and *everything that seems extraordinary* in the mountains, the forests, the rivers, the lakes, the rocks, and the hills.[2] The Todas of central India call their deities *Der*, and Colonel Marshall tells us that amongst them there is a tendency for everything mysterious or unseen to ripen into Der. In the Fiji Islands the word *kalu*, which is used to signify the gods, is also applied to everything great or marvellous.[3] "The Negroes," says a traveller, "worship everything extraordinary and rare." When first the Negroes of the Guinea coast saw a pump on board a European vessel, they thought it a very marvellous creature, "since it could make water rise up whose natural property is to descend."[4]

For the most part, however, the sphere of the extraordinary extends, for the savage, far beyond what we should consider its due limits. It includes, for instance, all the wild animals which excel man in strength, agility, or cunning, and whose proceedings always have something mysterious in them. It includes the plants,

[1] *Royal Commentaries*, bk. ii. chap. iv.; C. R. Markham's translation (Hakluyt Society), London, 1869, 1871, vol. i. p. 116.

[2] Léon de Rosny, *Les origines du Taoisme*, in the *Revue de l'histoire des réligions* for Sept. Oct. 1890, vol. xxii. pp. 171, 172.

[3] T. Williams, *Fiji and the Fijians*, London: Hodder and Stoughton. 1870, p. 183.

[4] Sir John Lubbock, *History of Civilization*, London, 1870, p. 202.

whose slow growth and periodical blossoming depend upon forces alien to the intervention of man. It includes the sun who, defying all interference, pursues his course, dealing out alternate life and death; the moon, that strange and changing being, which the popular imagination is still unable to disentangle from the affairs of our planet; the atmospheric phenomena, beginning with the thunder-storm, whose sinister rumblings throw all animated nature into terror; running waters, that sometimes fertilize and sometimes lay waste, and whose continuous and spontaneous movement nothing can arrest.

There is nothing, even down to the rocks, which may not become an enemy or an ally according to the associations which chance events have thrown round it; nothing which may not acquire a character all the more active and mysterious in proportion to the barriers the imagination has had to pierce in order to draw it into the category of conscious and animated beings. "The Á-shi-wi, or Zuñis," says Mr. Frank Cushing, "suppose the sun, moon, and stars, the sky, earth, and sea, in all their phenomena and elements, and all inanimate objects, as well as plants, animals and men, to belong to one great system of all-conscious and inter-related life, in which the degrees of relationship seem to be determined largely, if not wholly, by the degrees of resemblance. In this system of life the starting-point is man, the most finished, yet the lowest organism; at least, the lowest because most dependent and least mysterious. . . . . The animals . . . . are considered . . . . more nearly related to the gods than is man, because more mysterious. . . . . Again, the elements and phenomena of nature, because more mysterious, powerful, and immortal, seem more closely related to the higher gods than are the animals."[1]

It seems clear that the reason why living man is seldom worshipped is precisely because he is too well known. The only exception is in the case of certain persons withdrawn by the prestige of their authority or their wisdom from the ordinary conditions of humanity—that is to say of savage or primitive humanity. Sir John Lubbock points out that the adoration of the king is only found in cases where he is powerful enough to withdraw himself from the common life.[2] The French say that no one is a hero to his valet-de-chambre; and in the same way we may assert that no one is a god to his familiar companion. The traveller Battel, speaking of a king of Loango who is worshipped as the equal of a god, adds that no one is allowed to see him eat or drink. This is a wise precaution for a royal deity to take.

On the other hand, certain men may be worshipped, even when alive, on account of some extraordinary characteristic which exhibits them in a mysterious light. Thus whites have often been regarded as superhuman beings by the red, yellow, or black savages who see them for the first time. But just the same thing may happen in the case of a hitherto unknown animal, as in Mexico with the horse ridden by Cortez, or on the west coast of Africa with Monteiro's ass. However *ondoyant*

---

[1] *Zuñi Fetiches*, in the *Publications of the Bureau of Ethnology*, "Smithsonian Institute," 1883, vol. ii. p. 9.

[2] *Origin of Civilization*, p. 234.

et divers man may be, he is far less mysterious to the savage than the celestial bodies, trees, or even stones are.

<small>The place of fear in worship.</small> To say mystery is to say fear. Man, like the animals, fears the unknown, even though a kind of fascination draw him towards the object of his terror, that he may learn to give himself some account of it. This two-fold feeling unquestionably lies at the root of religion; and, in this connection, the Latin poet might well say that fear was the first creator of the gods:

> "Primus in orbe deos fecit timor."

But it was not fear alone that created them. It is not only evil that man expects from his deities, nor does he confine his adoration to the maleficent powers of nature. Nature herself has always a two-fold aspect, the one fruitful and propitious, the other cruel and destructive, both reflected in one of her most complete and transparent personifications, the great goddess of the Phœnicians:

> "Diva Astarte hominum deorumque vita salus
> Rursus eadem quæ es pernicies mors interitus."

If man dreads the beings who may injure him, why should he not be equally capable of hope, trust, love, and gratitude, towards those from whom he hopes to receive benefits or has already received them. Whether we turn to the most rudimentary or the most elaborate religions, we always find the superhuman powers, taken collectively, arousing sentiments at once of dread and of attraction in the worshipper. The former may sink to the most abject terror, the latter may rise to the most

II. THE GENESIS OF THE IDEA OF GOD.

exalted love; but, in whatever proportions, they always combine to produce what we mean by *veneration*.

No doubt man may disentangle this mingled character of his deities. But whenever he conceives of certain superhuman beings as absolutely evil, you may be certain that he will counterbalance them with others that are absolutely good, even if, for obvious reasons, he devotes his chief attention to the former. One can conceive Ormuzd without Ahriman, and the Persian theology looks forward to the time when the latter shall be destroyed; but no one ever conceived Ahriman without Ormuzd, even amongst the sects who reserve their homage for Ahriman on the ground that Ormuzd does not need it.

You perceive that the sense of dependence is not enough to produce religion; otherwise man would have to adore everything that he is dependent on, from his own limbs down to the force of gravitation which prevents his forthwith knocking his head against the stars of heaven. As M. Réville observes, the sense of dependence furnishes no issue from opposition and antithesis, whereas the very purpose of religion is so to harmonize opposition as to solve the antithesis.[1] The religious sentiment is not fully satisfied until man feels himself one with his deities.

The sense of the Infinite as a factor in Religion. On the other hand, neither is the sense of mystery, of the great Beyond, the Infinite, the Supra-sensible, enough in itself to produce religion, unless man assigns some positive content to this purely negative conception. The savage standing

[1] A. Réville, *Prolégomènes de l'histoire des religions*, Paris, 1881, pp. 25, 26.

on his coral island, to take Professor Max Müller's example, might have speculated to his heart's content on what there lay beyond the horizon, but he could hardly have worshipped that invisible continuation of the tossing ocean or the azure firmament, had he not attributed to it the power of interposing in his own affairs. I am ready to admit that the perception of the finite really implies the conception of the infinite; but it is only a relatively advanced philosophy which succeeds in making the implicit idea explicit; and if the savage speculates on what lies beyond—whether that "Beyond," the boundaries of which he cannot apprehend, stretch behind the sights of nature or retreat within the inner consciousness of beings—it is only because he suspects the existence in it of a power with which he is, or can be, in some actual relation.

I ought to add, however, that the eminent Indian scholar whose views I am discussing has done much in his recent Gifford Lectures to meet the objections which have been urged, in this connection, against the definition of religion which he gave from the Chair which I have the honour of occupying at this moment. "The infinite *per se*, as a mere negative, would have had no interest for primitive man; but as the background, as the support, as the subject or the cause of the finite in its many manifestations, it came in from the earliest period of human thought."[1] To put this explanation above the reach of criticism, it is only necessary to insist on the part played by the practical element in the

[1] F. Max Müller, *Natural Religion*: the *Gifford Lectures* for 1888: London, 1889, p. 149.

II. THE GENESIS OF THE IDEA OF GOD.

genesis of religion—that is to say, the influences which the mysterious agents thus deified were supposed to exercise upon human affairs, and man's desire to enter into such relations with them as might turn to his own advantage.[1]

Confusion of concomitance and causality. Amongst the factors which contributed most actively towards increasing the number of the primitive deities we must give the first rank to the confusion of concomitance, or rather succession, with causality, together with the assimilation of dreams to reality.

Post hoc, ergo propter hoc, is man's first argument as he endeavours to get at the reason of things. Do we not, in our own day, hear causation defined by the most advanced psychologists as "a constant and uniform relation of succession"? The savage omits the qualifications of uniformity and constancy, or at best accepts a few accidental repetitions as enough. That is all the difference, but it is vital.

Roemer tells us of a Negro who once showed him a stone, amongst his domestic fetishes, to which he attached great value, because he once stumbled against it at the threshold of his hut as he was setting out on an important expedition. Mr. E. F. im Thurn says of the Indian of British Guiana: "If his eye falls on a rock in any way abnormal or curious—and none such escapes his notice—and if, shortly after, any evil happens to him, he regards rock and evil as cause and effect: and here

[1] The succeeding volume of *Gifford Lectures*, viz. *Physical Religion*, London, 1891, has contributed still further towards dispelling the misconception.

again he perceives a spirit in the rock."[1] This explains how peoples so far distant from each other as the Finns and the Redskins, can unite in attributing the fertilizing showers of spring to the cuckoo; for the former accompany or closely follow the latter. Perhaps this same coincidence explains the origin of the Cretan myth in which Jupiter transforms himself into a cuckoo to impregnate Juno.

This tendency to attribute events to some phenomenon with which they are associated, but with which they have really nothing to do, recurs amongst all uncivilized peoples—civilized peoples, too, for that matter, as is testified by the "fetishes" of gamesters in our own days, and other similar superstitions.—But this idea of the good or ill luck attached to some talisman is not in itself in any way religious, and it is a mistake to place the origin of religion in fetishism so understood. It is all very well to declare that the deity grew out of the amulet, but we have to be shown how men passed from one idea to the other; and here our teachers, in their turn, point to a concomitance in lieu of a cause. The idea that a material object can exercise a certain influence or produce certain events in virtue of some mysterious connection it has with them, can only be called a religious belief when this connection is ascribed to the intervention of a superhuman being incorporated in the object or using it as its tool. The Negroes themselves distinguish between their fetishes (gris-gris, jou-jou, mokissos), which they regard as superhuman beings, or rather as *possessed* by such, and their amulets, or talismans

[1] *Journal of the Anthropological Institute*, vol. xi. p. 370.

II. THE GENESIS OF THE IDEA OF GOD.

proper (mondas), which they do not regard as living and conscious.[1] But who does not see that this already presupposes a belief that such superhuman beings exist?

It is easy to understand how, when once the idea of mysterious superhuman personalities has been formulated in the imagination, this unwarranted extension of causality may indefinitely increase the number of the gods. Any conceivable object may happen to be associated with any conceivable event, and so may come to be regarded as its cause. Then follows, by a process already familiar to the human mind, the personification of that cause; and the primitive pantheon is enriched by a new god.

The assimilation of dreams to reality. The fantastic associations which occur in dreams contribute to the result as much as the real associations which casually occur in the waking life. Animals dream, but do not remember their dreams; the savage not only remembers them, but believes they are actual experiences. Travellers are all agreed on this point, and it would be wearisome to repeat the proofs of the fact, since it is not contested. The places which he has visited, the things which he has seen, the people he has talked to—in a word, all the details of his dreams, appear to the savage as real after he has awaked as they did while he was dreaming. If some of these people or things have played the part he is accustomed to assign to his gods, why should he hesitate to rank them henceforth amongst the superhuman powers which he must conciliate or serve?

[1] Compare du Chaillu, *Transactions of the Ethnological Society*, London, 1861, vol. i. p. 307.

In brief, under the action of this two-fold influence, the savage ends by deifying everything in nature. This is the stage at which, as Bossuet puts it, "everything was a god except God himself." In truth, whether we take the savage of our own time or his pre-historic counterpart, the difficulty is not to say what he worships, but to find anything that escapes his adoration.

The function of the first deities. The same associations, real or imaginary, which have thus indefinitely multiplied the number of the gods, have also served considerably to extend the sphere of action originally attributed to each of them. Men probably began by demanding of each being or each object which they had deified only those services which it was really suited to render in virtue of its actual nature. Thus they invoked the sun for warmth or fertilization; the moon, to dissipate the darkness; the spring, to slake or inflict thirst; the cloud, to drop its waters or to drift away; the wind, not to throw down the hut; the tree, to bear abundant fruit; ferocious beasts, to spare the life and property of the suppliant. But one day it was observed that the clouds before breaking gathered round a certain peak. It was this mountain then that made the rain. At the moment of the full moon the savage would fall ill; it was the full moon then which had sent his disease, and which could therefore take it away. As he started out on a successful hunting expedition he met a serpent; serpents then had the power of securing game; and if they could bring success in the chase, why not in war and other enterprizes as well? Or the savage had dreamed that the sun made him promises or presents;

II. THE GENESIS OF THE IDEA OF GOD.

this must have happened, and therefore might happen again. Another night he had seen a neighbouring rock change itself into a roaring lion, and hurl itself upon the enemies of the tribe; henceforth he will know where to turn in order to secure victory.

Here is an example in which the dream combines with a purely accidental coincidence as a factor in the result. M. E. de Backer, in his work on the Indian Archipelago, tells us of a native who had found a stone covered with small fishes, and next night saw a genius in his sleep. This genius told him that he was the stone itself, and that if he received due homage he would send him abundance of fish. The author adds that the fetishes or idols of the Dyaks—scraps of wood or stone, hollow crocodiles' teeth, little figures painted on sticks, human statuettes cut in bark—were almost always made in consequence of some dream in which the native had seen a gigantic "Kambi" or a hairy and terrible "Antung" appear.[1] In the same way, Mr. Powell tells us that amongst the Redskins every Indian "is provided with his charm or fetish, revealed to him in some awful hour of ecstacy, produced by fasting, or feasting, or drunkenness."[2]

Thus men not only come to deify all manner of different beings, but to invest them with powers so varied and so extensive that they no longer know what superhuman being they may not require under any given

[1] Valentyn, cited by De Backer, *L'Archipel Indien*, Paris, 1874, p. 222.

[2] Powell, *Myths of the North-American Indians*, in the *Publications of the Bureau of Ethnology*, "Smithsonian Institute," 1881, vol. i. p. 41.

circumstances; and in doubtful cases nine gods out of ten are ready to aid the worshipper, as the Californian savage gave to understand when he was asked what it was he muttered in order to secure the recovery of a sick man, and answered: "I talk to the trees, and to the springs, and birds, and sky, and rocks, to the wind, and rain, and leaves; I beg them all to help me."[1] "The cold has spoken to me," cries the author of the song which serves as a prelude to the Finnish Kalevala, "and the rain has told me her runes; the winds of heaven, the waves of the sea, have spoken and sung to me; the wild birds have taught me, the music of many waters has been my master."[2]

Might one not fancy one was listening to the premature echo of a great contemporary poet who calls every detail of nature to bear witness to his vanished joy?

> O lac, rochers muets, grottes, forêt obscure,
> . . . .
> Que tout ce qu'on entend, l'on voit ou l'on respire
> Tout dise : Ils ont aimé ![3]

But what is mere play of imagination or figure of speech in the modern poet, is to his savage contemporary of to-day, and was to the primitive savage of ancient times, the expression of a general belief in the animation of all nature and the possibility of entering into relations with its personified manifestations.

---

[1] Bancroft, *Native Races of the Pacific States*, 1875, vol. i. pp. 358, 359.

[2] Kalevala, chant i. As quoted in A. Lang's *Custom and Myth*, London, 1884, p. 165.

[3] Lamartine, *Le Lac*.

II. THE GENESIS OF THE IDEA OF GOD. 77

The belief in the reality of dreams acts on the development of religious ideas in yet another direction, as we see from the conception of the "double" and the idea of survival.

The idea of the "double." The man who in his dreams has just encountered the most extraordinary adventures, wakes again in the very spot and in the very position which he occupied when he fell asleep. He remembers having traversed immense spaces, accomplished difficult enterprizes, perhaps received blows or wounds, and yet his limbs, far from being fatigued, have found fresh strength and subtlety. He has just been conversing with individuals who will deny the existence of the interview, and in case of need will support their denial by an incontestable *alibi*, and perhaps he himself will pay them back in their own coin of denial the next day. Hence the only possible explanation—an explanation which must present itself spontaneously to the mind of the savage as soon as he endeavours to remember his dreams and to give himself some account of them—is that man is composed of two parts, one in some way enclosed in the other—one external, formed of the body which remains stationary during sleep; the other internal, which could cast the body like a garment and go its way, as the Greenlander expressed it, "to hunt, dance, and pay calls."

The Australian Kurnai who was asked whether he really believed that his *yambo* could "go out" while he was asleep, immediately answered: "It must be so, for when I sleep I go to distant places, I see distant people;

I even see and speak with those that are dead."[1] We have but to open the first treatise on ethnography that comes to hand, and we shall see that the same reasoning prevails amongst the Negroes, Kaffirs, Polynesians, Redskins, Greenlanders, and natives of South America. At the outside, some of them, such as the Karens of Burmah, have observed that in dreams one can only visit the places and people one has already known. Some peoples, such as the Tagals of Luçon, refuse to wake a sleeping man suddenly, because, they say, you must give his soul time to get into its abode again.

Here we see an opposition beginning to shape itself between the body and what we have come to call the soul. The savage is doubtless far from regarding his interior personality as an immaterial entity, conceived by force of abstraction, and reduced to a pure psychic force. He can conceive neither a being nor a force except under a material, or at any rate a sensible, form; he will therefore endow his *ego* with the traits under which his own personality and that of his companions appear in his dreams. It will thus be a reduction, or rather a reflexion of the body, vaguer, paler, half-effaced. This is what has been called the *double*, identified by many peoples with the shadow produced by the body, with its reflexion in water, with its image seen in the pupil of the eye, and so forth.

The sorcerers of Greenland describe the soul as a pale soft thing, without nerves, without bones, with-

[1] W. Howitt, *On some Australian Beliefs*: in the *Journal of the Anthropological Institute*, 1884, vol. xiii. p. 189.

out flesh. When one would seize it, one feels nothing. Is not this exactly the *animula vagula blandula, hospes, comesque corporis*, under the traits of which Hadrian conceived his own spiritual principle?[1] And in our own day, too, does not the description precisely correspond to the physiognomy of the spirits which our mediums profess to bring before us?

Worship of the dead.
This "double" of the personality has no religious significance in itself; but the deductions drawn from it go much beyond its mere existence. Amongst the beings with whom the savage enters into communication in his dreams, some have passed from life. Perhaps he himself has slain, not to say eaten, them! What conclusion can he arrive at but that man does not altogether die, and that the disappearance of the body does not involve that of the "double"? Thus when Achilles has clasped the shade of Patroclus and has seen it dissolve under his embrace like smoke, he does not fail to cry, "Verily, there is a certain soul and semblance even in the abode of Hades, though substance there be none."[2]

Animals do not appear to have arrived at the abstract idea of death. Primitive man, too, must have begun by confounding death with sleep, fainting and catalepsy. Hence the efforts to revive the corpse and ensure its preservation which we find even amongst the animals,

---

[1] Ælius Spartianus, *adrianus*, cap. 25. In the *Scriptores Historiæ Augustæ*.

[2] *Iliad*, xxiii. 103, 104. ψυχὴ καὶ εἴδωλον· ἀτὰρ φρένες οὐκ ἔνι πάμπαν. The word φρένες must be taken in its physical sense, midriff, vitals, substance or body.

and which survive in the customs of many peoples long after the idea of death has established itself in their minds. Even in the times of Marco Polo the Mongols sometimes kept their corpses as long as six months, and offered them food every day.[1] Obviously it was the dissolution of the body which finally revealed the difference between the apparent suspension and the definitive cessation of the vital functions.

The *double*, however, continued in the neighbourhood of the living, and maintained relations with them during sleep. According to some, such as the Yorubas of Western Africa and the Veddahs of Ceylon—it is the dead who come to visit the living; according to others, like the Maoris of New Zealand, it is the living who go to visit the dead. Again, the *double* has mysterious powers in dreams which it does not possess, or possesses in a less degree, when united to the body. It can assume the most diverse and terrible forms, can transport itself, or can act at a distance, with the rapidity of lightning—in a word, can produce results absolutely disproportioned to its previous powers, and that too by the most extraordinary means. Polynesians sometimes kill themselves in order that, when in the spiritual state, they may be able to take a fuller vengeance on a powerful enemy.[2] The same thing has been observed amongst the Hindus, who have likewise been known to kill some

---

[1] *The Book of Ser Marco Polo*, by H. Yule, second edition: London, 1875, vol. i. p. 208.

[2] Gerland, quoted by Réville, *Religions des peuples non-civilisés*, vol. ii. p. 92. May we not trace a survival of the same practice in the *point d'honneur* of the Japanese who kill themselves when insulted?

chance-met victim in order to get the assistance of his spirit. The case is reported of a Brahman who slew his mother so that her spirit could catch and punish a thief. M. Letourneau says that on the Congo likewise the son often kills his mother to secure the assistance of her soul, now a formidable spirit.[1] The Alfurus of Molacca bury children up to their waists, and expose them to all the tortures of thirst, until they wrench from them the promise to hurl themselves upon the enemies of the village. Then they take them out, but only to kill them on the spot, imagining that the spirits of the victims will respect their last promise.[2] On the other hand, Philander Prescott says that amongst the Redskins fear of the departed spirits often prevents murder more effectually than the fear of hanging does amongst white peoples.[3]

Relations of nature-worship and the worship of the dead. In any case, the *double* thus conceived unites in itself all the characteristics of those superhuman beings whom the savage believes to exist in nature, whom he endeavours to conciliate by the methods in vogue in his relations with the great ones of the earth, and whom he surrounds with testimonies of his affection and dread.

Did the worship of the dead precede or follow the worship of natural objects and personified phenomena? It is possible that in certain localities the worship of the dead manifested itself the first, or that the two

[1] *Sociologie*, pp. 240, 241; Eng. trans. p. 253.

[2] Rosenberg, *Der Malayische Archipel*, Leipzig, 1878, pp. 59, 60.

[3] In H. R. Schoolcraft, *Indian Tribes of the United States*, Philadelphia, 1851—1860, part ii. pp. 195, 196.

conceptions formed themselves *pari passu*, with a preponderance of the one or the other. It seems that in China the worship of ancestors grafted itself upon a previous nature-worship. Amongst the Polynesians it has been successfully established that the worship of the dead, native to the eastern archipelagos, sporadically overlaid the ancient mythological nature-worship, while it hardly penetrated into the most western islands of Micronesia.[1]

All I maintain is that neither of these two forms of worship necessarily presupposes the other; but that man, having been led by different routes to personify the souls of the dead on the one hand, and natural objects and phenomena on the other, subsequently attributed to both alike the character of mysterious superhuman beings. Let us add that this must have taken place everywhere, for there is not a people on earth in which we do not come upon these two forms of belief side by side and intermingled.

(ii.) PRIMITIVE RITES.

We have now to supplement the picture of primitive beliefs by that of primitive rites; that is to say, the *acts* which man's primitive conception of the superhuman beings and his relations with them led him to perform.

Probably the cultus was originally extremely simple. When the chief objects of nature are looked upon as quasi-human personalities, the man who desires their support will evidently approach them as experience has taught him to approach the mundane powers. Obviously, then,

[1] A. Réville, in the *Revue de l'histoire des Religions*, 1882 (vol. iv.), p. 16.

II. THE GENESIS OF THE IDEA OF GOD. 83

the request must be couched in the terms most calculated to persuade; and usually a present, or at any rate definite promises, must be added. And such are the motives actually revealed in prayer and sacrifice, or rather—to escape the misleading associations of the mystic sense often given to these terms—let us say, of petition and offering.

Prayer. Prayer at first is and can be nothing more than the demand for wealth and favours, beginning with the things most indispensable to existence, such as our "daily bread." I do not suppose there is a single tribe in which prayer of this nature is unknown, for all have something to gain from the superhuman powers. "Be greeted!" say the Hottentots to the new moon. "Let us get much honey!" "May our cattle get much to eat, and give much milk!"[1] Soon, however, the circle of requirements expands. Supplications are offered to the superhuman beings—often in identical terms by the most widely separated peoples—to make the rain fall, to put diseases to flight, to appease the storm, or to secure victory over enemies. "Great Quahootze!" cries the Nootka Indian, "let me live, not be sick, find the enemy, not fear him, find him asleep, and kill a great many of him."[2] You perceive that anything like a moral idea, or even a feeling of chivalry, is absolutely wanting at this stage of religious education. The suppliants do not even take the trouble, as they would do later on, to transform the national enemy into an enemy

---

[1] Tylor, *Primitive Culture*, vol. ii. p. 272.

[2] Brinton, *Myths of the New World*, second edition, p. 316: New York, 1876.

of the gods, in order to justify the demand for their intervention. Their help is secured by the best offer.

<small>Sacrifice.</small> The primitive theory of sacrifice answers to the same ideas. The Karens of Burmah go so far as to say that it is useless to demand anything of the gods without at the same time giving a proof of generosity; and in the interior of Africa, where the custom of *hongo* prevails (a toll more or less forcibly levied by the petty local chieftains on travellers), the Negro declares that you must never pass before the abode of a spirit without leaving a sacrifice, if it is but a little spittle.[1] The Negroes of Sierra Leone offer cattle in order "to make god glad very much, and do Kroomen good."[2]

> Munera, crede mihi, capiunt hominesque, deosque
> Placatur donis Jupiter ipse datis.[3]

How many people, civilized though they be, are still at this point in their conception of worship! Worship indeed is to them but a contract entered into on the principle "do ut des," in which man serves the gods in consideration of a reciprocity formally or tacitly accepted by them. We read in an Indian hymn addressed to the sacrificial spoon: "Well filled, O Spoon, descend below; well filled, ascend towards us, as at a price agreed. Let us exchange strength and vigour: give me, I give to thee; bring me, I bring to thee."[4] All this is naïve

---

[1] J. L. Wilson, *Western Africa*, p. 218.

[2] R. Clarke, *Sierra Leone*, p. 43; cited by Tylor, *Primitive Culture*, vol. ii. p. 394.

[3] Ovid, *Ars Amatoria*, iii. 653, 654.

[4] *Taittirîya Samhita*, i. 8, 4, 1.

enough; but as an example of the length to which men may go on this path, we note the following passage from the Taittiriya Samhita of the Yajur Veda: "If you wish to injure any one, say to Surya, 'Smite such a one, and I will give you an offering;' and Surya, to get the offering, will smite him."[1] Here the god descends to the level of a vulgar *bravo*, and lets himself out to a man whom the ideas of our own time would stigmatize as a contemptible craven. Yet this is the very Surya, "god amongst gods," who, according to the Rig Veda, "departs not from the right path." For the rest, there is not a religion in the whole of antiquity in which the deity allows negligence or parsimony in the matter of offerings to go unpunished. Did not the Brahmans go the length of proclaiming that the huge universe was created for the sake of sacrifice?

We can trace back, in the same fashion, the motives which underlie the other forms of sacrifice. When subjects have obtained a favour of their chief, they reward him by making him a present. This is the thank-offering. When they think he is enraged, they offer a gift to appease him. This is the sacrifice of propitiation. If they have really injured him, they attempt to disarm his wrath by paying a fine, or inflicting a penalty on themselves. This is the sacrifice of expiation.

Man naturally offers his deities what he believes is most necessary to them, or what he imagines will please them most. First comes food. Gods, however, like men, when once their appetite is satisfied, have more refined tastes to gratify. The Negro offers strong drinks to his

[1] *Taittiriya Samhita*, vi. 4, 5, 6.

deities; the Siberian, furs; the Redskin and the Ostiak, tobacco. The idea that in the other world the same wants are experienced as in this, is evinced by the character of the sacrifices offered to their dead by all the peoples of the earth; and the gods, whatever the origin attributed to them, form a community, the conditions of whose existence are hardly conceived, at a certain stage of religion, to differ materially from those of the souls of the defunct.

Human sacrifices appear to us the most absurd and abominable of all; yet there is not a people that has not practised this custom at some period or other of its history. Hindus, Egyptians, Chinese, Greeks, Romans, even Israelites, differ, in this matter, from the Negroes of our own times in nothing save the object they assign to this kind of sacrifice.

The aim is sometimes to assure to the distinguished dead the continuance of the services which had been rendered them in this world by the slaves and women slaughtered at their tombs; sometimes—as with the Polynesians, whose gods are particularly greedy of human flesh—it is to offer the present most worthy of the divine majesty, if not most agreeable to the celestial palate.

Intimidation of the gods. Good-will, however, is not the only sentiment on which one can rely in seeking to extort benefits from one's equals or one's superiors. Even the most powerful of men are sometimes susceptible to fear. Attempts will therefore be made to intimidate the superhuman beings by threatening words or gestures, with the view of extracting a favour from them or averting their wrath. When the storm rages, the peasant of the Palatinate offers the wind a handful of meal to appease it; but it is not every race that is so good-natured. The Payaguas of Brazil rush to meet the tempest, brandishing lighted torches. The Botocudos of Brazil and the Namaquas of Kaffirland shoot arrows at it. The Negroes of the Gold Coast and the Papuans of Malaynesia throw offerings into the sea to calm it; but the Guanches lash it with cords, just as Xerxes beat the Hellespont with rods for dispersing his fleet. To this very day, our peasants employ the same two-fold method with their saints. No doubt at a more advanced stage of civilization such attempts at intimidation are confined to the inferior spirits, the souls of the dead, the saints, and the demons; but at first the distinctions of the superhuman hierarchy are too fluctuating and undetermined to offer any obstacle to the general application of such methods. Does not Herodotus tell us that the Getæ shoot arrows at the Heaven itself?[1] Yet surely this deity, if any, must be above all violence.

Sorcery.   Side by side with these attempts to influence the will of the superhuman beings indirectly, we observe others intended to act directly upon them. There is no potentate on earth so great that he cannot be brought to reason by a stronger than himself, and forced to surrender his power to his conqueror. Now the gods are generally exempt from physical coercion—except in the case of fetishism, where the spirit lodged in the object is henceforth the slave of him who possesses it;—but since the gods have mys-

[1] iv. 94.

terious means of making their power felt, man asks whether he, in his turn, cannot act upon them by analogous methods. The only difficulty is to find them out. Hence the practices of sorcery which, as one would expect, are as numerous as they are bizarre— from the 'cat's concert,' to which all uncivilized peoples, without exception, have recourse, to put to flight the assailant of the sun and moon in an eclipse, down to the sorceries of vulgar magic and the evocations of fashionable spiritualism in our midst.

We need not enter upon a course of comparative sorcery; but it is not beside the mark to point out a few examples of the reappearance in all ages and in every part of the world of certain rudimentary conceptions as to the means of forcing certain courses upon the superhuman powers. There is not a nation that has not believed in the efficacy of incantations; there is none that has not made use of lustrations, or that has not kindled fires to put the demons to flight, or to hinder the dead from tormenting the living.

It is especially on its pseudo-medical side that sorcery has had free scope. According as diseases are attributed by savage peoples to the departure of the soul or to the entry into the body of a spirit that does not belong to it, the treatment will aim, now at bringing back the soul into its envelope, now at expelling the spirit to which the evil is due. And this is effected by processes which present a strange resemblance amongst the Negroes, the Siberians, the Australians, the Japanese, the Chinese, the natives of India, and those of the two Americas.

Sometimes it is deemed essential to make the spirit

II. THE GENESIS OF THE IDEA OF GOD. 89

thus expelled pass into the body of a living being, a pebble, a scrap of wood, or some object which can be thrown away, or perhaps into a rag suspended to a branch or a nail fixed into the trunk of a tree.

It is a corollary of these beliefs that a malady may be inflicted on a man by compelling a spirit to enter into his body. In this connection we note, in the first place, the practice of wounding or destroying a figure made in the likeness of the intended victim. This custom, very common in our Middle Ages, was previously known to the Chaldæans and Greeks, and is still employed by the Hindus, the Negroes of the Congo, and the Chippeways of North America. Next comes the bewitching of some object which has previously belonged in an intimate manner to the enemy whose destruction is sought—a lock of his hair, the parings of his nails, his footprints, sometimes even his proper name. This superstition, which we meet with amongst the Negroes, the Kaffirs, the Patagonians, the Redskins, the Polynesians, and various branches of the Indo-European race, implies, besides the belief that death, like disease, is the result of enchantment, the idea that the part is equivalent to the whole, and that we may reach the person by means of his representation or his possessions.

Side by side with the magic processes affecting human health may be placed, as of equal importance, those intended to influence atmospheric phenomena, and particularly the production of rain. Amongst the Redskins the sorcerer is known as the medicine-man, but amongst the Kaffirs he is called the rain-doctor. I have already had occasion to point out the identity of certain processes employed to secure rain amongst the most widely separated peoples. The Bushman strives to obtain rain by driving the hippopotamus—the amphibious animal *par excellence*—over the fields; and in doing so he acts from the same motives which lead the Negro to throw pitchers into the river, the Aryan to pour the sacred juice of the *soma* upon the altar, the Samoans, the Apaches, the Keramins of New South Wales, the Britons and the Welsh to besprinkle certain magic stones, or the peoples in Southern Europe to plunge their saints into the river. In Russia, the sorcerer, or occasionally the priest, has to undergo this compulsory bath in person if he fails to secure the rain.[1]

All these analogies are explained by the fact that the processes of sorcery are generally the result, not of a simple caprice, but of some association between two facts or two objects. Such is the power of logic, that even at the bottom of unreason itself there is ever found a spice of reason,—or at any rate of reasoning.

The same remark applies to the methods of divination by which man seeks to penetrate the secrets of the superhuman beings. The belief that all events of any considerable consequence result from the will of the deities, carries with it the idea that that will must be determined and formulated more or less in advance of the event. Hence the desire to penetrate to it beforehand, and to take advantage of the knowledge so gained. And here the confusion between concomitance and causality has free scope. For the rest, divination at the outset is no more than a branch of sorcery.

[1] An. Leroy Beaulieu, *L'Empire des Tsars*: tom iii. *La Religion*, Paris, 1889, p. 284.

II. THE GENESIS OF THE IDEA OF GOD.

Symbolism.
Finally, we must bear in mind that man, experiencing, as I have shown above, a mixed feeling of fear and trust towards his deities, ever dreads them, as one dreads the unknown, but at the same time seeks to draw near to them and realize a closer union with them. Hence a series of attempts to seal an alliance with the gods by some external act, to live their life or become assimilated to their nature, from the sacrificial banquets in which the savage is supposed to partake of the food offered to the spirits, up to his elaborate attempts to imitate their deeds and exploits. When these attempts are supposed to have a direct and forceful action on the superhuman beings, they come under the category of conjurations; but when they are simply intended to simulate the presence of some deity, to reproduce his movements, or to represent the relations the worshipper desires to enter into with him, then they are symbols and come under the category of homage rendered to the divinity. Symbolism—that is to say, the representation of an idea by an action or by an object which recalls it, in virtue of a natural or conventional association—is found even at the lowest stages of religious evolution. I would classify symbols as subjective, when their object is to express any shade of sentiment; figurative, when they directly represent a being or an abstract quality itself; and imitative, when they aim at reproducing the supposed acts of the real or imaginary being.

Figurative symbols, aiming at representing the deity or one of his attributes, can hardly be expected before a people has reached the conception of the deity as distinct from material beings or things. Subjective symbols, on the contrary, are found even amongst the most backward peoples. They may be divided into symbols of submission, of distress, of repentance, of joy, of love, and so forth—if, indeed, any enumeration can exhaust material as diverse as the religious sentiment itself in all its most delicate shades. Sometimes these symbols consist in a conscious reproduction of the attitude which man spontaneously assumes under the domination of the sentiments he wishes to simulate or to express—groaning, leaping for joy, throwing kisses with the hand, falling flat upon the belly before the object of adoration, covering the head with cinders, and so on. And here, as in hypnotism, it often happens that the very fact of impressing on the members and the features the characteristic pose of a given emotion tends to produce it in the consciousness. Sometimes men attempt to express their spiritual state by the use of certain colours or the display of certain objects. In general, black is a colour of ill augury; white, the emblem of joy; but there are exceptions, notably in the case of the Negroes, who paint the images of their dead white because the spirits appear to them in a palish form. Finally, an elaborated symbolism, such as the language of plants and flowers, is sometimes found even amongst quite primitive peoples. The Tahitians plant leafless shave-grass on the tombs as the symbol of death; and other peoples equally backward symbolize their faith in the continuation of life by evergreen plants.

Amongst the races who worship personified natural phenomena, imitative symbolism chiefly consists in repro-

II. THE GENESIS OF THE IDEA OF GOD. 93

ducing the course of such phenomena as the phases of the moon, the movements of the planets and constellations, the death and resurrection of the sun, the contests of the luminous sky with the storm-cloud, the mysteries of germination and of generation, or the production of fire on earth and in heaven. Hence the considerable place occupied by dancing in savage rites. Elsewhere, death and resurrection are reproduced in pantomime as an affirmation of belief in survival after death. Thus certain Australian tribes celebrate initiatory rites in which one of the neophytes lies on the ground whilst the rest cover him with dust, after which he rises again amidst general rejoicings.[1]

Did conjuration precede propitiation ? The question has been much discussed whether worship sprang from sorcery, or sorcery from worship. You will now understand that this controversy is absolutely otiose. Conjurations and propitiations have probably been practised, though at first with ill-defined and vaguely marked distinctions, from the day when man first felt the need of putting himself in communication with the personified forces of nature. Even amongst the most backward peoples we find this two-fold category of actions, intended on the one hand to conciliate and on the other to compel the superhuman powers. This explains the complex nature of worship, which sometimes tempts us to despair of the possibility of retracing its psychological origins. This also explains the difficulty of determining in what category to place

[1] J. Bonwick, *The Australian Natives*, in the *Journal of the Anthropological Institute*, vol. xv. 1886, p. 206.

certain acts which partake, or may partake, at once of the character of homage, of symbolism, and of conjuration. For instance, when we see the Abipones of South America and the Negroes of Central Africa performing dances in imitation of the movements of the celestial bodies, how are we to know whether the rite rests on the belief that they can compel the stars to pursue their periodic course,[1] or on the desire to drink in their life and so share their destiny and power, or on the belief that they are helping them in the accomplishment of their task, or on the simple wish to pay them homage and give them satisfaction by the "sincerest flattery" of imitation? Not one of these notions is above or beyond the range of ideas which permeate the lower levels of civilization, as we may see by studying the complicated ceremonial observed by savages towards their gods and their chiefs, or even in their intercourse one with another. It is well to note that all these ideas reappear amongst peoples as advanced as the Aztecs, the ancient Egyptians, the Hindus, and even the Greeks.

A closely connected question is that of priority as between the priest and the sorcerer. The probability is that at first every man was his own priest and his own sorcerer; that is to say, he alternately invoked or conjured the superhuman beings, varying his methods according to the degree of power which he attributed to them or the nature of the service he expected of them.

---

[1] It is a common idea amongst savages that to prefigure an event assures its occurrence; hence the veritable pantomimes in which the Redskins represent the capture of game or the defeat of the enemy before starting on the chase or the war-path.

II. THE GENESIS OF THE IDEA OF GOD.

Little by little, a first line of demarcation was established between the religious operations which can be performed by any one, and those which require special preparation or even a special temperament. Every one continued freely to put himself into relations with the superhuman beings by whom he supposed himself to be surrounded, as is still the case with savages; but the paterfamilias began to sacrifice on behalf of his family and in honour of the most formidable or the most respected powers. Finally, the still undistinguished functions of the diviner, sorcerer and doctor, were assigned to individuals singled out for their performance by the command of more or less real information, or by a predisposition to hysteria, which is easily taken for inspiration.

In this sense it is quite correct to say that the priesthood, properly so called, issued from the domestic cultus, not from sorcery. But cultus and sorcery alike proceeded from a religious state in which their respective practices were indifferently conducted by any one, without need of special qualification. For that matter, the differentiation was never absolute. There are cases in which sorcery remains the appanage of the chief, and others in which the sorcerer takes advantage of his prestige to make himself the priest *par excellence*. We shall see that even in the bosom of the most highly developed religions the priest never completely renounces the practices of sorcery; but it is with the assistance of the higher divinities, and no longer in virtue of his personal power, that he now practises his exorcisms; and they are directed exclusively against evil spirits. Be that as it may, whatever solution we adopt as to the priority of these two institutions, it will affect neither our point of departure nor our conclusion, nor even, as we shall presently see, our view of the intermediate development of the religious sentiment.

LECTURE III.
POLYDEMONISM AND POLYTHEISM.

(i.) SPIRITISM, FETISHISM, AND IDOLATRY.

WE have seen that the worship of natural objects springs from the arbitrary extension of human personality to every apparent source of life or even of movement. If this explanation is correct, it follows that, from the very first, worship must have been addressed, not to the material object conceived as such, but to the personality supposed to be embodied in it; although this vague and instinctive appeal to beings psychologically modelled after man did not necessarily imply a conscious distinction between the internal personality and its envelope or body.

Worship addressed to the personality of things. At first sight, indeed, it might often seem that savages worship the objects themselves, without reference to any spiritual attribute. Prescott reports that the Dacotah will choose a round stone at hazard, place it on the turf, then offer it tobacco or feathers, and pray to it to avert some real or imaginary danger.[1] In the Hawaian islands, Mr. Andrew Lang informs us, the native enters upon athletic competitions, provided with a stone that he has chosen on a certain beach of the Archipelago. If he is victorious,

[1] Cited by Lubbock, *Origin of Civilization*, p. 212.

he will treat it as a god; if not, he will throw it away or make an axe-head of it.[1] The same custom is found in Africa. "If," said an intelligent Negro to the traveller Bosman, "any of us is resolved to undertake anything of importance, we first of all search out a god to prosper our designed undertaking; and going out of doors with this design, take the first creature that presents itself to our eyes, whether dog, cat, or the most contemptible animal in the world, for our god; or perhaps, instead of that, any inanimate object that falls in our way, whether a stone, or a piece of wood, or anything else of the same nature. This new-chosen god is immediately presented with an offering, which is accompanied with a solemn vow, that if he pleaseth to prosper our undertakings, for the future we will always worship and esteem him as a god. If our design prove successful, we have discovered a new and assisting god, which is daily presented with fresh offerings; but if the contrary happen, the new god is rejected as a useless tool, and consequently returns to his primitive state."[2] In India, to this very day, the workman worships his tools, the housekeeper her marketing-basket, the fisherman his net, the scribe his pen, and—a form of worship which reappears elsewhere—the banker his account-book.[3] These customs appear to have been in existence as early as in

[1] A. Lang, *Was Jehovah a fetish-stone?* in the *Contemporary Review*, March, 1890, p. 358.

[2] Bosman, cited by Lubbock, *Origin of Civilization*, p. 166.

[3] "Of this custom, the most sensational example was to be found among the Thugs, who used to worship the pick-axe which they carried for speedy burial of their victims on the spot of the murder."—Sir Alfred Lyall, *Asiatic Studies*, London, 1882, p. 15.

the Vedic epoch.¹ One is certainly tempted to say, in such cases, that a spirit can hardly be assigned to these things; yet whenever we succeed in piercing below the surface of the savage's thought, it appears that the object worshipped derives its whole religious significance from the internal personality attributed to it. A Negro who was asked how he could offer food to a tree, explained to Halleur that this food was not offered to the tree but to the spirit it contained, and that the latter would only eat the spirit of the sacrifice.² We shall have occasion to note the complete conformity of this interpretation with the religious ideas of savages in the old and the new worlds.

I do not maintain that man began by erecting this soul of a thing into a separate or independent entity. In our own day, as Waitz well says, "the Negroes make a distinction between the spirit and the material object in which it resides, although they combine the two and make a single whole of them." Mr. Im Thurn, again, tells us that the natives of Guiana regard men, animals, celestial bodies, atmospheric phenomena, and inanimate objects, as beings of the same nature, alike composed of a spirit and a body, and differing only in the extent of their powers.³ This combining of the body and the soul, or rather this absence of any clear distinction between

¹ A. Barth, *The Religions of India*; translated by J. Wood: London, 1882, p. 8. Compare Habakkuk i. 16, for the like practices amongst the Israelites.

² Halleur, cited by Waitz, *Anthropologie der Naturvölker*, vol. ii. p. 188.

³ Im Thurn, *Indians of British Guiana*: in the *Journal of the Anthropological Institute*, vol. xi. p. 377.

them, was probably the rule amongst pre-historic peoples, who were far behind even the savages above referred to in the matter of psychological speculation. But it results from what I have said in my last Lecture that man would never have come to invoke or adore any object, had he not believed that in so doing he was dealing with personalities modelled after his own.

<small>Extension to things of a sharper distinction between body and soul.</small> Little by little, whether from analogy with the double nature he had discovered in himself, or in consequence of dreams in which he saw distant or destroyed objects, he must have extended to *things* a more or less sharp distinction of soul and body; and, moreover, he must have accepted for these souls of *things* the same power of quitting their envelopes, or even surviving them, which he allowed in the case of his own soul. Before the Incas established sun-worship in the valleys of Peru, the natives adored stones, blocks of rock, or *huacas*. A Peruvian legend tells us that, as one of these stones was being broken, at the order of the Inca Roca, a parrot flew out of it and disappeared into a neighbouring stone, which latter inherited the veneration accorded to its predecessor.[1] Now if the new fetish had been treated in the same way, no doubt the parrot, or some other living creature, would have been seen to escape from it too, as representing the veritable object of the popular worship. Here we come upon the attitude of mind described by Prof. Tylor as animism, and by Prof. C. P. Tiele as polydemonism.

It is probable enough that, like human souls, the

[1] Girard de Rialle, *Mythologie comparée*, Paris, 1878, vol. i. p. 14.

spirits of things had the character of *doubles* in the first instance. The Tahitians believe that not only plants and animals, but natural and artificial objects also, have souls, like man. If they are broken or destroyed, their spirit survives and goes to the country of the dead. In one of the Fiji islands the natives even point out a certain stream running across the bottom of a hole, "in which you may clearly perceive the souls of men, women, beasts, plants, stocks, stones, canoes, houses, and all the broken utensils of this frail world, tumbling along one over the other, into the regions of immortality."[1] The Redskins, as we are told by the early missionaries, admit the existence of a personal spirit in the most commonplace objects. That spirit, when once the object itself is broken, goes, like the soul of man, to the land of the setting sun.[2] These peoples would have had no difficulty in accepting literally the humorous description in Scarron's burlesque:

"J'aperçus l'ombre d'un cocher
Qui, tenant l'ombre d'une brosse
Nettoyait l'ombre d'un carrosse."

Perhaps it is the same belief that gives rise to the custom, still widely spread among savages, and formerly prevalent, as we have seen, amongst pre-historic peoples, of breaking or burning the objects deposited near the deceased. Some writers have maintained that the purpose of this practice was to protect the offerings against thieves; but the interpretation of it given by all the

[1] Mariner, *An Account of the Natives of the Tonga Islands*, Edinburgh, 1827, vol. ii. p. 123.

[2] Père Lejeune, *Relation de ce qui s'est passé en la nouvelle France en l'année* 1634, pp. 58—60.

peoples who still observe it, shows that the real intention is to assure the transmission of the object in question to the spirit of the deceased. The superstitious fear inspired by the deceased would generally suffice to protect the offering against thieves, so that its destruction would be unnecessary on that ground; but since the animals destined to follow the deceased into the other world were unquestionably sacrificed, it would seem only natural and consistent to treat his arms, garments, and utensils of every kind in like manner.

Here we come to a distinction which exercises a commanding influence on the ultimate direction of the religious evolution.

Belief in spirits, and its origin. If the objects personified possess a determinate individuality and are practically unlimited in their duration, like the heaven, the sun, the moon, rivers and mountains, then their soul, when thought of as capable of quitting its envelope, will, in its turn, receive a strongly marked and distinctive character. It will long—perhaps indefinitely—retain, in the consciousness, its relations to the particular object from which it is supposed to have issued, and which it continues to guide from outside. But the souls attributed to objects not distinguished by any salient characteristic, easily confounded with a whole series of similar objects, and destined ultimately to disappear, such as men and animals, may indeed survive, in accordance with the general theory of survival, but the recollection of their connection with the objects from which they first issued will soon be lost. Nothing will then be left them but the vague character of semi-material beings, anonymous and independent, invested with extraordinary faculties and capable of arbitrary intervention in the course of nature and in the destiny of man.

It is the action of these "spirits" which now explains everything that cannot be attributed to the human will or to the intervention of some specific deity; and this ready explanation dispenses with all efforts to discover the connection of cause and effect. This spiritism—or, to adopt M. Albert Réville's excellent definition, this belief in spirits detached from their natural basis and without necessary connection with specific objects [1]—is the dominating factor in the lower stages of civilization generally, though it remains undeveloped, indeed, amongst the peoples at the very bottom of the scale, such as the Bushmen, the Tierra del Fuegans, and the Samoyeds. In Siberia, Castrén found many individuals who worshipped natural objects, but who had never heard tell of spirits.[2] Such evidence confirms the presumption that spiritism cannot be a primitive phenomenon.

The souls of man and of animals, when not despatched to a special world of their own, easily pass into the general mass of spirits, whether because the memory of the individuals to whom they belonged is lost, or because they are regarded as themselves forming a specific class of the spirits. Thus on the Congo the term *Zombi* signifies at once the spirits, and the souls of the dead. It is the same in the Marianne Islands, where both alike bear the name of *Anti*. In like manner the spirits appear to be

[1] *Religions des peuples non-civilisés*, vol. i. p. 79.
[2] Castrén, *Nordische Reisen und Forschungen*, vol. iii.; *Vorlesungen uber die Finnische Mythologie*, St. Petersburg, 1853, pp. 196, 197.

recruited from the dead amongst the Polynesians and the natives of the Indian Archipelago. In the Solomon Islands, a traveller tells us that the only worship is that of the dead. They become spirits "who do whatever they like with the living."[1]

<small>Spirits of nature and souls of the dead.</small> Mr. Herbert Spencer relies on these facts, and others like them, to support his thesis that spiritism issued from necrolatry, or, in other words, that the spirits are in every case dead men whose individuality has in process of time been effaced. But in many cases we can still recover the links which distinctly attach the spirits to an anterior personification of natural objects and phenomena. There are tribes who have but one word to signify these objects and the spirits themselves, though they perfectly understand the distinction between the two. On the Gold Coast there are the *Wongs* who live at liberty in the fields, forests, rocks, hollow trees, mountains, caverns and water-courses; and, on the other hand, the sea, the rivers, plants, ant-eaters, birds, and serpents, are also called *Wongs*, and are treated accordingly.[2] In Western Africa, the Wanikas, when asked by the Rev. J. L. Krapf what they meant by the word *Mulungu*, answered variously that it meant the thunder, or the celestial vault, or the author of diseases, or some kind of Supreme Being; or that the dead become *Mulungus*.[3] It is well to note that

[1] Lieut. F. Elton, *Notes on Natives of the Solomon Islands:* in *Journal of the Anthropological Institute*, 1888, vol. xvii. p. 97.

[2] Waitz, *Anthropologie*, &c., vol. ii. p. 183.

[3] J. L. Krapf, *Travels, Researches and Missionary Labours in Eastern Africa*, London, 1860, p. 168.

we are now speaking of populations who are sometimes represented as exclusively worshipping the dead.

Amongst the beliefs of the Redskins we may detect the different stages of the transition by which the personification of a thing passes to the status of a detached spirit. The missionary Marquette, when navigating a river of North America, was warned by his boatmen that they would have to pass the cave of a terrible demon. This demon, who devoured travellers, was simply and solely a rock which divided the current at a bend of the river. Here the spirit is still inherent in its material envelope, as with Scylla and Charybdis in the ancient tradition. The cataract of the River Peihono passed, in the same region, for the residence of terrible spirits whose roarings sounded afar. They, too, devoured passing travellers who ventured on the river, but they could also surprise any one rash enough to fall asleep in their neighbourhood. Here the spirits have already acquired a certain independence, since, like the German Lorelei, they can quit their retreat for a moment. According to Schoolcraft, the Redskins tell mocking tales during winter, because the spirits are frozen up under the ground and cannot hear.[1] We can hardly doubt that these must be spirits of nature, though in this case it is not so easy to attach them specifically to the various classes of phenomena. Finally, all trace of connection disappears. Schoolcraft says that the Algonkins believe the whole world to be animated by good and bad spirits, who rule the affairs of man and his future destinies. This is full-fledged spiritism.

[1] H.R. Schoolcraft, *Indian Tribes of the United States*, Philadelphia, 1853-60, part iii. p. 492.

Indeed, it is not difficult to explain the process by which the *doubles* of men and of things enter into the mass of anonymous spirits. Ancestors are generally regarded as the protectors of their descendants. On the other hand, the spirits of inanimate things have their respective spheres of action sharply determined by the character of the objects to which they are attached. Now let these attributes mingle, in a sort of cross-chassé, or rather by reciprocal extension of the powers reserved to the two categories of superhuman beings, let the manes of the sorcerer or the chief be invoked for the production of rain, the stoppage of an inundation, the averting of a storm, the fertilization of the harvest, and so forth (as with the New Zealanders, Siberians, and Negroes); and, further, let the spirits of nature be invoked to assure bodily health or to protect the house (as amongst the Finns); and you have only to remove from these two varieties of spirits the traces of their respective origins, for them to appear henceforth invested with analogous attributes, identical in natural functions, and even alike in aspect.

Form and functions of the spirits. In losing the record of their connection with individuals or with specific objects, the spirits naturally lose the character and form of *doubles*, and yet they are far from being regarded as immaterial in the sense which we attach to the word. On the contrary, the most varied features and appearance are attributed to them, and, in particular, forms borrowed from all kinds of animals. We must not forget that, to the savage, animals are not only man's equals, but his superiors. They possess, in his eyes, a prestige proportionate to their more mysterious habits and less intelligible motives. Hence in particular the representation of spirits under the form of serpents and birds, so widely spread amongst the peoples of the old and new worlds. Elsewhere spirits assume fantastic and monstrous forms suggested by visions of the night or even by the caprice of imagination. The essential point is, that the form chosen must imply life and activity. If the spirits of plants are never, or but very rarely, conceived under the form of doubles, it is not because those spirits are ancient human personages who bore the names of plants, but simply because the vegetable has not a sufficiently active and spontaneous physiognomy to represent a personality conceived after the model of our own.

We must note that the spirits become visible under certain circumstances and to certain persons; or that they reveal themselves to other senses than that of sight, by a whistle, a murmur or friction.

Our folk-lore is full of traditions crediting the spirits with every sound in the least degree unwonted, from the cry of the night-bird to the whistling of the wind in the forest; but it is chiefly by their direct action on the human body that the spirits manifest their existence.

They may either act at a distance or incorporate themselves in the body. Amongst the Dyaks, diseases are attributed either to the spirits inflicting internal wounds with invisible lances, or to their introducing themselves into the body of their victim and so causing the disease. The first case we shall call *obsession*; the second, *possession*. This two-fold process is applicable to things as well as to beings—that is to say, the spirits can act on inanimate things from without, using them as implements (in which case these objects are talismans or amulets), or they may embody themselves in a concrete object (which then becomes a *fetish*). This distinction is already recognized by the greater number of savage races.[1] In the second case, the object, having become the body of the spirit, will dispense the benefits of the latter, and whoever possesses it (if it be capable of private appropriation) will become the possessor of the power attached to it. This is the whole meaning of fetishism, which may be defined as the belief that the *appropriation of a thing may secure the services of the spirit lodged within it*.

Moreover, it is easy to imagine that there are means of attracting spirits into bodies by the aid of special methods and receipts. In old Calabar they manufacture fetishes out of straw, rags, or wood. Then they expose them in the open air to enable the spirits to come into them. Amongst other tribes of Negroes, fetish-shops are kept by certain sorcerers. The shopman, after inviting the customer to take his choice, makes the spirit enter the selected object by dint of the regulation hocus-pocus.[2] In like manner, the Finns manufacture a kind of dolls or *paras* out of a child's cap filled with tow and stuck at the end of a rod. The fetish thus made is carried nine times round the church, with the cry, "Synny para!" (Para, be born!) repeated every time, to induce a *haltia*—that is to say, a spirit—to enter into it.[3]

---

[1] See above, pp. 72, 73.

[2] J. Becker, *Vie en Afrique*, vol. ii. p. 306.

[3] Castrén, *Vorlesungen* u.s.w., p. 166.

Amongst ourselves, haunted houses and possessed objects, the witches known to our rustics, and the table-turning familiar in our drawing-rooms, clearly show that these superstitions are not yet extinct, though they have ceased, so to speak, to rank as religious phenomena.

Source of fetishism. Fetishism, as I have just analyzed it, implies the conception of spirits capable of existing unattached to material objects. No doubt, if we choose to apply the term fetish to every object capable of being appropriated, which is regarded as the body of a superhuman power, it becomes inaccurate to say that fetishism necessarily presupposes spiritism; for whenever man is led by some association to attribute a propitious or disastrous influence on his fate to any given object, he will pay his homage to the personality with which he invests it, whether or not he regards that personality as capable of separating itself from its material envelope. In the latter case, the spirit is bound up with the fate of its body. Castrén tells us that the Ostiaks worshipped a larch-tree, to the branches of which they hung the skins of animals as offerings; but in consequence of these skins often being stolen by travellers, they cut a block of wood out of the tree, deposited it in a safe place, and transferred their homage to it. In such a case, fetishism is absorbed into naturism or physiolatry, as I have defined it in the course of the preceding Lecture.[1] So, too, there are cases in which

---

[1] I have elsewhere proposed to distinguish between *primary* fetishism, in which man, personifying natural objects, chooses one as an auxiliary or protector; and *secondary*, or derived fetishism, which implies the incorporation of an independent spirit in a material object.

fetishism is absorbed in necrolatry; namely, when the fetish consists in the remains of the deceased, or even in one of his bones in which his personality is supposed to have taken refuge.

I think it is better, however, to reserve the name of fetish for objects which owe their supernatural powers to the fact that a spirit from outside has taken possession of them. Thus we may put an end to that veritable quarrel of words which has risen between Positivists of the school of Comte, and naturists like M. Albert Réville and even Prof. Max Müller. We may declare the naturists right when they say that fetishism (the worship of material objects, frankly regarded as such) does not constitute the whole religion of the Negro; and we may say that Comte's disciples are also right when, like M. Girard de Rialle, they lay at the basis of all religions the tendency to consider natural objects, beings, and phenomena, as possessing feelings and wills similar to those of man, and differing only in degree or activity.[1]

The idol an elaborated fetish.

The transition from fetishism to idolatry is easily established. The idol may be regarded as an elaborated fetish. The fetish is an object supposed to be inhabited by a spirit to which superhuman power is attributed, and the idol is the fetish so fashioned or re-touched as to reproduce

The first form obviously does not involve an anterior conception of the spirit as a distinct entity separable from its material envelope.—*Origines de l'idolatrie:* in the *Revue de l'Histoire des Religions*, vol. xii. pp. 4, 5, note.

[1] Girard de Rialle, *Mythologie comparée*, Paris, 1878, vol. i. p. 2.

the appearance of the spirit supposed to reside in it. It is now no longer the spirit that is conceived in the likeness of the body, but the body to which, by a sort of reflex action, the supposed traits of the spirit are given. I must not be understood to class as idols all images which represent superhuman beings, and are therefore worshipped; but only those which are regarded as conscious and animated. Even so there is no great religion, ancient or modern, without its idolaters. Doubtless enlightened Roman Catholics, Brahmanists, and Buddhists, are justified in repudiating the charge of idolatry as far as they themselves or even their official doctrines are concerned, in spite of the worship, to some extent symbolic, which they accord to their representations of superhuman beings. But the great herd does not always observe these distinctions, and a Saint or Madonna that rolls its eyes, drops tears, sheds blood, speaks, inflicts diseases or wards them off, and sends rain or fine weather to the fields, is as much an idol—that is to say, a fetish in human form—as the veriest fetish of fetishes amongst the Negroes, whether in human form or not, is a fetish.

In China, when an idol is tardy in rendering the services expected of it, it is torn from its temple and flung into the mud; but if the desired effect subsequently follows, it is cleaned up again, replaced, and perhaps promised a fresh gilding. Though pagan antiquity never went so far as this in the treatment of the idols, it could never completely free itself from the idea that its deities resided in the images. Need I record the case of Ramses sending to his father-in-law in Syria the statue of the god Khonsou to cure his sister-in-law? Of the Tyrians throwing chains on the statue of Baal Melkarth to prevent his going over to the enemy? Of the Romans bringing over the statue of the Magna Mater of Mount Ida, at great expense, from Pessinus, in order to secure them the victory over the Carthaginians? Of Stilpo, banished from Athens for maintaining that the Minerva of Pheidias was not the goddess herself? Even in the last days of paganism, its most intelligent apologists, according to Arnobius, made it consist in worshipping, not the gold and silver of the idols, but the deities which their consecration had brought down into them.[1] St. Augustine reports Hermes Trismegistus as holding that "attaching invisible spirits to visible and corporeal things by means of certain processes, in order that the latter may become, as it were, the animated bodies of the spirits to which they are consecrated, is making gods; a great and marvellous power with which men are endowed."[2] This is a definition which the Negro sorcerer, in his fetish-shop, and his Finn confrère animating a *para*, would readily accept.

In Polynesia, they make figures of carved wood into which the priests inject the souls of the dead or those of the gods according to taste; and when the spirit is in, it can be ejected again by drawing it out into certain feathers, which in their turn can pass it on to other figures. We may add that when these figures are without occupants, they retain a sacred character, but no

---

[1] *Adversus Gentes*, vi. 17, cited by Tylor, *Primitive Culture*, vol. ii. p. 163.

[2] Augustine, *De Civitate Dei*, viii. 23; apud Tylor, vol. ii. p. 164.

III. POLYDEMONISM AND POLYTHEISM. 113

kind of worship is rendered them. This is a typical example of the difference between an image and an idol, and also of the assimilation of the idol to the fetish.

This assimilation is often pushed so far that, but for the form, it would be impossible to distinguish between idol and fetish. It is true that idols are often the objects of public worship and would seem to escape individual appropriation; but the same may be said of fetishes also, if they belong to a tribe rather than to a family or an individual. Such, for example, were the Bethels, those "living stones," as Sanchoniathon calls them, which figured as palladiums in more than one ancient city. We may see in Western Africa how the transition from the private to the public worship of the idol-fetish takes place, without any modification in its nature in the process. It is often the domestic fetish of the chief which accomplishes on a large scale for the whole community, and under the direction of the official sorcerer, what private fetishes do on a small scale for individuals; presiding over atmospheric changes, healing epidemics, denouncing criminals, and foretelling the future. What more did the first idols of Greece, Egypt, India, or Assyria, do?

Springs of idolatry. The simplest origin of idolatry is as follows: Given the presence of a spirit in a certain object, the worshipper would feel himself in closer communication with it if the form of this object reproduced the likeness of the spirit.

But other origins may also be found. In the first place, any resemblance between a natural object and the supposed form of a spirit would raise a presumption that the latter was present in the former, just as the appearance

I

of a human body is evidence of the presence of the soul or internal personality. The Zunis of North America and the natives of the West Indies, when choosing fetishes, prefer stones and scraps of wood that present some resemblance to birds or animals.[1] Many peoples worship rocks or trees, the outlines of which recall the human features. From this to accentuating the resemblance by a few strokes of the axe or hammer is but a step.

In the second place, men would imagine that the spirit would come by preference to dwell in a body made after its own image. In Chaldea and in Assyria, where maladies were attributed to spirits that bore the form of fantastic animals, it was customary to carve these monsters round the palaces in order to offer the spirits an exact representation of their own bodies, and therefore an abode preferable to the body of the invalid.[2] It is the same with the Siamese, who represent the demons of disease in human or quasi-human shape, and make them pass into clay figures, which they hang on trees or expose in streams.[3]

Perhaps it is this superstition which reappears on the Congo in the custom of making images of the crocodile or the hippopotamus as a protection against the attacks of these animals while crossing rivers. So, too, we read in the book of Numbers (xxi. 6—9) that Moses had a brass serpent, the *Nehustan* (2 Kings xviii. 4), raised on a pole,

---

[1] Im Thurn, *On the Races of the West Indies:* in the *Journal of the Anthropological Institute*, 1887, vol. xvi. p. 195.

[2] C. P. Tiele, *Religions de l'Egypte et des peuples sémitiques*, Paris, 1882, p. 175.

[3] Tylor, *Primitive Culture*, vol. ii. p. 162.

for the Israelites to gaze at as a cure for serpent-bites.[1] In virtue of the same principle, many peoples believe that the souls of the deceased pass by preference into statues or portraits made in their own likeness.[2] Long before Mr. Herbert Spencer, the author of the *Wisdom of Solomon* connected idolatry with the worship of the dead. "For a father afflicted with untimely mourning, when he hath made an image of his child soon taken away, now honoured him as a god, which was then a dead man, and delivered to those that were under him ceremonies and sacrifices."[3]

The New Zealanders make images of carved wood in honour of the deceased, and place them in his house or by his tomb. They give these little statues clothes, and talk to them, under the conviction that the spirit of the departed dwells in them.[4] Amongst the Papuans, when

[1] It is interesting to re-discover the same belief in the depths of India. At Cowtha, near Koram, there is a temple dedicated to a serpent-god *Sufi-Nath*, whom the worshippers pray to guard them against the bites of reptiles. The legend declares that if any one is bitten, he has only to get himself carried to the temple to be cured (*Indian Messenger*, Dec. 16, 1888). Amongst the ancients, Æsculapius was the serpent-god, or at any rate his worship, which was of Phœnician origin, was connected with that of the serpent, regarded as the image of Eshmun. This belief in the curative virtues of the serpent reappears in the centre of Africa. According to Livingstone, "the serpent is an object of worship, and hideous little images are hung in the huts of the sick and dying."—David and Charles Livingstone, *Narrative of an Expedition to the Zambesi and its Tributaries*, London, 1865, p. 46.

[2] Cf. Herbert Spencer, *Sociology*, §§ 154—158.

[3] *Wisdom of Solomon*, xiv. 15.

[4] Tylor, *Primitive Culture*, vol. ii. p. 159.

any one dies, the survivors go to the neighbouring forest and cut a statuette or *Korwar* out of a bit of wood, and then they invite the spirit to come and live in it. The Ostiaks and the Samoyeds make rough statues in the likeness of their relatives, and offer them food. In the same way the ancient Egyptians multiplied statues in their tombs, as receptacles for the *double*. "These statues," says M. Maspero, "were more solid than the mummy, and there was no limit to the number of them that could be made. A single body offered the double one chance of survival; twenty statues gave him twenty chances."[1]

Sometimes this belief is combined with the idea that the double survives in the bodily remains. The ancient Mexicans made a paste of the ashes of their dead and human blood, and then made an image in the likeness of the deceased out of it. Amongst the inhabitants of Yucatan, the distinguished dead were burnt, and their cinders placed in statues, hollowed inside.[2] This is not unlike the proceedings of the Egyptians in covering the lid of the sarcophagus that contained a mummy, with the sculptured likeness of the deceased.

But we must not conclude that idolatry always had its origin in the worship of the dead. We have already seen that the idol often issued from the fetish. In other cases we may attach it still more directly to some natural object previously personified. Pausanias speaks of a sacred tree that the Corinthians worshipped in honour of

[1] Maspero, *Histoire des âmes dans l'Égypte ancienne*; in the *Bulletin de l'Association scientifique de France*, 1873, vol. xxiii. p. 381.

[2] Herbert Spencer, *Sociology*, vol. i. p. 327.

Bacchus at the command of an oracle. They made two statues to this deity out of the wood of the tree, and in the time of the writer these statues were still the object of special veneration in the agora at Corinth.[1] In the Antilles, where the sorcerers profess to understand the language of plants, they make idols out of the wood of trees supposed to have nominated themselves for the distinction.[2]

Moreover, we have already had occasion to point out that the form of the idols is not always human. Indeed, it may vary infinitely, provided it always represents something living, as we may see from the frequent occurrence of idols of animal or fantastic shape.

In the long run, however, the human form gained the preponderance in the representation of the most powerful spirits, whether because man had now come to regard himself as the most exalted being in nature, and knew not what better to do than to attribute his own features to the higher powers; or whether, by dint of attributing to the deities human sentiments and motives, he was instinctively drawn to lend them the human figure likewise. Perhaps the transition between the two forms is marked by those idols with a human head and an animal body, or an animal head and a human body, which we find in the temples of the Egyptians, Hindus, ancient Americans, and others.

Relation of idolatry to symbolism. Some authors have attempted to discover marvels of symbolism in these monstrous combinations. They maintain, for example,

[1] Pausanias, ii. 2. 7.
[2] Tylor, *Primitive Culture*, vol. ii. p. 197.

that the artist started with the human form in his representation of the gods, but introduced wings to indicate their power of transporting themselves through space, fins to show that they could live in the water, a lion's body to denote their courage, or a bull's head to represent their strength, just as he sometimes gave them a number of arms or heads with the same intent.

Unquestionably, the most enlightened exponents of the ancient worships thus interpreted the monstrous forms of their gods at a period when they began to cause scandal; but it is none the less evident that at first the reality of these representations was believed in. "Animal forms in which the gods were clothed," M. Maspero well remarks, apropos of the Egyptian deities, "have not an allegorical character. They indicate an animal-worship which reappears in more than one ancient and modern religion. The ambiguous forms themselves, half-man, half-beast, simply prove the ignorance and credulity of the ancients in the matter of natural history."[1] Since the presence of such creatures on earth was supposed to be possible, *a fortiori* the superhuman world might be peopled by them; for their very grotesqueness gave an extra assurance of the reality of their existence. At the outside, if we are to allow anything at all to the invention of the artist or the mythologist, we can only admit that the grotesque combination was due to a naïve desire to give a more adequate representation of superhuman beings, by combining with the traits derived from man, the forms of beasts consecrated by tradition, and, for that matter, necessary to

[1] *Revue de l'Histoire des Religions*, vol. i. p. 121.

indicate the individuality of the various deities. It appears that in the hieroglyphics of the first dynasties, the great deities of Egypt are invariably represented in the shape of animals.

But many writers have gone far beyond this. Indeed, the theory is still widespread that idols are symbols, the original significance of which has been lost by degeneration. According to this theory, which is outlined as early as in the *Wisdom of Solomon*, idolatry in general would represent, not an advance, but a degradation. Man, after having conceived the deity as pure spirit, figured it forth symbolically under material traits, and then came to regard these supposed portraits as divine individualities, the temporary or permanent abodes of the gods.

I am far from denying that in certain cases an image may have become an idol by its primitive meaning and purpose being forgotten. History shows us indubitable examples of religious decline in which idolatry, always latent in the popular superstitions, re-ascends, as it were, to the surface of worship.[1] In the bosom of the same system the image, which in the mind of its author or of its reproducer has a merely symbolic significance, may become a veritable fetish to others. But these facts, which are explained by survivals or local infiltrations,

[1] The example of Buddhism is familiar. Surely nothing can be more contrary to the teaching of Buddha than the idolatrous worship with which the masses now surround his images; and in like manner the emperor Si-tzong, in the 16th century, was obliged to combat a similar abuse by forbidding the erection of images of Confucius in the temples raised to his memory. De Harlez, *La religion nationale des Tartares orientaux*, &c., Brussels, 1887.

cannot weigh against the combined observations of ethnography and history, which everywhere show us idols issuing from fetishes by a series of easily-traced steps.

Idolatry a step in progress. The widespread worship of stones erected endwise is itself absolutely fetishistic; but no sooner is a spot of red painted on the stone, as in Southern India, than we stand on the threshold of idolatry. The same distinction may be drawn between the wooden stake to which sacrifices are offered by the Baguirmis of Africa, and the staff of the Brazilian sorcerers, surmounted by a gourd, pierced with a hole to represent the mouth. Sometimes they clothe the stick or stone, covering it with stuffs and ornaments, as in the Society Islands, where they worship a fragmentary column clothed in native costume. Then sculpture comes in. On the top of the pillar a rude head is carved; this brings us to the *hermes* and the doll, which already mark striking progress in the development of religious art. Next, the limbs are traced on the stem of the column, and then carved out and thrown into attitudes of life and motion.

All these steps may be traced amongst the Negroes of tropical Africa, where idolatry is no less clearly developed than pure and simple fetishism. So, too, amongst the Samoyeds, where we find, side by side with complete statues of a rude description, pillars surmounted by a human head, and mere stones dressed in coloured stuffs.

Perhaps you will ask me how I know that these parallel forms succeeded each other in this definite order. Apart from the logical necessity of supposing that in art and religion alike man advanced from more elementary to more highly developed forms, we have in this case the evidence of history, especially amongst that people in which idolatry received its fullest development.

The Greeks began, like the rest, by worshipping blocks of stone and scraps of wood, regarded as the bodies of their deities. Pausanias tells us, apropos of thirty shapeless stones worshipped as gods at Pharæ, in Achaia, that amongst the Greeks unhewn stones had in very ancient times received divine honours.[1] "The natural advance," says M. Maxime Collignon, "consisted in giving shapeless stones a regular form, however rudimentary. .... Zeus and Hera are thus presented on the coins of the island of Ceos. ... At Sicyone, the most ancient image of Zeus-Meilikhios was a pyramid, that of Artemis Patroa a column. Such, too, was the form of the ancient Hera of Argos; and perhaps we may discover a reference to these old representations of the deity in a painting in Pompeii, which represents a group of Eroses and a Psyche sacrificing before a column, attached to which are a tiara and a sceptre. ... As art advances, characteristic features are added to these pillars—a head, arms, or phallic emblems. This is the origin of the Hermes column surmounted by one or many heads."[2] The same development takes place in wood as in stone: witness the transition from the square blocks which represent the first deities of certain Greek cities, to the xoana which even in the best days of art were the most popular images amongst the worshippers.

It must not be supposed, for that matter, that even in

[1] Pausanias, vii. 22. 4.
[2] Max Collignon, *Mythologie figurée de la Grèce*, pp. 11—13.

the most advanced religions the credit of an image is proportionate to its artistic merit. A roughly coloured virgin, or an old saint who has almost lost the human shape, will often excite a deeper veneration in simple souls than a Madonna of Raphael's or a statue by Michael Angelo.

(ii.) The Divine Hierarchy.

The great nature-gods. It is amongst the populations of incoherent imagination, without stable social organization, and with little connection in their ideas, that fetishism and polydemonism reach their maximum of intensity, and smother all other forms of worship. The genii of nature—that is to say, the superhuman beings associated with the production of certain specific phenomena, and deriving some degree of fixity of sphere and function from the consciousness of this connection—are, amongst such races, relegated more and more to the background by the pullulation of the little anonymous and detached powers, which the Negro, the Redskin, or the Australian feels far nearer to him, which he understands how to manage, and which he possesses, or supposes he possesses, more direct and efficacious means of controlling. Not that the divinities of nature, as representatives of natural phenomena, entirely disappear. Their survival in the background is attested in the case of many peoples wholly given over to spiritism, by the belief in a supreme god—generally the heaven or the sun—who is sometimes made the creator, but from whom they withhold the attentions granted to the lowest of the spirits. The Odshis hold the heaven to be the mightiest of deities, but they think he has delegated the government of the world to the inferior spirits.[1] In Dahomey, it is the sun who occupies the supreme place; but there, too, his supremacy is purely theoretical.[2] The natives of Timor in the Indian Archipelago also regard the sun as their chief deity; but they expect neither good nor ill from him, and explain that he is too high to trouble about them, and too good to injure them.[3] Finally, the Californians concentrate their homage upon the inferior spirits, adding that the sun and moon used to love them, but that now these deities no longer concern themselves with man.

In this vague notion of a superior god who has lost his power or is inaccessible to emotion, the vanishing traces of a previous monotheism have sometimes been found; but I believe what it really implies is simply the existence of a phase of religion in which the regents of the heavenly bodies or the chief natural phenomena retained an importance proportioned to their real place in nature, while care for the destinies of man was left to other superhuman beings. It is not monotheism, then, but nature-worship, that is presupposed.

Amongst other peoples of better mental endowments, however, or more favoured by circumstances, the parasitical growth of spiritism has failed to stifle the worship

[1] Waitz, *Anthropologie*, vol. ii. p. 171.

[2] A. Réville, *Religions des peuples non-civilisés*, vol. i. p. 56.

[3] De Backer, *L'Archipel Indien*, p. 227. According to Du Tertre, cited by Lubbock (*Origin of Civilization*, p. 254), a similar notion prevails among the Caribs.

of the great natural deities, which directly springs out of the physiolatry explained in my last Lecture.

Prof. Pfleiderer justly remarks: "Though this belief in spirits had great vogue among the Latins, no less than among the old Iranians, Slavs, Germans, and Pelasgians, yet there never was a time in any of these peoples when the spirits took the place of gods, and were the highest or even the sole objects of worship."[1] In my opinion, not only the Greeks and Hindus, but the Egyptians, the Chinese, and even the Mesopotamians, might have been added to the list.

From the sky-god to the god of the sky.
Let us take, for example, the words which have served the Hindus and the Greeks respectively to designate the celestial vault and the ruler of the heavens: in the one case, Ouranos and Zeus; in the other, Varuna and Dyaus. It is probable that before their separation the Indo-Europeans already possessed the equivalents of these two terms to designate the heaven, under some such forms as *dyu* and *varana;* and whereas the Greeks apply the first of these names to the celestial lord, Zeus, and the second to the firmament properly so called, Ouranos, the Hindus differentiated the other way, making Varuna figure as the

---

[1] *Philosophy of Religion*, London, 1888, vol. iii. p. 111. Professor Pfleiderer has long contended that the religious sentiment must, in the first instance, have addressed itself to natural objects and phenomena, or rather to the quasi-human personality with which man invested them by analogy, though the distinction between this personality and its envelope or body was not very clearly drawn in the consciousness.—*Der Religion, ihr Wesen und ihre Geschichte*, Leipzig, 1869, vol. ii.

god of heaven, and Dyaus as the visible sky itself. This is enough to raise a strong presumption that the distinction between the personified heaven and the god of the sky is subsequent to the separate development of the two languages; and this presumption is decisively confirmed by the fact that Ouranos still continued to be a mythological personality amongst the Greeks; whereas amongst the Hindus, as Prof. Max Müller has luminously explained, traces are found in the Vedas of a period when Dyaus was not only personified but even received the epithet of Pitar, and was thus the full equivalent of the Hellenic *Zeus pater* and the Latin Ju-piter.[1]

The very epithets assigned to him, the Most High (ὕψιστος), the Thunderer (κεραύνιος), the Rainer (ὑέτιος), the Cloud-gatherer (νεφεληγερέτης), and so forth, show that the Greeks never lost the reminiscence of the time when Zeus was identical with the sky and its brilliant or stormy manifestations. The same may be said of the Latins, amongst whom such expressions as "sub Jove vivere" for "to live in the open air," enlighten us as to the primitive nature of the divine being, to whom an old poet thus alludes:

"Adspice hoc sublime candens quem invocant omnes Jovem."

Here, again, the parallel with Varuna is complete. In the Vedas, he is sometimes said to have created the sun, and sometimes it is called his eye. Some of the hymns would depict him as a king and a judge, the universal creator; others say that he clothes himself alternately in white and black garments, that the celestial waters flow

[1] Max Müller, *Hibbert Lectures* for 1878, p. 143.

from his mouth as from the hollow of a reed, and that the celestial fire springs from his belly in the clouds.[1] Amongst the Persians, Ahura Mazda, the omniscient lord, is a deity so completely disentangled from nature that it has often been doubted to what phenomenon he could be attached. Yet the hymns describe him as clad with a luminous, shining body, visible from afar; they call him the firmest of the gods because he is clad in the firm stone of the heaven.[2] And, for that matter, Herodotus calls attention to the fact that the Persians worship Zeus—that is to say, their supreme god—on the summits of mountains, "giving the name of Zeus to the whole sphere of heaven."[3] Amongst the Egyptians, side by side with the solar disc, Aten, we find the lord of the Disc, and even "the hidden soul of the lord of the Disc." Horus, too, according to Maspero, before typifying the rising sun, was previously the part of the universe situated on high (hori), the actual substance of the firmament, the heaven-father of the gods, who was insensibly transformed into a separate god, living in the heaven.[4]

In Mesopotamia, Anu, "the hidden," represents the god of heaven, side by side with Ana, "the exalted one," who personifies the heaven itself.[5]

So, too, amongst the Chinese we find Tien, the per-

[1] *Rig Veda*, viii. 41, 10. v. 85, 3.

[2] James Darmesteter, *Essais Orientaux*, pp. 120, 121.

[3] Herodotus, i. 131.

[4] *La Mythologie Égyptienne*, in the *Revue de l'Histoire des Religions* for Jan.-Feb. 1889, vol. xix. p. 5.

[5] Tiele, *Histoire des religions de l'Égypte et des peuples sémitiques*, p. 187.

sonified heaven, and Shang Ti, the celestial emperor. Amongst the Finns, Ukkho, the grandfather, and Yumala, the god of Thunder, who provided the generic name for deity when supplanted by Ukkho in his specific relations with the firmament.

This seemingly contradictory duality of conception, which applies to many other divine personifications, may be explained either as a juxtaposition of the beliefs of several communities who mingled their traditions at some period or another, or, more probably, as the mingling of the beliefs of different epochs superposed one upon another without any mutual exclusiveness. But in either case it bears witness to a direct connection between the god of the object and the deified object itself. Admitting, then, an early period in which nature-worship prevailed, is it not obvious that the worship rendered to the rulers of nature springs direct out of the worship offered to the personified phenomena themselves? What need is there, then, to postulate an intermediate period in which the gods of these phenomena, having become simple spirits, were absorbed into the general rank, only to regain their primitive importance once more at a later period?

Not only is evidence of any such interregnum totally wanting, but it even appears that the very doubling of heaven, of earth, of the sun, of the moon, of the dawn, of the storm, &c., into a visible or sensible phenomenon on the one hand, and the spirit presiding over that phenomenon on the other, has served to increase the religious preponderance of the deities in question, by leaving the god thenceforth free from the limitations of his body, and so enabling him to fulfil more general functions, and to exercise his activity in a more extended sphere. Thus the Zeus, father of men and gods, ruler of all things, guardian of the family and of the city, inspirer of wisdom, and avenger of perjury, is a far more august personage than even the Zeus who scatters the rain over the fields of the Athenians, or makes Olympus tremble with the nodding of his brow.

Spirits promoted to deities.
On the other hand, it is probable that even amongst the peoples most predisposed to the worship of nature, when certain spirits (from whatever cause) had acquired marked pre-eminence, they frequently took their place at the head of the superhuman world side by side with the great deities of nature. This must have been the case with the spirits to whom the production of the abstract phenomena most closely concerned in the destiny of man had been ascribed. It is probable that the gods of disease, of war, of death, of plenty, and of certain moral qualities, were in many cases not nature gods, but spirits directly created on the analogy of the superhuman powers whose action was supposed to be manifested in natural phenomena and the ordinary events of life. Even the most backward peoples are not without their abstract deities, or rather their deities who produce abstract phenomena. The Mintiras of Malacca attribute every disease to its own *hantu*. It was the same with the early Chaldeans. In Polynesia, as formerly in Mesopotamia, every part of the body has its special spirit. The Iroquois, the Arancans, the Museronghis of the Lower Congo, the Khonds, and the Maoris, all have gods of war. The Iroquois have a spirit of sleep, and the Ojibways a god of death represented as a

walking skeleton. In Shintoism, which affirms the existence of eight million deities recruited from the souls of heroes, the rivers, the mountains, the waterfalls, and the great trees, the only gods particularly adored throughout the empire, apart from the great solar deities, are the genii of Pity, of Wealth, and of Medicine.[1] It is no great step from these abstract personifications to the Pantheon of the Romans, where, as M. Preller points out, we find deities of all the events alike of nature and of humanity, all the vicissitudes of human life and activity, all the relations and all the enterprizes of civil life.[2] It was the same with the Greeks, though there the tendency was restrained by their anthropomorphism. Plutarch tells us that Themistocles, having levied a contribution on the island of Andros in the name of two deities, Persuasion and Force (Πειθὼ καὶ Βίαν), the inhabitants refused, invoking the commands of two quite equally potent deities, Poverty and Incapacity (Πενίαν καὶ Ἀπορίαν).[3] We must note, however, that where such personifications mount to the first rank, as amongst the Parsees and the Brahmans, it is generally by dint of a very advanced system of metaphysical speculation.

Apotheoses of men. Under the category of spirits promoted to a higher grade, may likewise figure the souls of illustrious personages who have actually lived—chiefs, sorcerers, warriors, and others. Generally speaking, savages accord the dead a worship proportionate to the

---

[1] Isabella Bird, *Shintóism*, in *Religious Systems of the World*, London, 1890, pp. 98, 99.

[2] Preller, *Römische Mythologie*, Berlin, 1858, pp. 45, 596—631.

[3] *Themistocles*, xxi.

vividness of the recollection they have left behind them. They mostly confine themselves to invoking the relatives whom they have personally known. "Ask the Negro," says M. du Chaillu, "where is the spirit of his great-grandfather, he says he does not know, *it is done*. Ask him about the spirits of his father or brother who died yesterday, then he is full of fear and terror."[1] But on the shores of the Tanganyika and the neighbouring country, Lieutenant Becker tells us that the shades of certain illustrious dead escape this oblivion. "They make public sacrifices to them, and the tribe considers them its permanent protectors."[2] Amongst the Ama Zulu, Bishop Callaway tells us, the worship of ancestors does not extend beyond the father. They do not so much as know the names of more distant ancestors. Nevertheless the whole nation places at the head of its innumerable spirits a superhuman being named 'Mkulukulu, the great-great-father, who is regarded as the creator, the legislator, and the first ancestor. No doubt it would be hard to say whether in this case it is a real progenitor who has been raised to the dignity of universal creator, or a nature-spirit that has been promoted to the rank of ancestor; but the same difficulty exists with regard to almost all the gods who have been regarded as founders of the race, or even of the state, such as the Hindoo Yama or the Peruvian Manco Capac.

Certain natives of Siberia pay honours to the figures of the dead for three years; after which they are buried and heard of no more; but if the deceased is a celebrated

---

[1] Du Chaillu, *Transactions of the Ethnological Society*, vol. i. p. 308.
[2] J. Becker, *La Vie en Afrique*, vol. ii. p. 298.

shaman, his statue becomes the object of permanent worship.[1] We may cite for comparison the history of Æsculapius amongst the Greeks. Homer simply speaks of Æsculapius as a faultless physician (ἰητὴρ ἀμύμων).[2] Subsequently, as Herbert Spencer has pointed out, he has altars and temples dedicated to him; his worship extends from Asia Minor over the whole Greek world, and at last he is hailed as "The guider and governor of the Universe, preserver of the World, and guardian of the Immortal Gods."[3] The question always remains whether we have to do with a historical personage, or whether we are to see in this god of medicine an ancient serpent-god, or a representative of some natural phenomenon, or even, as M. Maury supposes, an ancient personification of fire, an analogue of Agni, the succourer.[4]

In any case, when we think of the important place occupied by the worship of heroes in Greece, we need not be surprised to find the dead establishing themselves even amongst the great gods of Olympus by securing the attributes of more or less effaced naturegods. We may say that in the classical mythology there is a continual cross-stream of influence between the gods and the heroes. When gods are represented as magnified men, it is no wonder that magnified men should come to be regarded as gods.

[1] Ad. Erman, *Travels in Siberia*, Cooley's translation, London, 1848, vol. ii. p. 51.

[2] *Iliad*, iv. 194, and elsewhere.

[3] Ælius Aristides, *Opera*, Oxford, 1722, vol. i. p. 37: ὁ τὸ πᾶν ἄγων καὶ νέμων σωτὴρ τῶν ὅλων, καὶ φύλαξ τῶν ἀθανάτων.

[4] A. Maury, *Religions de la Grèce antique*, Paris, 1857, vol. i. pp. 448 sqq.

At this very day, India shows us the process of apotheosis in the very act, at least in the case of the secondary deities, whose ranks are constantly opened to the manes of di-tinguished men, and, above all, such as have made themselves objects of terror during their lifetime.[1] It is true that their deification only rises to the secondary rank; but at the time when Hindu mythology and Hindu society alike were in course of formation, the secondary divinities in their turn may have had facilities for reaching the higher places in the Pantheon.

Genii of Species. There is yet another category of divinities which has exercised a certain influence on the development of polytheism, though it does not suffice to furnish all its elements, and still less, as Auguste Comte would have it, to explain the conception of spirits detached from bodies.[2] I refer to the genii of species.

The conception of a species implies an effort of generalization too great for many of the peoples who have reached the phase of spiritism. The Kamtskadals seem to have no general name for "fish" or "bird," and they distinguish between the different kinds of living things by the name of the month in which they most abound.[3] The Damara of South Africa "has no one name for a river, but a different name for nearly every reach of it."[4] The Australians have a name for every species of vegetable and animal, but no general term for "tree," "bird,"

[1] Sir Ch. Lyall, *The Religion of an Indian Province*, in the *Fortnightly Review* for 1872, p. 133.

[2] *Philosophie Positive*, second edition, vol. v. pp. 74 sqq.

[3] S. S. Hill, *Travels in Siberia*, London, 1854, vol. ii. p. 402.

[4] F. Galton, *Tropical South Africa*, London, 1853, p. 176.

or "fish."[1] It is probable that primitive humanity was equally incapable of forming such conceptions. In time, however, by dint of noting the identical characteristics of certain objects, man came to classify them under ideal categories respectively determined by the traits common to all their members, and thereupon the observation of certain properties shared by a whole group of species led to the formation of collective ideas still wider in their scope.

Thus from the existence of traits common to all the trees massed on certain spaces, the existence of the collective individuality we designate by the name of wood or forest was inferred, and hence the existence of a genius of the forests to govern the whole mass of trees. In the same way the similarity of the ears of corn gave birth to the idea of wheat, just as their common destination produced the conception of harvest; hence the belief in a genius of wheat or harvest. The universal attributes of water inspired the conception of a liquid element, and thence of a god of water; the general attributes of flames, the conception of an igneous element, and thence of a god of fire. The "Earth" herself only seems to have been conceived, and therefore only deified, by peoples who had already reached a certain stage of mental development. On the lower levels of evolution, islands, mountains, and special portions of land are deified; but the spirit of generalization could not reach beyond some clearly determined portion of the soil.

Each member of these collective totals may preserve its individuality, and therefore its special spirit; but the

[1] *Encyclopedia Britanica*, vol. iii. p. 112. Sub. "Australia."

genius of the species, from the very fact of its governing the whole, acquires a superior authority. Sometimes, indeed, even though the idea of species or element has been distinctly realized, the individual spirits nevertheless retain their independence, and are not subordinated, but are merely divided into certain great categories corresponding to the objects or to the phenomena, the directive principle of which they represent. Thus among the Botocudos of Brazil, the Esquimaux, the Chinese, the Proto-Chaldeans, and others, the spirits are divided into spirits of the woods, waters, earth, air, &c., as in the Indo-European traditions. The Finns recognize these divisions, but also believe in the existence of general spirits, the *haltias*, who preside over the destinies of species. There are *haltias* of rye, oats, grass, &c., and they occupy an intermediate position between the ordinary spirits and the great deities of nature.

An analogous conception has been pointed out amongst the ancient Peruvians. They believed that every kind of animal had a representative in heaven, charged with watching over the species and providing for its reproduction. This belief reappears in North America. The Iroquois hold that every species of animal and every variety of vegetable, has its special genius; and they declare that the *Manito* adored under the form of an ox is not the ox itself, but the Manito ox which is under the ground and animates all oxen.[1]

Professor Sayce, in his profound and subtle analysis of the Mesopotamian religion, has shown that Merodach, Ea, Mul-lil, and other great gods of the Chaldean Pan-

[1] De Brosses, *Du culte des dieux fétiches*, Paris, 1760, p. 58.

theon, may well have been in their origin the ox or bull, the fish, the antelope, and so forth, venerated for the services they rendered to the local populations, subsequently regarded as the tutelary deities of the individual and the city, and finally confounded with the spirits of the planets and the great natural phenomena.[1] In that case we are evidently dealing, not with an ox or a serpent, but with the representatives of the respective species.

What the Vedic Rishis adored on their hearths was not the flame itself, but fire personified under the name of Agni, who, "scattered in all places, remains one sole and only king," as the hymn expresses it.[2] Amongst the Greeks, Hestia was present in every flame; and amongst the Romans, Ovid hints that when the ancients gathered round the hearth for their repasts, they believed themselves to be in the presence of the deity itself.[3]

The gods of human groups, from the family up to the state, came into existence in virtue of the same principle that gave birth to the genii of species. Every group, however arbitrary, as soon as it had a distinct individuality, had a claim to a personality which could represent and direct it. Here, however, it seems to have been the exception for that personality to be created *de novo*, like the Dea Roma. Sometimes the part was taken by the patron spirit of the principal member or family, as we have seen in the case of the tribal fetishes of the

---

[1] *Hibbert Lectures* for 1887, pp. 280—300.

[2] *Rig Veda*, iii. 55, 4.

[3] *Fasti*, vi. 305, 306.

Negroes. Or it was the soul of some illustrious chief, the tribal hero or the founder of the city, that was raised to this position. We are justified in asking whether amongst all those *Baalim* which divided amongst them the cities and petty states of the Semitic world, there might not have been some who had actually lived upon the earth, had afterwards assumed the posthumous government of their cities, and had finally acquired the ordinary attributes of the nature-gods. Or, again, the function of national or tribal patron may have been deliberately assigned to one or another of the gods representing the heaven, the sun, or the moon, in forgetfulness of the fact that these divine beings shine over all the world alike; or to some other superhuman power connected with natural phenomena of a character more susceptible of national appropriation, such as the genius of some species, or an archetypal animal. This is what we actually find to be the case amongst the peoples addicted to totemism.

Totemism. I must not expatiate on the strange custom of totemism, the study of which has been popularized by several eminent writers in England. From the religious point of view, it may be defined as the worship rendered to the genius of some species of animal by a tribe which regards it as its progenitor and its patron. We should note that even amongst the Redskins the totem or *dodaim* is not just an animal amongst the rest, but an ideal individual which rules all the representatives of its species, "a Manito ox under the earth which animates all the oxen."

The inspiring motive of totemism, I take it, is found

in the desire to give the tribe a representative of its collective personality to serve as its protector. This representative at the same time (by the usual ὕστερον πρότερον) explains the separate existence of the tribe itself. It is obvious that in the choice of a totem, as in the choice of fetishes, chance and even caprice take a large share. We may, however, form an approximate judgment of the probable genesis of tribal totemism by observing what takes place in the case of individuals. Sometimes at the moment of birth the women of the family repeat the names of a number of animals one after another, and the child's totem for all his life will be the animal whose name is being uttered as he gives his first cry. Sometimes the child himself, when he has reached the age of puberty, goes to a solitary place, and after offering a sacrifice chooses as his totem the first animal he sees, dreaming or waking; and he then seals his contract by drawing a few drops of blood from his person.[1]

On the other hand, it may well be that families or tribes designated by the name of some animal may have finally reached the conclusion that this animal must have been their progenitor and is still their protector. There is nothing foreign to the mental and religious habits of the inferior peoples in such reasoning. Totemism, then, is met with amongst almost all the races of the two worlds that live in isolated tribes; but that is no reason for making it the primitive and neces-

[1] Bancroft, *Native Races of the Pacific States of America*, vol. i. pp. 740, 741. Cf. De Brosses, *Du culte des dieux fétiches*, pp. 46, 47.

sary phase of all religious development, as some writers have done.

In a word, four categories of superhuman beings must have taken precedence of the common herd of spirits at an early stage, especially amongst the peoples predisposed to a polytheistic conception of the universe; to wit, the great deities of nature, the spirits that preside over the most important factors of human destiny, the genii of species and of the chief groups, and the souls of the illustrious dead.

Subordination of spirits to gods. In order, however, that this first differentiation should result in polytheism, we need another factor, the necessity of which has often been overlooked, namely, the subordination of the spirits to the gods; in a word, the establishment of a hierarchy amongst the superhuman beings.

Practically, no doubt, the gods of polytheism are often distinguished from the spirits simply by their greater power, but that power is exercised on the mass of superhuman beings as well as upon the mass of men. The ordinary spirits become their servants, their vassals—nay, even a kind of serfs attached to the soil or invested with subordinate functions; unless, indeed, having failed to find a place in the ranks of the divine army, they are treated as enemies and rebels and laid under the imperial ban.

At the same time that this subordination is being developed, the gods themselves undergo a parallel movement of co-ordination. A certain number, sometimes determined by special circumstances, is singled out for distinction: three (the family triad), seven (the

III. POLYDEMONISM AND POLYTHEISM. 139

seven planets known to the ancients), nine (the enneads of the Egyptians), twelve or thirteen (the months of the year), thirty-three (perhaps, amongst the Hindus, the year, the four seasons, and the twenty-eight days of the month). These special deities, whatever may be the beings or the phenomena which they properly represent, are not only put at the head of the Pantheon, but have a certain authority over the lower ranks of the divine hierarchy, and may consequently come to be regarded as ruling over the whole superhuman society.

This organization is demanded by the human mind, which cannot be content to leave the government of the universe a prey to anarchy; but it is not so much the result of philosophical speculation as a deduction from the examples furnished by the organization of terrestrial communities. We may note, in fact, that the different peoples conceived and developed this divine hierarchy *pari passu* with their own approximation to political unity.

The divine societies modelled upon those of earth. The idea of shaping the society of the gods on the model of their own little communities on earth, appears to have occurred at an early stage to peoples still in quite a backward state of civilization. The Jesuit Molina tells us that amongst the Araucans the god Pillan is the grand *Togui* (regent) of the invisible world. As such, he is surrounded by his Apo-Ulmenes and his Ulmenes, to whom he confides the less important affairs. "These ideas," adds the sagacious observer, "are certainly very rude; but it must be acknowledged that the Araucanians are not the only people who have regulated the things of heaven by those of the earth."¹ The Yorubas of Western Africa, says the missionary Bowen, have only one god of heaven, just as they have only one king of the nation; and as petitioners have to approach the king through the intervention of his servants, so men in approaching the supreme deity have recourse to the mediation of the *oresas* or spirits.² The Kimbundas of the Congo say that Suku-Vanange, probably a personification of the celestial vault, hands men over to the Kilulu; and as there are more bad than good amongst these spirits, life would be intolerable to the poor Negro, were it not that from time to time Suku-Vanange, driven to desperation, issues from his constitutional neutrality and strikes the worst of the Kilulu with lightning."³

Whether these first attempts to construct a superhuman hierarchy are really due to the influence of Christian doctrines concerning the rôle of the deity and his agents, or whether they are to be attributed to the spontaneous development of local spiritism, in any case they retain traces of a certain casual and precarious character, like the Negro empires which, in every district of Africa, rise and fall with equal facility, without resulting in the smallest progress towards a permanent national unity or political centralization even within a limited area. These divine hierarchies are seldom found amongst peoples in the pastoral or nomadic stage of civilization, or even amongst those agricultural populations

[1] Ignatius Molina, *History of Chili*, English translation, vol. ii. p. 84: London, 1809.

[2] E. B. Tylor, *Primitive Culture*, vol. ii. p. 316.

[3] R. Hartmann, *Les peuples de l'Afrique*, Paris, 1880, p. 184.

in which the village group is the nucleus of social organization. Even in such cases, however, a kind of Platonic belief in a supreme deity is not rarely professed. But polytheism of a really organized character is only found amongst races who have attained a sentiment of national unity superior to the village and clan divisions, possessing a sufficient degree of culture to co-ordinate their religious traditions, and above all enjoying a centralized administration, without which no permanent sovereign power can be secured.

The Polynesians, when first discovered, were at a relatively advanced stage of civilization, and had an exceptionally rich Pantheon, in which the gods of the elements were the heroes of adventures comparable to those of the Greek mythology of pre-Homeric times. They even distinguished the *tikis*, or spirits, from the *atuas*, or gods. The former comprise certain animals, the souls of the dead, the guardian-spirits of families and individuals, the genii of diseases, and finally innumerable fetishes. The latter include the gods of the celestial bodies and natural phenomena, to whom the forms of animals were sometimes attributed, at any rate when they visited the earth.[1] In New Zealand, the first place was occupied by the cosmogonic couple Rangi (Heaven) and Pepë (Earth), with their children, the gods of the winds, of the plants, of the fishes, of the forests, of men, and so on; together with Tangaroa, the god of the

[1] This is the explanation of zoolatry given by the Manguians. On animal gods, cf. W. W. Gill, *Myths and Songs from the South Pacific*, London, 1876, p. 35.

sea, Maui, the god of the sun, a kind of Polynesian Heracles, and his grandmother, perhaps a personification of the night. In the Hervey Islands, other cosmic deities appear: Vatea, half man and half shark, god of the sea and of vegetation, or of heaven. In the Sandwich Islands there is a goddess of the moon, Hina, "the woman of the white locks;" in Hawai, Pelë, the goddess of the great local volcano. And, finally, there are gods of war, of the harvest, of fish, and what not. The relative power of these deities, however, varies in the different archipelagos, and in no case do we find that the tikis have been subordinated to the atuas, or even that any attempt has been made to co-ordinate these latter, any more than the host of little insular states into which the Polynesian archipelagos are divided.[1]

The mythology of the Polynesians has sometimes been compared with that of the Finns, in regard to its stage of religious development. Amongst the latter, however, the subordination of the spirits begins to appear, inasmuch as the inferior spirits of forests, waters, and the soil, are respectively grouped, as children or servants, round the presiding couples of the element to which they belong. The water spirits depend on Ahti and Wellamo, god and goddess of the waters; the forest spirits on Tapio and Mielliki, who preside over plants; and the spirits of the soil on Tuoni and Tuona Akka,

[1] On the religion of the Polynesians, consult Albert Réville, *Religions des peuples non-civilisés*, vol. ii. chaps. ii.—vi. Sir George Grey, *Polynesian Mythology:* London, 1855. W. W. Gill, *Myths and Songs from the South Pacific:* London, 1876. Williams and Calvert, *Fiji and the Fijians:* London, 1870.

III. POLYDEMONISM AND POLYTHEISM. 143

who rule over the subterranean world.[1] But inasmuch as the Finns were still in the pastoral age at the introduction of Christianity, this organization of the divine society never passed the patriarchal type. Their Olympus was formed after the model of the house, their Pantheon after that of the family; Ukko himself, the supreme god, was no more than a majestic shepherd who led the clouds, his sheep, to their pasture.

The divine societies of the Indo-Europeans. Even the Indo-Europeans do not seem to have possessed a regularly organized polytheism before their dispersion. Indeed, amongst the Slavs, who were perhaps the most backward of all the branches of the race, we see that even the great gods drawn from the common fatherland—Perun (perhaps the Vedic Parjanya, god of thunder), Svarog and Ogon (the respective equivalents of Svar the heaven, and Agni the fire), and even Bogu, the god of heaven—hardly rose above the crowd of spirits in the popular worship. And, on the other side, the very history of the terms (already recounted) that respectively served the Aryans of India and those of Persia to designate their great gods, *Devas* and *Ahuras*, shows us that amongst the Eastern Aryans the same terms were originally applied more or less indifferently to every category of superhuman beings.

Amongst the Aryans of India, in the Vedic period, social organization does not appear to have advanced much beyond the patriarchal rule of clans; at any rate we can discover nothing like the rigorous divisions of caste or

[1] A. Réville, *Religions des peuples non-civilisés*, vol. ii. chaps. ii. and iii.

the organization of great unified monarchies which prevailed subsequently. The society of superhuman beings, still closely attached to the phenomena of nature, manifests a correspondingly unstable character, almost amounting to anarchy, corrected and perhaps to a certain point maintained by what Prof. Max Müller has called henotheism—that is to say, the religious disposition to ascribe to each god at the moment of invocation all the attributes of supreme power. This division, or rather this alternation, of sovereignty only extends to six or seven great natural deities. The hymn of the legendary Manu Vaivasvata says that amongst the gods "there are neither great nor small, neither old nor young, all are equally great;" but practically, Varuna and Indra, gods of the heaven; Surya, the sun; Ushas, the dawn; Agni, the fire; Soma, fermented drink; and Aditi, space,—are, turn by turn, raised above all other gods, and are still more clearly distinguished from the innumerable spirits to be found in the popular cultus.

Amongst the Germans we find the mythological systematization carried out much further. At the bottom of the scale are the giants and elfs, then the Vanir, and finally the Ases or Æsir, ranked on a system which corresponds well enough with that of German society. Odin, who presides in the council of the Æsir, like the German chief in the assembly of free men, is no more than the president of a republic. His power is almost equalled by that of Thor, and even of Loki, until the latter becomes a rebel spirit.

Amongst the Greeks of the Homeric epoch, the celestial state is still more directly modelled on that of

III. POLYDEMONISM AND POLYTHEISM.

earth. The great gods correspond to the local kings, whose assembly is presided over by the King of men, just as the Olympians gather under the presidency of Zeus; and the power of the latter over his divine colleagues—though clearly enough established in the sense of his boast that he is the mightiest of the gods[1]—is no more absolute than that of Agamemnon over his allies. On the other side, the popular assembly of the Agora has its counterpart in the gathering of all the divine beings to learn the will of Zeus. We may even add that just as Greece was never able to attain a national unity, so all the efforts of the philosophers failed to give currency in the popular theology to a more advanced conception of the divine unity.

It is extremely difficult to reconstruct the worship of the Latins before the historical development of Rome, but it is probable that their *numina* were hardly superior to the mass of spirits, in spite of the presence amongst them of certain great deities of nature, drawn in some cases from the common fund of Indo-European traditions. The organizing faculty which characterizes the Roman genius found scope in the cultus earlier than in theology, and, with the exception of Jupiter, Mars, Neptune, the old Janus, Juno and Vesta, the greater part of the deities who took the first place in the worship of the Romans were foreign importations, in some instances relatively late. It is especially as the president of this divine oligarchy that the old Jupiter Optimus Maximus of the Capitol became the special patron of Rome and assumed the supreme government of the universe.

[1] *Iliad*, viii. 17.

III. POLYDEMONISM AND POLYTHEISM.

Amongst the Persians, monarchy was firmly established at an early date, perhaps under the pressure of a terrible struggle with the Turanian populations. Ahura Mazda, "the omniscient lord," naturally assumed the absolute sovereignty over the propitious powers since his immediate function was that of generalissimo of the armies of light in their contest with the powers of darkness. Here the hierarchy is complete. The old deities of nature, and certain great abstractions, personified by stress of circumstances, are the generals and captains of the celestial army. They include, firstly, the six Amesha Çpentas, the "Beneficent Immortals;" then, the Yazatas or "Worshipped ones," and amongst them Mithra, god of light; Naïryo Sanha, god of fire; Apam Napat, god of fire concealed in the waters; Haoma, god of the drink of immortality; Vayu, god of the wind, he who throws the storm against the wind; Tistrya, genius of the dog-star; and Anahita, goddess of fertility. Lastly come the mass of Fravashis, including the divine protoplasms of the just, and the genii of pure things.[1]

The divine society in Egypt. Quitting the Indo-European peoples to study the polytheism of other races, we find the same correspondence between the forms of political institutions and the organization of the divine society. Egypt before Menes appears to have been divided into independent nômes, in each of which a certain number of gods, properly so called, appear beside and above the spirits. It seems that before the

---

[1] Tiele, *Outlines of the History of Religion*, &c., translated by Carpenter, London, 1877, §§ 102—104, pp. 168—172. J. Darmesteter, *Ormazd et Ahriman*, Paris, 1877, chap. vi. Eug. Burnouf, *Commentaire sur le Yaçna*.

beginnings of history these little local Pantheons had undergone a certain concentration by the establishment of triads and enneads, the principal member of which often received the title of supreme god. But, as M. Maspero well observes, "the supremacy of these highest and even unique gods was confined to the limits of their respective nômes. Divine feudalism," continues this acute historian, "is the primordial fact of the religion of Egypt, as human feudalism is the primordial fact of its history."[1]

The divine societies of the Semites. In Mesopotamia, the first inhabitants of Chaldea appear to have placed a certain number of superhuman powers (*an* or *dingir*) above the spirits, before the epoch at which their history begins. These beings were the rulers of the principal natural phenomena, but were supposed to have made the world and to be man's protectors against the attacks of evil spirits. Above all stood Ana, the personification of heaven; Ea, the spirit of the earth; Mul-lil, ruler of the subterranean world; the Sun; the Moon; Istar, the evening star; perhaps the gods of the other planets then known; and finally, the gods of fire and the storm. The mere uttering of their names was enough to put the demons to flight; and the power of the name rose with the rank of the deity. "The most irresistible of all the powers resides in the mysterious name which Ea alone knows. Before that name, everything in heaven, on earth, and below, must yield. The gods themselves are chained by that name and obey it."[2]

[1] *Revue de l'histoire des Religions*, vol. xix. p. 11.

[2] Fr. Lenormant, *La Magie chez les Chaldéens*, Paris, 1874, p. 40.

This, however, is only a magical exaggeration, and at the outside amounts to nothing more than henotheism. "Thou alone art exalted," says the hymn to the Sun; "amongst the gods thou hast no equal."[1] The Prefect of Kalakh, in an inscription bearing the date of King Raman-ninari III., does not hesitate to say: "Put your trust in Nabu [the god of the scribes], and trust in no other god."[2] Elsewhere Bel is called the lord and the creator of the gods. Gradually some kind of order is introduced amongst the host of deities (there are passages which speak of sixty-five thousand[3]) by grouping them into triads, the members of which vary according to the city, the province, or the state. Sometimes it is Anu (the ancient Ana, god of heaven), Bel, and Ea transformed into a god of the ocean. Sometimes Sin, god of the moon, the god of gods; Shamas, god of the sun; and Rimmon, god of the wind. But even these triads appear to be rather a juxtaposition of deities than a combination tending to unity. It was otherwise with the Assyrians, whose bent was to form a military monarchy, the type of which is reflected in the organization of their divine world. At the bottom of the scale is the innumerable host of spirits; then come the gods, who may be likened to officers and imperial functionaries; above them are the chief deities, varying in number on the different inscriptions, sometimes thirty-six, sometimes thirteen or twelve, sometimes seven. These are

[1] Schrader, cited by De Pressensé, *L'ancien monde et le christianisme*, p. 63.

[2] Tiele, *Outlines*, &c., § 47, Eng. tr. p. 78.

[3] Sayce, *Hibbert Lectures* for 1887, p. 216.

what we might call the ministers and generals of Assur, who himself is the celestial prototype of the all-powerful despot who presides over the destinies of Assyria.

The religion of the Assyrians, however, had been modified by contact with Proto-chaldean beliefs, and for a pure type of Semitic religion we must turn to the populations of Syria. Here we find, not, indeed, the monotheism so long supposed to be proper to the genius of the Semitic race, but something very like monolatry, inasmuch as it often reveals the adoration of a local god regarded as supreme, and so far exalted above all other gods as to sink the latter even lower than the spirits. But here we have occasion to distinguish between the populations of the shore, where the easy conditions of life early developed a rich mythology, and those of the inlands, amongst whom the rugged aspects of nature produced a severer conception of the divine order. Amongst these latter, the imagination was more impressed by the imposing unity of the forces of nature than by the incessant variety of their manifestation. The idea of force dominates that of matter, and thus the superhuman beings are much less varied if not less numerous. Nothing is more like one Eloh, says M. Renan, than another Eloh; whence all that is required is to give these elohim a chief to direct them, and we have a god whose pre-eminence no rival will dispute.

For the rest, amongst all the western Semites the very names of the gods express a general and abstract idea of force and power rather than a determinate individuality. It was long supposed that the names of Baal, Adon, Moloch or Melek, El, Çedeq, Rabba, Asherah, &c.,

denoted so many divine personalities, worshipped by the whole race. Now we know that they were simply generic names, titles in a word—master, lord, king, the mighty, the just, the lady, &c.—under which each group of populations designated its chief deity.[1] It is probable that in every state the divine king adopted as supreme patron was surrounded by a court of secondary deities or subordinate spirits fulfilling all the offices of the government and the household. Yahveh himself, the Yahveh Çebaoth, god of the celestial armies, was surrounded by a veritable *divan*, in which the first place was held by a kind of "seraskier" or generalissimo, as M. Renan has it, the archangel Michael, and a grand vizier, the Mal'ak, the angel charged with communications to man. Then came the other angels, the cherubim and seraphim and the benë-elohim.

The conception of the superhuman world probably differed very little from this type amongst the Philistines, the Moabites, and the other more or less independent peoples that covered the Syrian region bordering on the desert, and even some of the cities of Phœnicia. At Beyrout, they specially worshipped the seven Kabires, probably planetary deities; but there came a time at which they placed the eighth (Eshmun) above them, and he became the chief deity, whether his name conceals a god of nature, or whether we should see in him a pure creation of theological speculation.[2]

---

[1] Tiele, *Religions de l'Égypte et des peuples sémitiques*, Paris, 1882, pp. 281 sqq.

[2] *Ibid.* p. 307.

III. POLYDEMONISM AND POLYTHEISM. 151

The divine societies of the Aztecs and Incas. The new world, at the period of the first European invasion, presented every degree and type alike of religious and social organization. Side by side with rudimentary forms which have survived to our own day in the customs and beliefs of the aboriginal peoples, the Spaniards found civilized communities at various levels of polytheism. This polytheism was still in an early stage, though the peoples of Central America and Mexico had a highly developed mythology. They worshipped the *teotl*—that is to say, the chief personifications of the elements, conceived under names and in forms which varied from centre to centre of civilization; but while raising some of these deities to the rank of official protectors and mythical legislators, they never seem to have enrolled them in any regularly classified hierarchy. This is because, as M. Albert Réville has shown, these peoples never had a unified and centralized empire, but only great federations, and states exerting a temporary preponderance.[1]

Further south, on the other hand, the Peru of the Incas presents the type of the most centralized state which our planet has ever known; and this centralization has its counterpart in the organization of the divine world. The Inca was supposed, not only to be descended from the sun, but to be commissioned to apply the government of the solar deity on earth; and just as everything in the empire was subordinated to the Inca, everything in the heavens was subordinated to the Sun. The latter had a court in which the moon, the great

---

[1] Réville, *Les Religions du Mexique*, &c., p. 23: Paris, 1885. Cf. the same author's *Hibbert Lectures* for 1884, pp. 28, 29.

planets and principal constellations appeared. Others, gods who must once have been almost as important as himself — Viracocha, Pachacamac, and Catequil — had become his children or his ministers.

The divine society in China. In the official religion of China, the parallelism of which I have given so many examples, is carried still further. From an early date we find a divine state closely modelled upon that of earth, and the different stages of the respective organizations are closely connected one with the other. At the head stands Shang-ti, the celestial emperor who watches over the general interests of the world; the terrestrial emperor, the "son of heaven," is his deputy for the government of men, and, moreover, has exclusive charge of the worship demanded by his superior. In like manner the chief functionaries preside over the worship of the great spirits of nature; the governors of provinces and cities, over that of chief local deities of their respective areas; and finally, the father of the family over the worship of the manes of his ancestors and the rank and file of spirits. Confucius declares that the functionaries of the State are the servants of heaven, just as the Li-ki says that the spirits are the functionaries of Shang-ti.

It is interesting to note that men have, in every case, been conscious of this parallelism spontaneously established between the celestial kingdom and the states on earth; but, by a common illusion of perspective, it is always the human society which has been supposed to be modelled on that of the gods.

Lecture IV.

DUALISM.

(i.) The Struggle for Order.

So now we have the gods arranged in a society like that of man. What will be the object of the organization? What will be the goal it proposes to itself? I was going to say, what will be its platform?

In the first place, it will be the interest of its own members. The gods pursue their own good, and have no scruple in naïvely avowing an egoism copied from that of their worshippers. The important point to notice, however, is, that the interest of the gods may in various ways coincide with that of their worshippers. *(Contracts of alliance with the super-human beings.)*

On the one hand, the latter might enter into a treaty with their gods founded on reciprocity of service; whence the two-fold consequence, that the gods would be interested in the prosperity and aggrandizement of the nation that had adopted them, and that they would be opposed to the gods of the neighbouring nations whenever their respective subjects fell into conflict. Even savages show a tendency to put themselves under the protection of their own ancestors and fetishes, as a defence against those of neighbouring peoples. And if they rank the spirits in general amongst these hostile powers, it is because, being more or less detached and anonymous, they represent the stranger, and to that extent the enemy. In polytheism we have no longer to deal with isolated powers, but with pantheons organized by nations or groups of nations; and the relations between these superhuman communities are again modelled on those of earth.

The gods as regulating powers. Mythology favours yet another order of conceptions which directly tends to turn the efforts of the gods towards the good of man, or at least towards one of the most necessary conditions of his existence, namely, an established order in nature.

I mean by mythology the transformation of natural phenomena or abstract events into personal adventures ascribed to superhuman beings. It does not enter into the scope of my plan to expound the rules by which we must interpret mythology; and still less to fathom the principles of the rival schools which trace the mythological stories respectively to oblivion of the primitive meaning of words, to distortion of history, or to the purely fantastic action of the savage imagination. But, whatever its origin, we discover at the base of all the myths a tendency to personify the details as well as the forces of nature, and to attribute to these imaginary personalities conduct like that of human beings, but powers far transcending those of man.

In nature-worship—that is to say, as long as personified objects are looked on as the bodies of spirits which act through them—we perhaps get no further than dramatizing the most characteristic of the actual relations between the objects concerned. The storm will be regarded as a fight between heaven, or the sun, and the storm-cloud. The occultation of the heavenly bodies will be represented as their consumption by a monster. The creation will be attributed to a union, or perhaps to an original separation, of the heaven and the earth.

May be the formation of these first myths was preceded by a period in which man simply depicted the phenomena of nature by isolated analogies drawn from his own experience. Thus, before representing the storm as the marriage of the heaven and the earth, or as the battle of the sun with the storm-cloud, with the wealth of detail that constitutes the charm of Indo-European mythology, he must have conceived of the rain as seed, the production of crops as birth, the clouds as an army of monsters or giants, the sun as a dart-hurler, the lightning as a celestial weapon, and the thunder as the voice of an invisible warrior or the shock of arms in the sky. Mythical elements remain at this undeveloped stage amongst peoples whose imagination is too poor (like that of the Chinese), or too random (like that of the Negroes), to group these rudimentary conceptions into a general whole; but elsewhere they early combine into complete dramas of nature, like those which we trace in the earliest religious texts of the Chaldeans, the Egyptians, and the Indo-European peoples.

When, as human thought advances, men reach a juster conception of the impersonality of things, they find a growing difficulty in making celestial or earthly objects take the part of quasi-human persons. But we must not forget that the personality of these objects has not disappeared; it has simply escaped from its envelope to rule from outside. Thus it preserves its former attributes and its old relations on the one hand, and on the other hand, as its new personality approximates to the human form, it lends itself more readily to combinations modelled on the life of man. Was it not in Greece that the deities of nature approached the human type most closely both physically and morally? And was it not there too that mythology acquired its widest extension and exercised its deepest influence?

In the long run, however, when the bonds connecting the spirits of things with the things themselves were once broken, these superhuman beings would inevitably be credited more and more with actions that had nothing in common with the mutual relations of the phenomena. The gods would tend to transform themselves into historical personages, and to annex the exploits of real heroes and even of the creatures of the popular fancy. The myth would be lost in the tale or legend, or might even tend to attach itself to any casually determined personality, till it became impossible to distinguish between a god transformed into a hero, and a hero transformed into a god.

Relations of mythology and religion. These adulterations have given rise to a distinction between mythology and religion; the latter including the sentiments that man cherishes with respect to his gods; the former, the stories which he accepts concerning them, or rather the deeds and exploits which he attributes to them. But do not the sentiments we experience towards any one largely depend on the idea we have formed of his nature, disposition, and doings?—that is to say, precisely on what mythology has to tell concerning the gods?

IV. DUALISM.

If we make a distinction at all—and, seeing how small an influence many myths exercise on the religious feelings and on the worship, I am inclined to think we should—it should be based on the fact that a whole class of myths simply minister to human curiosity, without affecting man's relations to the gods. Such notably are the myths professing to explain the first origin of phenomena, without concerning themselves with their maintenance or their reproduction. For in truth it is the future, and not the past, that awakes the hopes and fears on which the religious sentiment feeds; so that, from this point of view, the traditions connected with the present and future course of phenomena have vastly greater importance than those that refer to the formation of the universe, though the latter no less than the former present themselves in mythological guise, as recording the definite events of a given moment in the past. Again, to feel this importance, men must believe the traditions to be something more than stories invented for their pleasure—more even than a faithful record of historical facts which are now past and done with. Then, but then only, will mythology become religion, when it represents the most important deities as strengthening the action of the beneficent phenomena, over which they preside, against the efforts of the beings who regulate or produce the maleficent phenomena opposed to them.

Hence grows a dualism which finds its first application on the field of the conflicting forces that affect the two great primary necessaries of life, light and food. But, with the aid of mythology, it soon comes to embrace the whole mass of superhuman beings. These latter are divided into two camps, according to their nature or affinities. Man himself soon falls into line, and not only offers his divine defenders sympathy, but actively co-operates with them, encouraging them by his prayers and praises, strengthening them by his sacrifices and incantations, and abstaining from all that might hamper or enfeeble their action. Hence another bond of union is contracted between man and the gods, whom he now feels to be fighting in the same army and espousing the same cause with himself.

<small>Progress and systematization of natural dualism.</small> This dualism based on natural phenomena appears but little developed amongst peoples at the first stage of polytheism, such as the ancient Mexicans, Polynesians, or Finns. Amongst the Proto-chaldeans dualism manifests itself not so much in the sphere of natural phenomena as on the field of man's daily struggle against evil spirits, especially the spirits of disease; but the death of Tammuz, the descent of Istar into hell in search of her lost lover, the incidents of her quarrel with her sister Allat, queen of the subterranean world, and, on the other side, the legend of the Deluge, of the fight of the moon-god with the seven evil spirits, to say nothing of the story of the creation itself, prove clearly enough that natural dualism was not entirely absent from the Assyrio-chaldean mythology. We may remark that the seven evil spirits at the head of the infernal armies represent the seven principal winds, and that the great gods, invoked to keep them in check, are unquestionably planetary deities, or at any rate personifications of natural phenomena of some kind.

According to Prof. Sayce, the texts show traces of a period when all the superhuman beings were at once good and evil. It must have been by gradual steps that the Chaldeans came to separate the two phases of this mixed character, and to make the superior gods the dispensers of all benefits, while the lower spirits assumed the exclusive rôle of the agents of evil.[1]

Amongst the Egyptians there were originally three kinds of deities—the gods of the elements, the gods of the dead, and the solar gods. The first, such as Sib and Nut, appear half-effaced in the worship; the second, with Osiris at their head, were gradually assimilated to the sun below the earth, that is to say, the sun after sunset; and thus the whole religion of Egypt became, as M. Pierret expresses it, a "solar drama;"[2] that is to say, it was entirely concentrated in the struggle of light against darkness, and, by extension, of life against death. The luminous gods embark in full strength in the solar boat, "the good boat of thousands of years." They are joined there by the souls of the just, thus assimilated to Osiris. One Horus places himself at the helm, another at the prow, with couched spear; the oars are grasped by the Akhimu Urdu, "who cease not to exist," and the Akhimu Soku, "who are never destroyed." The crew, however, quit the luminous fields of heaven to penetrate the darksome region of the world below. At the sixth hour of the night begins the daily fight in which the serpent Apap, with all his army of monsters, strives to arrest the course of the boat. But the gods

[1] Sayce, *Hibbert Lectures* for 1887, p. 205.
[2] Paul Pierret, *Le Panthéon Égyptien*, Paris, 1881, p. xv.

of light overcome all obstacles. Ra triumphs. "Apap is slain." And therefore the sun rises again, with renewed lustre, on the horizon of grateful Egypt.[1] The same dualism re-appears, in a quasi-historical form, in the myth of Osiris as told by Herodotus, and as read, with its anthropomorphic traits still further emphasized, on the inscriptions of the temple of Edfu.[2]

You are aware of the importance assumed in the worship of the Syro-phœnicians, by the scenic representations which reproduced the passion of a deity alternately slain and resuscitated. In Phrygia, it was Attis, mutilated by the jealousy of Cybele, and then transformed into the pine with evergreen foliage, who wakes from his winter slumber at the beginning of the spring. At Byblos, it was Adonis, slain by a wild boar and recalled to life by the enamoured Astarte. If we may judge by the dates at which the feast of his death and resurrection were respectively celebrated, Adonis (amongst those Syrian populations who suffer most from the parching sun) represents the spring sky, slain by the sun when the heaven grows scorching, and born again at the approach of autumn, when pregnant nature re-finds her lost lover.[3]

[1] G. Maspero, *Histoire Ancienne des peuples de l'Orient*, Paris, 1886, pp. 280 sqq.

[2] H. Brugsch, *Die Sage von der geflügelten Sonnenscheibe*, in the *Abhandlungen der Königlichen Gesellschaft der Wissenschaften zu Göttingen* (vol. xiv.). *Historisch Philologische Classe*, Göttingen, 1869, pp. 173—236.

[3] C. P. Tiele, *Histoire comparée des anciennes religions de l'Égypte et des peuples Sémitiques*, book iii. chap. iv. *La religion de Gébal ou Byblos*, pp. 291—298.

IV. DUALISM.

Amongst the Greeks, the "mysteries" clearly betray the influence of Oriental religions; but under the smiling climate of Hellas the Aryan genius had conceived a view of the universe too serene and harmonious to fall in with the tragic emotions of nature-worship. It chose rather to relegate the fight with the chaotic forces of nature to the origin of things. The Titans were enchained once for all in their dark dungeons, and, but for the menacing predictions of a Prometheus, there would be nothing left to trouble the Olympian quiet of Zeus. But when the Greek religion had overstepped its frontiers, it finally took a more sombre tone, and under the influence of theories of emanation the $δαίμων$, which had once simply meant spirit—sometimes even the good genius of man, as in the case of Socrates—gradually became a synonym for an evil power, the *demon*, whose name Christianity took, in this new signification, and applied it to the whole body of pagan divinities.

Amongst the Germans, also, it is easy to see how dualism became accentuated as religion developed. The giants of the frost, the wolf Fenris, the serpent Nidhugr gnawing the roots of the cosmic tree, were always evil spirits; but the organization of the army of darkness and the frimas is not complete until Hel and Loki have placed themselves at its head to lead it to the attack of the Æsir. Now Hel and Loki were originally conceived with less antipathetic traits. Prof. Tiele points out that as we ascend towards a remoter antiquity, Hel, the personification of twilight, occupies an ever loftier position, though she sank at last into the goddess that enchains the dead and terrifies the living. As to Loki, the god of fire, he was at first the brother and companion of Odin; nay, he rendered signal services to the gods in their fight with the giants; but subsequently he was looked upon as the father of the evil powers, and it is he who strips the goddess of earth of her adornments, who robs Thor of his fertilizing hammer, and causes the death of Balder, the beneficent sun.[1]

With the Hindus, dualism takes a yet more important place both in worship and in mythology. They are never weary of telling how the Maruts, Indra, Agni, and Vishnu, waged war with the serpent Ahi—alternately named Vritra (the enveloper), Cushna (the parcher), and Dasa (the slayer)—to deliver the celestial cows or spouses, that is to say, the waters held captive in the caverns of the clouds. Elsewhere it is the fire, the dawn, or the sun, whose fate is the stake of the battle. The history of the asuras, or rather of the word which serves to designate these personified evil influences, bears striking evidence to the progress, or, if you will, the systematization of Hindu dualism, as mythology developed. At first the term *asura* (being or spirit) is applied indifferently to good and evil beings. In fact, Varuna himself is the Asura *par excellence* in the Vedas. On the other hand, the devas of the Vedic songs sometimes play the part of demons in retaining the light or the water for themselves.[2] It is in the brahmanas and the puranas, compositions of a later date, that the dualism attains its

[1] C. P. Tiele, *Outlines of the History of Religions*, § 118, pp. 194, 195.

[2] Abel Bergaigne, *Religion Védique d'après les hymnes du Rig-Veda*, three vols., Paris, 1878—1883, vol. iii. pp. 78, 79. Vol. xxxvi. of the *Bibliothèque de l'école des hautes études*, Paris.

IV. DUALISM.

height, and the devas are represented on the one side, and the asuras on the other, as fighting for the possession of the *amrita*, the heavenly water which assures fertility to the earth and immortality to living beings.[1]

Whether Zoroastrianism be attributed to a natural evolution of the old Indo-Iranian religion, or to a violent reaction against the nature-worship of which we find the earliest traces in the Vedas, it is certain in any case that there too we find a dualism which must have strengthened greatly after the separation of the two peoples. Indeed, we may safely say that it has not been carried out more completely in any known religion. Opposed to Ormuzd, and the superhuman beings grouped around him to maintain all that is good in the world, we find Ahriman and his daevas, whose object is absolutely to thwart the work of the Omniscient Lord, whether by destroying what he makes, or by producing, in their turn, counter creations. Here the opposition is complete. Not only have we two hierarchies, exactly corresponding to each other, but the correspondence extends to all their respective acts; and all the details of nature are divided between the two powers. Nothing has a mixed, neutral, or equivocal character. Everything that does not come from Ormuzd proceeds from Ahriman. If a being or a phenomenon has no actual counterpart in the antagonistic forces of nature, the blank is filled up by a process of abstraction. This

[1] Moor, in his *Hindu Pantheon*, reproduces a picture of an episode introduced into the *Mahabharata*, representing the churning of the ocean, for the recovery of the beverage of immortality, by means of the mountain Mandara. The serpent Vasuki girds the mountain as a cord, and one end is pulled by the devas and the other by the asuras.— Edward Moor, *The Hindu Pantheon*, London, 1810, p. 182 and plate 49.

explains the singular conglomeration of abstract genii and deities of nature which characterizes the religious system of the Persians.[1]

Even the Jewish religion attests, in the course of its development, the growing accentuation of dualism. In early times, no superhuman being was recognized in opposition to Yahveh. Beyond the national deity and the gods of foreign peoples, we find little more than spirits subordinate to the supreme God, such as angels, seraphim, cherubim, and those benë-elohim, or sons of God, whom the book of Job represents as coming from time to time to pay their court to the Eternal. Even Satan was but a kind of public minister, an inspector, or rather *agent provocateur*, who had no power to torment or tempt save by permission of his master. It is only quite at a late period that we find the revolted angels organizing themselves into an army of darkness under the guidance of Satan, to struggle against the soldiery of heaven under the direction of Yahveh; and we may even ask whether this phenomenon, when it does appear, is not due to the influence of Iranian demonology. We see Yahveh surrounded by six archangels, like Ahura Mazda with his Amesha Çpentas; and, as in Iranian mythology, the introduction of evil and death into the world becomes the work of the rebel spirits.

You will observe that though dualism becomes more pronounced as its organization is perfected, yet it never goes the length of setting the powers of good and the

---

[1] Compare James Darmesteter, *Ormazd et Ahriman*, Paris, 1877, part ii. chap. vi. pp. 242—314. Vol. xxix. of the *Bibliothèque de l'école des hautes études*, Paris.

powers of evil on a footing of absolute equality, still less of admitting the possibility of the final triumph of evil. Even in the religion of the Persians, Ahura Mazda is anterior to Ahriman and will survive him. Three thousand years after Zoroaster, the evil spirits will be destroyed, while the just will behold the definitive kingdom of the Omniscient Lord, in which disease and evil will be banished for ever from nature.

<small>Conception of the cosmic order, and idea of law.</small> This confidence in the permanence, the return, or the triumph of the forces that have assured the actual development of the world, finally took the shape of the conception of law, that is to say, of a natural order sustained by the superhuman powers.

Conceive, if you can, the mental state of infantine peoples beginning to reflect on the great phenomena of nature. For them, everything is chance, caprice, or, at the outside, mere habit. They are never sure that the day once gone will re-appear on the morrow, or that the summer will return after the winter. If the sun returns in the spring from his retreat, if the moon reassumes her lost form, month by month, if the rain puts an end to the drought, if the wind is appeased, it is these phenomena themselves who will it so; but who shall say whether they will always be of the same mind?

The Abipones, who believe that their race sprang from the constellation of the Pleiades, suppose that when it descends below the horizon, at the approach of summer, their grandfather is sick; and they celebrate his re-appearance in autumn with great demonstrations of joy.¹ Here we find the explanation of the festivals celebrated by all the ancient peoples in connection with the re-birth of the sun at the winter solstice, still perpetuated in the popular traditions of Christmas in Europe.

But are we sure that the being who re-appears at intervals is always the same? The Bechuanas of Southern Africa do not say that the sun sets, but that he dies.² The French term of *Noël* takes us back to the *dies natalis solis invicti* of Pagan antiquity—to an epoch, that is, in which men must have believed that the sun was re-born each year. And to this day we speak of "new moons" in witness of the times when it was supposed that moons grew old and died.³ Certain tribes of Australia declare that the sun kills the moon every month. The Bassutos have got beyond this stage, for they say that the sun chases the moon every month and eats her, little by little; but she is clever enough to escape him when she is reduced to a mere thread, and so gradually recovers her former shape.⁴ Certain favoured peoples however, by comparing repeated observations, gradually discovered

---

¹ Martinus Dobrizhoffer, *Historia de Abiponibus*, Vienna, 1784, vol. ii. p. 77.

² Max Müller, *Chips from a German Workshop*, vol. ii. p. 83.

³ In the Walloon provinces of Belgium they still tell the children that the stars are made out of bits of the old moons.—*Questionnaire de Folklore wallon*, Liège, 1890, p. 87.

⁴ Albert Réville, *Religions des peuples non-civilisés*, vol. i. p. 143, and vol ii. p. 151.

that the days and the seasons succeed each other at regular intervals; that the sun, moon, and stars re-appear periodically at the same points of the horizon, and invariably traverse the same course; that the storm always comes to put an end to the drought, and the blue sky replaces the clouds. This constancy at last re-assured mankind. They said that the phenomena which acted thus must have their own superior reasons for doing so, drawn either from an unalterable affection for earthly creatures, or from the necessities of their own existence. Thus men were led by an act of faith, in which religion anticipated science, to regard the course of celestial phenomena as a path traced out once for all. Then was born in the human spirit the first idea of a natural order, in which the past is a guarantee of the future. It is this " immutable way" which the Aryans of India called Rita;[1] the Persians, Asha;[2] the Chinese, Tao or Tien;[3] the Egyptians, the Ma or Maāt.[4]

[1] Max Müller, *Hibbert Lectures* for 1878, p. 237.

[2] James Darmesteter, *Ormazd et Ahriman*, part i. chap. i. §§ 11—17, pp. 13—18. M. Darmesteter points out that the Persian Asha, like the Hindu Rita, bears the two-fold signification of the cosmic order and the liturgical order, whence he concludes that the idea is anterior to the separation of the Indo-Iranians. Prof. Max Müller, mounting still higher, attempts to prove that it had its origin before the formation of the Indo-European languages.

[3] Albert Réville, *La Religion chinoise*, Paris, 1889, pp. 102, 120, 137, 138. Ch. de Harlez, *Les Religions de la Chine*, Leipzig, 1891, p. 47.

[4] Le Page Renouf, *Hibbert Lectures* for 1879, pp. 119 sqq. P. Pierret, *Panthéon égyptien*, p. 20. Eugène Grébaut, *Hymne à Ammon-Ra*, Paris, 1873, p. xix., in the *Bibliothèque de l'école des hautes études*.

IV. DUALISM.

Results of the belief in a natural order. We may easily imagine what new light this idea—concrete and quasi-material as it was—must at once have thrown upon the spectacle of the universe. Certainly it alone made the development of science possible. The explanation of phenomena by the capricious intervention of superhuman beings gives so easy a solution, that it discourages all attempts to inquire into the natural causes of events, as we see clearly enough from the uncivilized peoples of our own time. But when, instead of having to deal with fantastic and arbitrary beings, man believes in superhuman agencies who govern the world according to laws, he will no longer hesitate to search for these laws by a rational study of the facts, and he will even be stimulated in such a course by the thought that he will thus gain a new means of bringing the divine wisdom and power into relief. The pursuit of science will become a conscious act of religion.

Doubtless the natural order, as conceived at that epoch, only applies to the most regular phenomena, and, on the other hand, includes a number of supposed facts which we regard as absurd and impossible. Moreover, it is still admitted that this order may be violated, within certain limits, by the caprice or passion from which the gods are not yet entirely free. But this arbitrary element is more and more regarded as exceptional and anomalous; and the very fact of its being set in opposition to the normal course of affairs shows the existence of a well-established belief in that order itself, and at the same time marks the beginning of a struggle in the human mind, which will not end until the supernatural,

IV. DUALISM.

or rather the anti-natural (which must not be confounded with the supra-sensible), has been banished from the reason and the conscience.

Widening of the religious horizon. Nevertheless we must not conclude that the elasticity of the religious sentiment has been weakened by this gradual suppression of the arbitrary element. It is, indeed, evident at a glance that the conception of a natural order must result in restraining within ever narrower limits the independence of the personified phenomena, and even of the gods which rule them. "Surya," says a Vedic hymn, " does not transgress the places indicated;"[1] and Heraclitus formulates the same thought with respect to Helios. But we must note that this very order itself is regarded as the work of personal agents, to whom a veneration intensified by the increased grandeur of their functions is straightway directed. In a word, the problem of the Author of things does but shift its ground.

Who has established the order of nature? We have seen that the Incas worshipped the sun, whom they regarded as their father and first legislator; yet we are told that the Inca Yupanqui, who lived shortly before the Spanish conquest, once said: "If [the sun] was a living thing, he would become tired as we do; and if he was free, he would visit other parts of the heaven which he never reaches. He is like a tethered beast that always makes the same round, or like the dart which goes where it is sent, and not where it wishes." And a little later, the Inca Huyana Capac is said to have remarked to the high-priest at a great festival of the sun at Cuzco: "Our

[1] *Rig-Veda*, iii. 30. 12.

father the Sun must have another Lord more powerful than himself, who orders him to make this journey day by day, without resting."[1]

One may well doubt whether these words have not been put into the mouths of the Incas in order to make them precursors of Christianity, but the naïve reasoning attributed to them re-appears amongst many other peoples. "Who," asks the Zend-Avesta, "was from the beginning the father of the pure world? Who has made a path for the sun and for the stars? Who makes the moon to increase and to decrease?"[2]

This question has been answered in divers ways. The simplest is to say that each celestial body is directed by its own deity. The Polynesians declare that the sun used to follow a capricious course, but the sun-god Maui caught him in a kind of lassoo which compelled him thenceforth, in spite of his struggles and cries, to remain above the horizon long enough to allow man to pursue his occupations.[3] Not so many centuries ago, in Europe itself, a genius was placed within each planet to direct it through space as a kind of pilot. As soon, however, as the regular phenomena which in their entirety constitute the cosmic order have been brought into relations one with another, that cosmic order itself will come to be regarded either as the movement proper to the personi-

---

[1] Garcilasso de la Vega, *Commentarios Reales* (first part), Lisbon, 1609, book viii. chap. viii., and book ix. chap. x. Translated by Clements R. Markham, London, 1869: "Hakluyt Society," pp. 354, 446.

[2] See Max Müller, *Science of Religion*, London, 1873, p. 240.

[3] *Mélusine*, vol. i. (1878), p. 13.

IV. DUALISM. 171

fied firmament, which serves as their theatre, or as the result of an impulse due to the god who governs the sum of the celestial phenomena. The first of these two notions prevailed in the ancient religion of the Chinese, in which the majestic succession of the cosmic phenomena is regarded as the immediate manifestation of the celestial activity. The second prevailed in the Semitic religions, particularly in that of the Israelites, in which the book of Genesis makes the Eternal say, " Let there be lights in the expanse of heaven to part the day from the night, and to serve as signs of days, seasons and years." Amongst the Chaldeans, it is Bel who fixes the stars, and establishes the places of the planets and the sun, "that they might know their bonds, that they might not err, that they might not go astray in any way."[1] Among the Egyptians, it is Ptah-Ptanen who prescribes to heaven and earth the path which they transgress not.[2] With the Persians, it is of course Ahura Mazda who takes this part.

The two conceptions are in a certain way united in the Vedas, where we are sometimes told that the unshaken laws rest on Varuna as upon a rock; and sometimes this same god is represented as the author, the guardian, and the guide of the Rita: " Varuna has laid down the course of the sun, he has thrown out the impetuous torrents of the rivers, and he has hollowed the

---

[1] Fifth tablet of the creation story. *Apud* Sayce, *Hibbert Lectures* for 1887, p. 389.

[2] Le Page Renouf, *Hibbert Lectures* for 1879, p. 223.

great courses in which flow in seemly order the loosened flood of the days."[1]

Finally, the natural order may be personified under the features of an abstract deity—the Gathu, the "Broad Way," which figures amongst the Hindus as one of the deities of the morning; the Rita itself; the Asha Vahista, the genius of purity, or rather of regularity, amongst the Persians; the goddess Ma, the Egyptian personification of truth, that is to say, conformity to the reality; perhaps the Moira of the Greeks, to say nothing of Nomos, their personification of law, and the Erynnyes, those daughters of Zeus and of justice, who not only forbid the sun to exceed his orbit, but likewise refuse to allow the horse of Achilles to speak the language of men.[2]

These abstract personalities may maintain themselves against the gods in cases where the latter retain, from their mythological past, a capricious or arbitrary character. In such cases, the ancient deities will either be gradually relegated to the background by this new conception of the superhuman power, or else their wills will be gradually assimilated to the irrevocable decrees of the new power, which is summoned to rule the destinies of the universe. In China, Taoism, degraded as it now is by vulgar superstitions, originally defined the *Tao* as having existed even before the deity,[3] whereas the official religion of the empire sees in the order of nature the will of heaven itself. In Egypt, we learn from the texts that

---

[1] *Rig-Veda*, vii. 87. 1.   [2] *Iliad*, xix. 418.

[3] Ch. de Harlez, *Les Religions de la Chine*, Leipzig, pp. 174 sq.

Mā is sometimes called Lady of the Heaven and Ruler of the World, who "knows no lord or master;"[1] whilst other passages, perhaps more faithful to the prevailing conception, declare of Osiris: "He maintains order in the universe and makes the son succeed the father." Whilst the Brahmans, as we have just seen, attribute the creation of the Rita to Varuna, Buddhism recognizes nothing in the universe but the action of the *Karma*, the residue of acts, that is to say, the action of effects and causes. In the Buddhist writings, Çakra, the chief of the thirty-three gods who inhabited the Vedic Olympus, declares his inability to act in opposition to the consequences of the Karma.[2] So, too, with the Greeks, Moira is superior even to Zeus; but the opposition pales in proportion as the will of the lord of Olympus comes into more constant harmony with the requirements of universal order, until the time is reached when Cleanthes can exclaim: "Oh Zeus! in conformity to law dost thou conduct all things."[3]

[1] Le Page Renouf, *Hibbert Lectures* for 1879, p. 122. M. Eugène Grébaut notes, rightly enough, that this conception of the Truth as a supreme law of the universe is anterior and superior to monotheism in Egypt. Indeed, when once it becomes the foundation of the whole theodicy and of religion itself, it places the relations of the faithful to the superhuman world on bases independent of the questions of pantheism, dualism, and creation properly so called.—*Hymne à Ammon Ra*, Paris, 1875, p. xix.

[2] S. Beal, in *Religious Systems of the World*, 1890, p. 84.

[3] Stobæus, *Physica*, bk. i. c. ii. § 12. From Homeric times downwards, M. Jules Girard points out a tendency to make the gods, in virtue of their very being, the representatives of stability, endurance, fixed principles, obvious or hidden laws of the universe.—Jules Girard, *Le sentiment religieux en Grèce d'Homère à Eschyle*, second

We are now in a position to judge whether this assimilation of the cosmic to the divine order—the reign of law in the whole series of observable facts—implies, as certain superficial thinkers declare, the first step towards atheism. On the contrary, it surely leads to the recognition of the rational principle in the universe. The Vedic poet well understood this when he cried: "The sun and the moon move in regular succession in order that we may believe, O Indra!"[1] Is it not in the same sense that we must take the words of the Psalmist, "The heavens declare the glory of God"? "It is because of law that we believe in the gods," says Euripides;[2] and the Egyptians went further still in declaring that "the gods live by Maāt."[3]

What lessons have we here for those who still continue to require some violation of the natural laws as a proof of the omnipotence and even the existence of God! How much more truly was Kant on the line of religious progress—nay, in the stream of our ancient Indo-European tradition—when he urged us to seek that proof in the spectacle of the heavens and in the voice of conscience, rather than in the miracles of Joshua stopping the sun, or Jesus raising the dead!

The conception of universal order thus formulated, however, implies yet another step of progress, viz. the assimilation of the divine order not only to the cosmic but also to the moral order.

edition, Paris, 1879, p. 52. Pindar had already sung, Νόμος ὁ πάντων βασιλεὺς θνατῶν τε καὶ ἀθανάτων, cited by Plato, *Gorgias*, § 87.

[1] *Rig-Veda*, i. 102, 2.
[2] νόμῳ γὰρ τοὺς θεοὺς ἡγούμεθα.—*Hecuba*, 800.
[3] Le Page Renouf, *Op. cit.* p. 120.

(ii.) THE STRUGGLE FOR GOOD.

Immorality of the myths. How can peoples professing relatively advanced views as to the nature and functions of the deity—the Hindoos and Greeks, for example—accept accounts of their gods as absurd and gross as the stories of their respective mythologies are? And, moreover, how could peoples whose morals were so relatively pure as those of the Germans attribute vices and even crimes to their gods at which they would have blushed themselves? The views developed in the preceding Lectures have already put us in a position to give a partial answer to the question. Such facts as the destruction of the twilight by the sun, the removal of the clouds by the wind, the apparent union of the heaven with the atmosphere, the earth, the clouds, or the dawn—have no immoral character in themselves, even when respectively called parricide, theft, or adultery; but they quite change their character when the beings to whom they are attributed are no longer looked upon as heavenly bodies and as natural objects (whether personified or not), but are regarded as heroes, of a human or a quasi-human physiognomy, living in a society similar to that of man.

This explanation presented itself to the minds of the ancients. Thus in the sixth century before our era, Theagenes of Rhegium taught that the wars of the gods signified the conflict of the elements. Socrates explained that if Orithyia was carried away by Boreas, it simply meant that she had been hurled from the rocks by the north wind. And, in like manner, a Hindu commentator, Kumarila, explains the scandalous chronicle of the Vedic gods as follows: "It is fabled that Prajapati, the Lord of Creation, did violence to his daughter. But what does it mean? Prajapati, the Lord of Creation, is a name of the sun..... His daughter Ushas is the dawn. And when it is said that he was in love with her, this only means that, at sunrise, the sun runs after the dawn, the dawn being at the same time called the daughter of the sun, because she rises when he approaches. In the same manner, if it is said that Indra was the seducer of Ahalya, this does not imply that the god Indra committed such a crime; but Indra means the sun, and Ahalya .... the night; and, as the night is seduced and ruined by the sun of the morning, therefore is Indra called the paramour of Ahalya."[1]

Numbers of myths, however, and especially mythic episodes, do not lend themselves so easily to this treatment as simple metaphors. When interpretations from nature have done what they can towards explaining mythology, we still have a residuum which represents the free play of popular fancy. Why has imagination here, too, allowed itself so free a course in directions which reason and morals, as we understand them, would have prohibited? The anthropological school explains this anomaly by throwing back the formation of the myths to an epoch at which their authors were still at the intellectual and moral level of the savages of to-day. Mr. Andrew Lang has contributed much to the illustration of this theory by comparing the classical mythologies

[1] See Max Müller, *History of Ancient Sanskrit Literature*, London, 1859, pp. 529 sq.

IV. DUALISM. 177

with the traditions of uncivilized peoples in both hemispheres.[1] We cannot insist too often on the point that the god of the savage is simply an idealized chief or sorcerer. Why should he not comport himself as the worshipper supposes a chief or sorcerer endowed with increased faculties would do? But if this theory accounts for the absurdity and the crudity which make the more cultivated nations blush for their mythology, it does not explain why the authors of the myths have ascribed acts to their deities which they themselves would regard as blameworthy or degrading. The only possible explanation is, that at first morals had no influence whatever on the conception formed of the gods. Ethics and religion were absolutely independent of each other.

Original independence of morals and religion. I am not now to discuss ethical origins. Whatever theory we profess in this matter, one fact is certain, namely, that even amongst the most primitive peoples the right of the strongest is limited by certain obligations that custom has consecrated, and the violation of which at any rate involves public disfavour, and arouses in the mind of the victim a sense of injustice. Indeed, were this not so, no society at all could exist beyond the limits of the family, in which possibly parental authority might suffice to maintain the social ties. No doubt peoples differ much in their definitions of good and evil, but they all admit the distinction itself, and declare that we must do good and shun evil.

You will observe that this has nothing to do with the belief in superhuman beings, whose support, if not the

[1] See, especially, his *Myth, Ritual and Religion*, London, 1887, 2 vols.

result of pure caprice, is proportioned to the generosity with which they are treated or the skill with which they are served.

Even groups which have already reached the first stage of polytheism, such as the ancient Mexicans, the Polynesians, or the Shintoists of Japan, show no trace as yet of a connection between religion and morals. We must not be misled by the prayers in which the worshipper implores pardon for his sins, and prays, often in very exalted terms, that the stain may be taken from him. "From a distance," says a Japanese prayer, "I reverently worship with awe before Ameno Mi-hashira and Kunino Mi-hashira (the god and goddess of wind), ... I say with awe, Deign to bless me by correcting the unwilling faults which, heard and seen by you, I have committed."[1] Yet the very author who translates this prayer adds that Shintoism does not bear so much as a trace of an ethical code.

In the ancient Chaldean civilization it hardly seems that men's moral conduct influenced their relations with the gods in any way, and yet their religious literature contains hymns which M. Lenormant rightly describes as penitential psalms. "Oh Lord," cries the worshipper of Bel or Istar, "my sins are many, my transgressions are great! . . . The sin that I sinned I knew not. The transgression I committed I knew not. . . . The Lord in the wrath of his heart has regarded me; God in the fierceness of his heart has revealed himself to me. . . . O Lord, destroy not thy servant! When cast

[1] Isabella Bird, *Shintóism*, in *Religious Systems of the World*, London, 1890, pp. 93, 98.

into the water of the ocean, take his hand. The sins I have sinned, turn to a blessing. The transgressions I have committed, may the wind carry away. Strip off my manifold wickednesses as a garment."[1] But as soon as we look below the surface, we see that these despairing cries of a conscience a prey to the agonies of remorse, refer to faults committed, not against men, but against the gods, by ritual omissions or legal impurities sometimes contracted by the worshipper even without his knowledge.

<small>First entry of religion into social relations.</small> Nevertheless, religion must have exercised a favourable influence on the consolidation of social relations from the first. To begin with, it developed the spirit of subordination, prevented the scattering of the tribe, and formed a link between successive generations; and in the next place, it favoured the sacrifice of a direct and immediate satisfaction to a greater but more distant and indirect good.

<small>The oath.</small> The transition from the purely interested intervention of the superhuman beings in the affairs of men to the exercise of their moral or judicial functions, may perhaps be found in their anxiety to make the oath respected. In general, the spirits are indifferent enough to the lies which their worshippers tell one another; but the latter, in order to inspire confidence in their promises, often have occasion to close the possibility of breaking their word with impunity against themselves. This object may be secured by giving a pledge, or more simply by calling upon the gods, and especially the most powerful or the most dreaded of them, as witnesses to

---

[1] Sayce, *Hibbert Lectures* for 1887, pp. 350, 351.

the promise; so that if either of the parties breaks his engagement, the divinity in question may feel himself personally affected, and may therefore take vengeance.[1]

Amongst the Greeks, the importance of the oath varied with that of the deities invoked.[2] The most solemn were those made in the name of the Eumenides or of Zeus Horkios. Every oath implies a promise made to the deity, and we know with what rigour Yahveh himself exacted the accomplishment of vows, however imprudent, as, for instance, that of Jephtha. Now, when the gods have thus been made the champions of truth on solemn occasions, an easy transition leads to their being supposed to love the truth for its own sake, and to desire its prevalence on all occasions.

The ordeal. Another institution in which the deity began to assume the character of a justiciary power is found in the "Judgments of God" in which the superhuman beings sometimes punished the culprit and sometimes simply helped in his detection.

Every one knows of the ordeals of the Middle Ages in which the accused had to submit to the test of fire or water. Some of these customs apparently go back to the common era of the Indo-European races, since traces of them are found in the code of Manu, whereas it is amongst the Germans that we probably find the

[1] The bare fact of lieing in the presence of a deity in itself shows want of respect. Mrs. Murray Ainsley tells us that in certain parts of India the merchants refuse to take up their positions under a *pipal* tree, because, if they did, they could not ask more than the right price for their wares.—*Revue des traditions populaires*, Jan. 1889, p. 19.

[2] A. Maury, *Religion de la Grèce antique*, 3 vols, Paris, 1857, vol. ii. p. 167.

earliest explanation of them. For in ancient Germany their efficacy is attributed, not to the intervention of a god from outside, but to the inherent sentiments of the personified element. Thus, if the culprit could not sink in the water, it was because it rejected him; and the fire, of its own accord, spared the innocent victim who trusted it, and threw himself into the flames or walked upon burning torches. It is very significant that analogous customs are found wherever some kind of social justice is beginning to germinate—for instance, amongst the Negroes, the Malagassy, the Polynesians, the Redskins, and others. Under the kinglets of pagan Africa, the ordeal generally consists in drinking a poisonous draught; and here, with the complicity of the sorcerer charged with the preparation of the drink, it often constitutes the whole machinery of government.

M. Albert Réville represents the ordeal as a proof that the savage thinks the spirits of justice and truth superior to those of evil and error;[1] but I cannot help asking whether this is not forcing moral dualism prematurely to the front ere the corresponding stage of religious development has been reached, and I am tempted to regard it as simply a tribute to the keener sight and intellect of the superhuman beings, who are supposed to be more capable than man of discovering the authors of certain crimes. To whom, indeed, can the savage turn for help in such investigations better than to the powers supposed to be acquainted with the past and the future? Lieutenant Becker once saw an idol at Boma, in East Africa, with several heads. When he

[1] *Religions des peuples non-civilisés*, vol. i. p. 103.

asked the meaning of this polycephaly, he was told that it enabled the god the better to discover criminals.[1] At any rate, it is certain that the gods thus employed as informers or detectives naturally become the terror of criminals, and finally get the reputation of hating crime itself.

Crimes against the gods of the community. Again, when a man believes in the gods of the community, he cannot but allow that their protection extends to all the members of the tribe, and consequently that they will insist on the rights of his neighbour being respected as much as his own. Yet more: there are certain crimes which directly affect the interests, if not the very existence, of the tribe itself, such as treason, breach of customs, and so on. The repression of such attempts naturally concerns the gods of the community, and all the more so because they are regarded as the authors of the violated custom, and the organizers of the threatened society; and this is actually the case even amongst populations as backward as the Araucans, the Andamans, and the Australians.

Conception of a moral order on the model of the cosmic order. Finally, the time comes when the idea of law, already applied to those phenomena which in virtue of their periodicity or permanence *ought* to recur, is extended to all acts imposed by the voice of conscience which *ought* to be accomplished by men. Hence the assimilation of the course which man is bound to follow in his conduct, to the course which the celestial bodies ought to follow in their movements. "Malefactors," says the Rig-Veda,

[1] *La vie en Afrique*, vol. ii. p. 304.

"do not follow the path of the Rita."[1] Even in our own language, such terms as "regularity," "rectitude," "right," and "righteousness," imply that the moral idea which they express was at first accepted in a physical sense. Amongst ourselves, as in ancient Egypt, to respect the prescriptions of custom or of morals is still translated into *conforming with the rule*. To abide by the principles of justice is for us, as for the poets of the Rig-Veda, *to follow the right path*.

Nowhere was this assimilation of the moral and the cosmic order pushed so far as in the ancient religion of China. The entire ritual, and even the whole system of ethics, rests upon the idea that, since the heaven moves by fixed rules, man must do the same; and on the other side it is admitted that the crimes of man re-act almost fatally upon the course of nature, by releasing irregular phenomena or evil spirits, who in their turn intervene to punish man. In the Kia-iü, Confucius lays it down that if the people cease to follow Tao, the heaven in its turn will disturb the cosmic order;[2] and twenty-seven centuries afterwards, in 1731, we find the same theory embodied in a proclamation addressed by the emperor Yong-Tcheng to his people after a long drought. "Justice," it says, "originally aroused by heaven and man, answers more swiftly than the echo. The floods and droughts or disasters which trouble all the earth come from the acts of man."[3]

[1] *Rig-Veda*, ix. 73, 6.
[2] J. Happel, *La Religion de l'ancien empire chinois*, in the *Revue de l'histoire des religions*, vol. iv. 1881, p. 264.
[3] De Harlez, *Les croyances des premiers Chinois*, Bruxelles, 1888, p. 55; vol. xli. of the octavo series of *Mémoires* of the "Royal Academy" of Belgium.

Superhuman champions and opponents of the moral order.

Naturally, it is the gods charged with maintaining physical order who are likewise entrusted with the maintenance of moral order; and their importance increases in proportion to their task. They are, however, often aided by special deities, particularly amongst the peoples who deify abstract qualities and moral virtues. These virtues sometimes act as inspirers of man, and sometimes as avengers of the offences that particularly concern them respectively.

"Justice," says Hesiod, "is the virgin daughter of Zeus, honoured and revered by the gods who hold Olympus. Should any outrage her, slighting her by crooked doings, straightway she takes her seat by Zeus, the son of Kronos, and chants of the evil mind of men, that the people may be punished."[1] Such, too, was the part taken by Mā amongst the Egyptians; for it is she whom we see introducing the departed to the tribunal of Osiris and acting as assessor at their judgment. Her image is even represented as a weight in one scale of the balance, the other being occupied by the heart of the deceased.[2] The Persians were impelled to deify the moral qualities of man, and to place them in the ranks of Ahura-Mazda's army. We need only mention the Good Mind, the Best Purity, the Desired Kingdom, and the like.[3] Amongst the Romans, the virtues constituted a special class of deities, but they were merely hypostases of more ancient deities; that is to say, divine attributes detached

[1] *Works and Days*, 256—261 (254—259).
[2] P. Pierret, *Panthéon égyptien*, Paris, 1881, p. 64.
[3] Tiele, *Outlines of the History of Ancient Religions*, p. 168.

for separate personification. Thus, according to Preller, *Fides* was attached to Jupiter, *Concordia* to Venus, *Pudicitia* to Juno, &c.[1]

By an analogous evolution, it is the spirits in revolt against the cosmic order which come to be represented as striving to overturn the moral order. Amongst the Persians, with whom the conflicts of the Indo-Iranian nature-worship were transformed into an ethical struggle, we may still recognize in the two conflicting armies the ancient champions of light and of darkness, or of the storm, which the Vedas have preserved as personifications of natural forces.[2] Amongst the Jews, in like manner, the angels of darkness became essentially the angels of evil. In Egypt, the struggle of Osiris and Set was originally the myth of death combined with a solar myth. "Set," says M. Maspero, "represented material evil; .... but material dualism everywhere brings moral dualism in its train. Just as Osiris becomes the Good Being (Unnofir), Set becomes the Evil Being."[3] Finally, amongst the Teutons, dualism, at first purely physical, likewise tends to take a moral turn when Loki, rejected from the ranks of the gods, has become the head of the armies of evil.[4] Thus a kind of assimilation is established everywhere between the forces representing light, life, order, truth, justice, on the one hand, and darkness, death, disorder, falsehood,

---

[1] Preller, *Römische Mythologie*, second edition, Berlin, 1865, pp. 622, 623.

[2] J. Darmesteter, *Ormuzd et Ahriman*, passim.

[3] *Revue de l'histoire des religions*, vol. xix. (1889), p. 24.

[4] Tiele, *Outlines*, &c., §§ 118, 119, pp. 194—198.

and iniquity, on the other. The drama which has hitherto been confined to nature now embraces the conscience, and man feels more than ever bound to bring his aid to the gods who are fighting for the good of the world.

He who fails in this duty takes sides with the evil powers, and condemns himself henceforth to share their fate. The gods withdraw from him the protection which alone assures the enjoyment of the universal order, or they even inflict direct punishment on him, proportioned to his fault. Sometimes they themselves hurl the thunderbolt at conspicuous criminals, as amongst the Jews, Greeks, and Hindus; more often they act through the medium of special agents who personify punishment. "For the (king's) sake," we read in the code of Manu, "the Lord formerly created his own son, Punishment, the protector of all creatures, (an incarnation of) the law, formed of Brahman's glory."[1] The Greeks had a whole series of beings representing the celestial punishments; Nemesis sprung from the union of Zeus with Themis; the Poinai, represented by the poets as the attendants of justice; Ate, dark remorse; the Erinnyes, who pursued the culprit, and executed the decrees of Minos. Amongst the Persians and Jews, it was the spirits of evil who were charged with tormenting the criminal until the day of the final chastisement.

The problem of unpunished crime. Meanwhile it was impossible not to note that vice sometimes escaped unpunished and virtue went unrewarded. The poignant question addressed by Job to the Eternal, "Wherefore do

[1] Manu, vii. 14, p. 218, in Bühler's translation, Oxford, 1886. Vol. xxv. of *The Sacred Books of the East*, edited by Max Müller.

IV. DUALISM.

the wicked live, become old, yea, are mighty in power?" (Job xxi. 7), appears again on the lips of Theognis addressed to Zeus: "How canst thou, O son of Saturn, put the sinner and the just man on the same footing?"[1] It is the ever-recurring and terrible problem which reduces the thinker to the alternative of denying the omnipotence or the absolute justice of the divinity, and which has always been the citadel of atheism. "May neither I nor my son now be just amongst men," cried Hesiod, "since it is an evil for a man to be just, inasmuch as the unjust shall secure the larger rights. Yet I do not hold that Zeus, who exults in the thunderbolt, is closing the account as yet."[2]

Attempts have been made to explain this anomaly by saying, with the Chorus in Æschylus, that suffering is a lesson; or with Solon, that the children pay the debts of their father; or with Confucius and the Prophets, that the good pay for the evil; or, finally, with Job, that the decrees of Providence are inscrutable; but these answers have never fully satisfied either the reason which seeks the wherefore of things, or the conscience which revolts against the idea of throwing upon the innocent the consequences of the sins of others. Thus most peoples have sought in doctrines of a future life the means of repairing the evils and the injustices of the present.

<small>The theory of continued life after death.</small> At the threshold of our investigations we found man admitting, on the strength of his dreams, not only the continuance of the human personality after death, but even its posthumous intervention in the affairs of the survivors. This per-

[1] Vv. 377 sq.   [2] *Works and Days*, 270—273 (268—271).

sonality, henceforth conceived as a *double*, sometimes pictured under traits of an animal, wanders around its last home and walks among its descendants, joining in their life and even sharing their repasts. Or perhaps it re-encases itself in another body. And, on this point, while allowing due influence to dreams, as suggesting such transformations, I am not disinclined to believe that the theory of human re-incarnation often has its origin in anthropophagy, and that the belief in metempsychosis may be due to the custom of leaving human bodies to be consumed by animals.[1]

Or sometimes the soul was relegated to the tomb in company with the body, which it still frequented till it was reduced to dust; and, by a natural extension, the peoples who bury their dead conceive them as wandering with their fellows in the deep caverns of the subterranean world. In like manner, those who commit their dead to the waves suppose them to have gone, like the sun, to a distant land beyond the sea. Finally, those who practise cremation suppose that the dead ascend to the heights of heaven with the smoke of the funeral pyre. Hence insensibly arises the conception of another world situated under the earth, on a distant island, on the summit of a mountain, beyond the firmament, or even in the stars, the mysterious abodes to which almost all peoples despatch their dead to continue the life of this world.

The word "continue" is strictly in its place, for the future life is at first represented as a continuation, or

---

[1] On all these points Mr. Herbert Spencer's exposition in chaps. xii. to xv. of his *Sociology*, vol. i., is as lucid as it is exhaustive.

IV. DUALISM.

rather a copy, of the present existence. Eating and drinking, hunting and fishing, harvesting and other work, go on just as in this world, and so do war and love; although, says the Araucan, "they have no more children, for they are but souls."[1] In the other world, every one retains his ancient rank. The Polynesians believe that the departed are divided into the social classes to which they respectively belonged in their own country. The same belief prevails amongst the Kaffirs, in Dahomey, and amongst the Indian aborigines. When he has descended into Hades, Achilles still, apparently, plays the part of a powerful prince amongst the dead.[2] When Eabani goes down to hell, he discovers the great kings of old still wearing their crowns,[3] just as Isaiah (xiv. 9) represents the kings of the earth sitting on their thrones in Sheol above the crowd of shades. You are aware that the Egyptians reproduced all the scenes of public and private life in the interior paintings of the tombs, supposing that this would secure their recurrence for the defunct in the other world.

The future life conceived as better or worse than the present. It often happens that, while still modelled on the terrestrial life, the future life is conceived of as notably worse or better. Sometimes, doubtless by an inference drawn from dreams, it bears the character of a vague, pale, half-effaced and miserable copy. Nothing can be more dismal than the fate of souls in the Hebrew Sheol, the Assyrian Arali, or the Greek Hades. "A corner in this world is better than a corner in the world of spirits," say the

[1] Tylor, *Primitive Culture*, vol. ii. p. 76.
[2] *Odyssey*, xi. 490. [3] Sayce, *Op. cit.* p. 62.

Yorubas of Western Africa.[1] This was also the opinion of Achilles, who would have preferred to be a slave on earth rather than king amongst the dead. The Finns believed in the subterranean region of Tuonela, where there was a sun, fish, and bears, as on the earth; but the luminary was paler, the soil more ungrateful, and the water colder.[2]

Elsewhere, on the other hand, the future life is supposed to satisfy the aspirations which have never been realized here below. Man—and this is an indication of his superiority over all other known beings—frames for himself an ideal of happiness duly related to his mode of life and his stage of education. Whether that ideal is purely material or prevailingly moral, in either case every one admits his inability to realize it on earth; or if by chance the modesty of his aspirations or the unlooked-for kindness of fortune should enable a man to do so, he immediately feels the boundaries of his desires expand, and is more keenly conscious than ever of the inadequacy of things as they are. Hence the restless feeling, which must early have impelled man to look beyond this life, for a little more happiness, while the day was coming in which he should look there for a little more justice. He represented the future life, then, as destined to provide him with enjoyments and compensations for which he longed in vain below. "For the men who pronounce these prayers," says a poet of the court of Assurbanipal, "may the land of the silver sky, oil unceasing, and the wine of blessedness, be their food, and a good moon-

[1] Tylor, *Primitive Culture*, vol. ii. p. 80.
[2] Réville, *Religions des peuples non-civilisés*, vol. ii. p. 204.

IV. DUALISM. 191

tide their light."¹ "Place me, O Soma," said the Vedic poet, "where celestial light reigns eternal, where the mighty waters abound, where life is free, where the worlds are radiant, where the desires of my desires are accomplished."² The Greenlanders imagine that in the other world there will be no night, good drinking water everywhere, and plenty of fish. The Redskins conceive of the better world as a vast hunting-ground, where the game comes of its own accord to meet the blow of the hunter. In the Tonga islands, they suppose the dead to dwell in a spacious and shady abode, where they amuse themselves with dancing when they are not sucking sugar-cane.³ The Patagonian sorcerers say that they sometimes see, in the very depths of the earth, the cave where the souls are glutted with cattle and strong drink. In the depths of Amenti, the Egyptians describe the kingdom of Osiris, the fields of Talu, where wheat grows seven feet high. You know by reputation Mahomet's Paradise, and the Elysian Fields of the Greeks. How many Christians of the present day have conceived an idea in no way more elevated of the Paradise where they believe they will pass their time in doing nothing—unless it be taking pleasant walks and joining in religious music!

The superiority and the inferiority of the fate which awaits the dead in the future life, though apparently contradictory conceptions, are nevertheless simultaneously held by many peoples; for the popular imagination is not

¹ Sayce, *Hibbert Lectures, 1887*, p. 357.
² In Belgium, the Walloon populace still sing that in Paradise "they eat sugar with a ladle" (on magne dè souc al losse).
³ Condensed from *Rig-Veda*, ix. 113, 7—11.

daunted by trifles. Sometimes the souls are divided between the two posthumous realms, according to the rank, profession, or mode of life of the deceased. And where a better world alone is believed in, as in the Tonga islands and Samoa, the future life sometimes exists for the chiefs and the priests alone. It was observed, however, that in the present life success is not always the privilege of birth and of rank, but often falls to the most insinuating or the most courageous. Thus the better world would be assigned to the heroes who fell on the field of battle, as is notably the case with the Tupinambas of Brazil, the Comanches, the ancient Mexicans, perhaps the Assyrians, and the Germans, whose Walhalla was open to warriors who fell with their weapons in their hands. The natives of Nicaragua despatched all who died in their beds to the under-world; violent death alone gave access to the country of the sun. It is curious enough to find the same superstition actually appearing in the Russia of to-day, where the sect of the "Smotherers" take the words of St. Matthew (xi. 12) literally, "The kingdom of heaven is taken by violence," and save their members from a natural death by anticipating their end when they are seriously ill.[1]

The Esquimaux, for their part, being a pacific and industrious people, promise heaven to those who have caught the greatest number of seals and whales; to those who have been drowned in the sea; to those, generally, who have worked hard; and finally, like the Mexicans, to women who have died in childbirth.

You will observe that the deceased thus privileged—

[1] Leroy Beaulieu, *L'Empire des Tsars et les Russes*, 3 vols., Paris, 1881—1889, vol. iii. *La Religion*, p. 367.

especially those whom the superhuman powers have snatched away in the flower of their age—have succumbed while rendering services to their community. It is but natural therefore that the gods of the community should reward or rather compensate them. However this may be, we can already note the germs of what is presently to become the theory of retribution thrusting themselves up through the mere theory of continuation.

The theory of posthumous retribution. At the stage of belief which I have called spiritism, or polydemonism, the dead form a class of spirits not subject to any higher authority; but when the existence of the gods is once admitted, they cannot be excluded from intervening in the fate of souls. Being generally installed in a kind of Paradise themselves, the gods admit thereto, by preference, such as have gained their good graces by praise and sacrifices, while those who have failed to render them their dues must go to the tortures of hell. *A fortiori*, when the gods have become the protectors of the moral order, they will reserve Paradise to those who have fought the good fight, done right, observed the truth, and followed justice. The idea of a judgment of the dead, to which the theory of rewards and punishments naturally leads as its culmination, appears to have found its way into the minds even of very backward peoples. Bosman declares that certain Negroes of Guinea imagine that when they cross the river of death they are questioned by a superhuman being, who asks them if they have observed the sacred days and if they have abstained from prohibited kinds of food. Doubtless the Egyptians, like all known peoples, had their own ritual prescriptions, the violation of which would involve chastisement in this world and in the next. But what a moral chasm between the Guinea Negro's catechism and the following apology which, thousands of years before our era, the believer must render to Osiris before the tribunal of the gods: "Verily, I know you, ye lords of truth and of justice. I have brought you the truth. I have destroyed lieing for you. I have not committed any fraud against man. I have not persecuted the widow. I have not lied before the tribunal. I have not broken faith. I have done no forbidden thing. I have not made the foreman carry out day by day more work than was due. ... I have not been anywise neglectful. I have not been idle. ... I have not done that which was abominable to the gods. I have not injured the slave with his master. I have not starved. I have not made to weep. I have not slain. I have not planned treacherous murder. I have not committed fraud against anyone. ... I am pure, I am pure, I am pure!"[1]

The theories of continuation and of retribution are sometimes found side by side in the beliefs of the same people. This co-existence is, for that matter, rendered all the easier by the belief in several abodes of the dead and several factors of the personality. If a little order must be brought into this parallelism, or rather superposition, of ideas which seem mutually to exclude each other, there is nothing to prevent the *double* being told off to continue the life of this world in one of the

[1] G. Maspero, *Histoire ancienne des peuples de l'Orient*, fourth edition, Paris, 1886, pp. 38, 39.

abodes assigned by popular tradition to the dead, and the soul or the spirit being allowed to go to Paradise or Hell according to the balance of its merits or demerits. This is notoriously what took place with the Egyptians, who appear to have believed at the same time that the *double* went on with the old existence in the tomb, and that the soul descended to Amenti, there to be judged. The Greek Hades, which originally received all the shades indiscriminately, afterwards had a special department, Tartarus, reserved for the punishment of great sinners; whereas the heroes and even virtuous men went, after death, to the Elysian Fields in the islands of the blest.

<small>Belief in remuneration in this life.</small> With the Hindus, the distribution of the souls between the various sojourns of the dead seems to have been rendered needless by the belief in metempsychosis. It was specifically upon earth that the theory of retribution sought to realize itself, in a graduated scale of animal re-incarnations; whereas the absorbtion of the personality into the bosom of the great whole became more and more the supreme recompence of the Brahman theology.

The Buddhists went still further in this direction. They suppressed the whole conception of a posthumous tribunal and judgment, or even judge, since they dispensed with gods in their moral system; but they retained from Brahmanism the theory of re-births, while holding that each re-incarnation was determined, in some sort mechanically, by the anterior conduct of the deceased. Indeed, strictly speaking, it is not the same soul which is re-incarnated, but the karma—that is to say, the resultant of all the acts of the individual, good and bad.

It is perhaps to their conception of the future life that the northern Buddhists owe the astonishing success of their propaganda amongst the Chinese populations, at the expense of the old official religion, or rather of Confucianism. The latter, indeed, admits the survival of souls, passed into the state of spirits, and so justifies the domestic worship; but it has nothing to say as to the conditions of their future state, or any posthumous retribution. "You do not yet understand life," said Confucius to one of his disciples, more than 2000 years before modern Positivism; "how then can you profess to understand death?"[1] The only punishment of the wicked which the great Chinese reformer appears to admit is, that their descendants, corrupted by their bad example, will shirk the duties of filial piety.[2] But the masses could not rest content with this philosophical solution; and as soon as they found themselves in contact with a religion as rich in revelations of future states as Buddhism, especially the Indo-Tibetan Buddhism already corrupted by the reaction of local superstitions, a great part of the nation superposed the amplified and degenerated doctrine of Buddha upon the traditional worship of ancestors, as well as on the official ceremonies of Confucian rationalism.

Jewish eschatology. The religion of ancient Israel appears to have been equally inaccessible to ideas of remuneration in another world. The conception of a future life does not advance beyond that Sheol in which "there are neither arts, nor work, nor knowledge, nor

[1] J. Happel, *Revue de l'histoire des religions*, vol. iv. p. 275, note.
[2] A. Réville, *Religion des Chinois*, p. 345.

wisdom;" and where the criminal and the righteous, the infidel and the saint, Assur and his assembly, Elam and his people, no less than Israel and his descendants, all lie confused.[1] To complete the analogy with the beliefs already traced amongst the Assyrio-Babylonians, there are certain chosen ones, such as Enoch and Elijah, who have been carried to heaven by the special favour of Yahveh, just as Eabani and Xisûthros, the Chaldean Noah, were snatched from the gloom of Arali and placed in the region of the silver sky by the grace of the gods.[2] But in Judea, where the moral sentiments finally became an essential factor of religion, these exceptions were not enough to satisfy the demands of justice, as it sought compensation for the persecuted righteousness and triumphant iniquity of this world.

The solutions of the Aryan and Egyptian religions were, however, closed against the Jews. The overshadowing greatness of Yahveh already precluded the existence of immortal beings at his side. While the Greek philosophy developed the idea of the soul as a spiritual entity, constituting the veritable man and using the body as an instrument, Jewish speculation refused to regard the body otherwise than as living flesh. The *ruakh*, the equivalent of our vital breath, was an emanation, or rather a free gift, of Yahveh, or even a fragment of his own divine *ruakh*, which alone existed in and for itself. "All living things," says the Psalm (civ. 29, 30), "wait upon thee; thou withdrawest thy

[1] Ezekiel xxxii. 22—32.

[2] F. Lenormant, *La divination et la science des présages chez les Chaldéens*, Paris, 1875, p. 153.

breath, and they die; thou sendest out thy breath, and they are created, and thou renewest the face of the earth."

Since, then, they could not put their hopes in the future life, the Prophets were compelled to seek their realization in this world, and accordingly it was on earth that they expected the coming of the kingdom of Yahveh, at first for the exclusive benefit of their own nation, but afterwards for the salvation of humanity at large. This, as M. Renan says, was the only way of vindicating the honour of Yahveh.[1] Hence rose the Messianic ideas, which from the Captivity onwards seem to have taken a two-fold direction. In some minds it was simply a question of a national restoration which would culminate in the assumption by Israel of the hegemony over all the peoples of the earth. This restoration would be the work of the Messiah, regarded sometimes as the descendant of the lawful dynasty, sometimes as a kind of angel sent by the Lord. Others conceived a complete social renovation, in which peace and justice should reign over the nations converted to the worship of the true God, the part of Messiah falling to the chosen people itself. "In that day Israel shall be a third with the Egyptian and the Assyrian. There shall be a blessing upon the earth. Yahveh Çebaoth shall bless it, and shall say, 'Blessed be Egypt my people, and Assyria the work of my hands, and Israel mine inheritance'" (Isaiah xix. 24, 25).

Blessed they who should see the dawn of that great day! But the others? They who had died in the past or who should succumb during the waiting-tide? Is it right that

[1] *Histoire du peuple d'Israel*, vol. ii. pp. 437, 438.

just men persecuted in Yahveh's cause during their lives should be deprived of all share in the final triumph? Is it right that the wicked who died in wealth and impunity should escape all future punishment? The belief in the solidarity of the generations, and even the idea of expiation, whereby the sufferings of the just weigh against the offences of the sinner, could but imperfectly satisfy the demands of the Israelite's conscience. Then was conceived, or at least brought into prominence, a doctrine which we likewise meet in Mazdeism, viz. the resurrection of the body. The Persians believed that at the end of time the actual world would be destroyed, that Ormuzd would proceed to a new creation from which evil would be excluded, and all the just who had died from the beginning would receive a new body, whereas the souls of the wicked would be finally destroyed, together with Ahriman. The Jews could not accept this theory in its completeness, since they did not believe in the survival of the soul, but they adapted it to their own aspirations by picturing a resurrection of the dead on the day of the final judgment, or rather a re-construction of the dissipated bodies and their re-animation by the breath of Yahveh.[1]

You are aware how this dogma found its way into Christianity, in the moral conceptions of which it maintains itself side by side with the idea of a judgment immediately after death; but the religious spirit, as you have already seen from innumerable instances, does not shrink from placing the most divergent or even contradictory theories side by side. Indeed, it derives

[1] Ezekiel xxxvii. 7—10; Isaiah xxvi. 19; Daniel xii. 2.

certain advantages from this inexhaustible wealth of explanations; inasmuch as it is thereby enabled, without breaking the continuity of the religious development, quietly to drop theories which are superseded by the discoveries of science or the advance of the moral consciousness, and bring to the front such others as better answer to the needs of the age.

<small>Moralization of the divine types.</small> The union of morals and religion, or rather the belief that the moral order enters into the divine order, influences not only the conception of the future life, but also the idea of the deity itself. If we look how the diverse attributes were successively ascribed to the gods at the most advanced stage of polytheism, we shall see that man first recognized his deities as possessing the attributes of power, and then assigned to them, one after another, the qualities characteristic of intelligence, of love, and finally of morality. Many of the gods who are described as punishing the sins of men are still represented in the mythologies as debauchees and brigands; yet as soon as they are regarded as protectors of the moral order amongst men, they are like so many judges who abandon themselves in private life to the very abominations which they punish from their exalted tribunal. Hence a gradual tendency to moralize their character and their mutual relations, as well as their intervention in the affairs of man.

How can a scoundrel inculcate straightforwardness, or a perjurer veracity? How can an adulterer or thief enforce respect for the marriage-tie or property? How can a creature as grasping as a miser cultivate the spirit of self-devotion and self-sacrifice? First of all, the traditions which attribute criminal or simply gross actions to the gods are thrown into the shade, or allegorically explained, and only those passions which are regarded as noble are left to them. These, however, include not only courage, but resentment of injuries, jealousy, passion, love of praise, and partiality towards friends. Yahveh reserves his favours for the children of Israel, and their unfaithfulness throws him into paroxysms of rage. He determines to destroy all the human race, and then repents; he hardens Pharaoh's heart that he may have the opportunity of inflicting the plagues upon Egypt. Moreover, he deceives the Israelites themselves. When he seeks to punish them for their profanations, he gives them "statutes that are not good and ordinances by which they cannot live" (Ezek. xx. 25).

In this process of moralizing the deities, one or another of the traditional qualities which figure in the character of each god is selected and thrown into relief. Indra, Thor, Ares-Mars, in virtue of their mythological prowess, will come to be regarded especially as types of valour. Varuna and Osiris, as the heaven which sees all the acts of men, and the sun which throws light upon them, will become judges *par excellence*. Pallas Athene, who sprang all armed from the head of Zeus, whether originally the personification of lightning or of the dawn, will become the goddess of wisdom. Hestia, the pure flame of the hearth, will represent chastity and the domestic virtues. It was long before Zeus could venture to take upon himself personally the judgment of the souls of the dead. He wisely left this function to the incorruptible judges of Hades. But in the end he became the avenger of outraged right, and at the same time the moral regulator of the universe. "If the gods do aught that is base, they are not gods,"[1] says Euripides; and his vigorous utterance finds a practical illustration in the German mythology, for when the trespasses and treasons of Loki began to wound the moral sense of his worshippers, they debased him from the ranks of the Æsir.

Finally, as the human ideal becomes more exalted, the passions still assigned to the gods are further purified by the exclusion of all movements of the soul that seem inconsistent with the majesty, the holiness and the kindness, the justice and the love, from which they can no longer be conceived as departing. "I will not execute the decree of my wrath; I will not turn to destroy Ephraim, *for I am God and not man;* I am the Holy One in the midst of thee, and I will not come in wrath" (Hosea xi. 9). In a word, man comes at last to ascribe to his deity only the two loftiest sentiments of the human soul, justice and love. "God," says Plutarch, "being perfectly good, lacks not any virtue; and least of all in what concerns justice and love."[2] Going still further, we notice that the former of these sentiments is subordinated to the latter, inasmuch as the divine punishments are conceived as having for their object the improvement of the sinner, as when a father chastens his son; until at last chosen religious spirits learn to proclaim that "God is love," not excluding from this term the idea of justice, but realizing it therein under its sublimest aspect.

[1] Bellerophon Frag. xix. v. 4.   [2] *De defectu oraculorum,* xxiv.

IV. DUALISM. 203

Identity of human and divine good. Henceforth the bond between men and gods no longer depends on the analogy of their enjoyments or their passions, but on identity of aspiration and reciprocity of sympathies, which make the gods feel for what is endured by men. It is no longer through the duration of a single human life only that Osiris, Vishnu, Krishna, Buddha, or the Messiah, personally submits to the miseries of a life upon earth, in order to bring man happiness, justice and salvation; but everywhere and always, from the bosom of celestial glory, he feels the reaction of every injustice, of every fall, of every undisturbed misfortune. "Since I received the great wound," says Osiris, "I am wounded by every wound."[1] It is almost the very expression employed by Isaiah to describe the sympathy of Yahveh with the Israelites. "In all their affliction he was afflicted" (Is. lxiii. 9). The idea that all injustice, all cruelty to the poor, is inflicted on Yahveh himself, penetrates the whole Hebrew literature; and amongst the Hindus, the Vishnu Purana, extending the limits of the divine sympathy yet further, proclaims that whosoever injures a living creature injures God.

And reciprocally the qualities and virtues thus ascribed to the superhuman beings do not fail to exert a truly moral attraction upon the faithful. "Is it possible," asks Plato, "admiringly to investigate an object without striving to resemble it?"[2] Thus Religion and Morals react one upon the other, the idea of duty purifying the conception of deity; and the latter, in its turn, fortifying the feeling of obligation, while fructifying it with love.

[1] De Pressensé, *L'ancien monde et le Christianisme*, p. 124.
[2] *Republic*, bk. vi. § 13.

LECTURE V.

MONOTHEISM.

Gods attached to the land or the people.   WE have seen that every nation begins by admitting the real existence of the gods adored by its neighbours. The Israelites in the period of the Judges believed in the sovereignty of Chemosh over the people of Moab, just as much as in that of Yahveh over the people of Israel;[1] and when the armies of Rome besieged a city, they began by offering sacrifices to the local deities, perhaps hoping to gain them over to their side, or perhaps on the principle that leads savages to appease the spirit of the tree which they are about to fell, by offering it a sacrifice.

It naturally follows that the sphere of action of the gods is always limited either to the territory regarded as their patrimony or to the people which has accepted their suzerainty. If the country of Israel belonged to the twelve tribes, it was because the god of Bethel had promised it to Abraham and Jacob (Gen. xiii. xxviii. xxxv). In another passage of the Bible we find the Syrians believing themselves safe against the Israelite invasion

---

[1] Jephthah's envoys said to the king of Ammon, "Wilt not thou possess that which Chemosh thy god giveth thee to possess? So whomsoever Yahveh our God hath dispossessed from before us, them will we possess" (Judges xi. 24).

because, as they said, Yahveh is a mountain god and his power does not extend to the plain (1 Kings xx. 23). Yet more, a change of country implies a change of gods. When David is reproaching Saul with his exile, he complains that his enemies have compelled him to quit "the heritage of Yahveh," and have said to him, "Go, serve other gods" (1 Sam. xxvi. 19); and reciprocally when Ruth, the Moabitess, follows her mother-in-law to Bethlehem, she cries, "Where thou goest, I will go, and where thou dwellest, I will dwell; thy people shall be my people, and thy God my God" (Ruth i. 16). The God of Israel is so closely connected with the soil, that when the Syrian general Naaman, healed of his leprosy in the waters of Jordan, gratefully desires to raise an altar to Yahveh in his own country, he must carry away a certain portion of the Israelitish soil, "as much as the load of two mules" (2 Kings v. 17).

On the other hand, in his own domain, Yahveh is the lord of strangers as well as the lord of the Israelite. When the Assyrians have captured Samaria, carried off the Israelites into captivity, and replaced them by populations from beyond the Euphrates, the latter complain that they are exposed to the wrath of Yahveh because they know not how to render him the homage he desires, and they beg the king of Assyria to send them some of the former sacrificers to teach them "the way to serve the god of the land" (2 Kings xvii. 27). But the Bible tells us that these same peoples also retained the worship of the gods they had venerated in the land whence they had come. In fact, however closely the gods of the peoples may be bound to their own territories, in the end they must come to identify themselves so closely with the nations as to accompany them wherever they take up their abode. Yahveh himself was the God of the Jews in Babylonia, even when the Captivity had come to an end, and the exile of the colonists had become a voluntary residence. In the same way, Assur was at first simply the god of the city that bore his name. But when the Assyrians transferred the seat of their empire to Nineveh, the god of their ancient capital still remained the supreme god of the nation.

Deities share the lot of their peoples. Another consequence of this close connection between each people and its special gods is, that the latter share the fates of the people and even of the tribe or the province which originally fell to their lot. In pre-Assyrian times, Mesopotamia was divided into little states, each of which had its principal god drawn either from amongst the members of the local pantheon or from the common divinities of Chaldea, and the fortune of the god invariably followed that of the state or dynasty which had adopted him as its protector. Thus we see a temporary hegemony successively achieved by the lunar god Sin with the city of Ur, by the sea-god Ea with Eridu, the solar god Samash with Larsa, Anu with Urukh, Mul-lil with Agadë, Merodach with Babylon, and (as we have just called to mind) Assur with Assyria. It was the same in Egypt, where, as soon as the nomes were united into a state, attempts were made to identify the respective gods of the little local pantheons one with another, while choosing for the supreme deity the chief god of the dynasty in power or of the city which served as its capital—Osiris at Abydos, Ra at Heliopolis, Ptah at Memphis, Ammon at Thebes, Neith at Sais, and so forth.

When a nation lost its independence, its gods did not cease to exist, but passed into the service of the conquerors and became subordinate to their deities. Thus the deities of the countries annexed by the Roman armies successively swelled the ranks of the imperial pantheon, more or less disguised in Roman livery. The same thing took place in Peru, where the Incas collected in their great temple of the sun at Cuzco the images of the gods worshipped by all the various nations that they had absorbed into their empire.

The supreme god of the universe. Under such a system, if a nation rose towards supremacy over the known world, its chief deities, and especially its supreme god, must necessarily approach to universal monarchy. Thus Jupiter came to extend his empire from the Irish Sea to the basin of the Ganges in the train of the Greek and Roman armies. Or, again, it might equally well come to pass that, simply through the development of their own theology, peoples were led to regard their supreme god as the master of all the gods. In fact, by dint of constantly repeating that their own deity was the mightiest of the gods, they would come at last to believe that the latter were not only inferior to him in power and rank, but were his mere vassals or subjects. This was the point of view at which the Judean people had arrived at the end of the period of the Monarchy. Finally, there is a third path which may lead to the political unity of the superhuman world.

It is that of the reciprocal assimilation of the deities who form the several national pantheons. Indeed, we may wonder that this assimilation did not more easily and more often occur amongst peoples who adored the same manifestations of nature; but we must remember that the nature-gods, when once conceived as ruling from outside the phenomena from which they originally sprang, always acquired sufficiently distinctive features to give them separate individualities as well as different names. Thus it is only in syncretistic periods that any attempt is made to establish their identity, and even then it is its own gods that each nation takes as the standards to which to refer the gods of the stranger.

It is the Phœnician deities that Philo of Byblos re-discovers in the gods of Greece; and reciprocally, it is now to Apollo and now to Kronos that the Greeks liken Melkarth, the divine king of Tyre. You are acquainted with the process of assimilation by which Herodotus attempted to draw the gods of Egypt into the classical pantheon. Megasthenes applied the same method to the gods of India, and Cæsar and Tacitus to those of Gaul and Germany. Zeus absorbed not only a certain number of Thracian and Thessalian deities, but the rulers of far more important pantheons, such as the Lybian Ammon, the Egyptian Serapis, and the Babylonian Bel Merodach; while Herodotus even gives his name to the great god of the Persians, that same Ahura Mazda who was destined to survive the Lord of Olympus by so many centuries.

Divine families. Imagination did not confine itself to the conception of divine monarchies corresponding to all the independent states or diverse races on the earth. Within the limits of each of these smaller superhuman societies, it erected groups on the type of the family. We have already seen how man was brought by the necessities of language to attribute sex to every manifestation of nature. And therefore when these manifestations were personified, they naturally became male and female. After that, what could be more simple or more consistent, when two phenomena united to produce a third, whether by fusion or by reaction, than to consider the personification of this last as the offspring of its two factors, themselves regarded as husband and wife? By a similar deduction, phenomena which sprang from the same source, or were supposed to do so, or even had certain traits or properties in common, were regarded as brothers and sisters; as, for example, the sun and the moon, the two twilights, sleep and death, and so on.

The divine fatherhood. Presently these family relations of the gods were extended till they embraced the whole creation, and especially mankind. The confusion between the terms for creating and begetting, which still maintained itself in half-developed languages, must have led to a spontaneous fusion of the ideas of creator and father. Sometimes, as in Egypt and with the Incas, it was the reigning dynasty alone that laid claim to this exalted affiliation. "I call upon thee, O my father Amon!" exclaimed Rameses II. at the battle of Kadshu. "My many soldiers have abandoned me; none of my horsemen hath looked towards me; and when I called them, none hath listened to my voice. But I believe

P

that Amon is worth more to me than a million of soldiers, than a hundred thousand horsemen."[1]

The analysis of the identical name which the Hindus, Greeks, and Latins gave to their heavenly deity, Dyaush pitâ = Ζεὺς πατήρ = Jupiter, implies not only that the ancestors of the Indo-Europeans spoke the same language and worshipped the same god, but further that they addressed that god as a celestial father. "Be unto us easy of access," said the Vedic poet to Agni, "as a father to his son."[2] Side by side with Dyaush, "our father," another hymn invokes, Prithivi, "the good mother," and Agni, "our brother."[3] It is the same thought that the Greek poet expresses when he maintains that "gods and men are sons of the same mother."[4] In the West, this idea, no longer held in check by the regime of caste, could not fail to stimulate more generous feelings and to provoke democratic inferences. The divine paternity must culminate in the brotherhood of man. "Wilt thou not remember over whom thou rulest?" says Epictetus, addressing a master on behalf of his slaves, "that they are thy relations, thy brethren by nature, the offspring of Zeus?"[5]

Amongst the Semites, the idea of the divine paternity was at first kept in the background, hampered in its

---

[1] Le Page Renouf, *Hibbert Lectures, 1879*, p. 228.

[2] *Rig-Veda*, i. 1, 9.

[3] *Rig-Veda*, vi. 51, 5. Prof. Max Müller has shown that this idea presents itself at every step in the *Rig-Veda*. See *Hibbert Lectures, 1878*, pp. 222, 223.

[4] Pindar, *Nemea*, vi. 1, 2.

[5] Arrian, *Epicteti Diatribæ*, i. 13.

V. MONOTHEISM.

development by the very majesty of the deity, which could not brook the establishment of any such relation with the gods. But it is not altogether absent, as we may see from the invocation of a Mesopotamian hymn to Istar: "May thy heart be appeased as the heart of a mother who has borne children;"[1] and you are aware how it appeared amongst the Jews at the beginning and end of the Captivity, in the prophecies of Jeremiah and of the second Isaiah, to become, with its corollary of the brotherhood of man, the cardinal doctrine of the religion taught by Jesus.

The place of metaphysical speculation in the development of monotheism. The highest point of development that polytheism could reach is found in the conception of a monarchy or divine family, embracing all terrestrial beings, and even the whole universe. The divine monarch or father, however, might still be no more than the first amongst his peers. For the supreme god to become the Only God, he must rise above all beings, superhuman as well as human, not only in his power, but in his very nature.

The conception of this new and higher nature is the fruit of metaphysical speculation. Monotheism is hardly complete until man, having conceived the idea of a first cause, of eternity, of infinity, and of the absolute, makes them the attributes of one only being, the Being *par excellence*. And these conceptions are not formed all at once in the human mind; they are the products of a slow mental evolution which acts upon materials already in existence, furnished by previous conceptions of the deity.

[1] Sayce, *Hibbert Lectures, 1887*, p. 352.

Thus we see how the monotheistic evolution may have advanced along very different lines to the same end, and may have proceeded, in the majority of cases, without any rupture with religious tradition.

Simplification of the national pantheons. Metaphysical speculation early concerned itself with the theology of the civilized peoples. The way to the recognition of the divine unity had been paved almost everywhere by the identification of the chief gods representing the same phenomenon, or its diverse aspects. Thus the Egyptians found means of gradually drawing all their deities into the circle of the divine families already established in triads on the model of the human family represented by father, mother, and son. We have seen how they gradually assimilated the gods of the dead and those of the elements to the type of the solar divinities; and the latter were in their turn identified with the sun, or rather with the soul of the sun, which remains one in all its manifestations, and which thus becomes the universal soul of all the gods. In the Turin papyrus, this mysterious deity is made to say, "I am the maker of heaven and of the earth. . . . It is I who have given to all the gods the soul which is within them. . . . I am Chepera in the morning, Ra at noon, Tmu in the evening."[1]

In fact, this is really a new being appearing behind the ancient gods; but since this "hidden soul of the

---

[1] Le Page Renouf, *Hibbert Lectures, 1879*, pp. 221, 222. Compare the *Atharva Veda*, xiii. 3, 13: "In the evening Agni becomes Varuna, who becomes Mitra when he rises in the morning; when he has become Savitar, he traverses the firmament; when he has become Indra, he burns the heavens at the zenith."

Lord of the Disc" equally manifests himself in all the chief deities, the name of any one of them may be given to him indifferently. Hence comes the Egyptian henotheism, which alternately assimilates Ra, Osiris, Ptah, Ammon, and the rest, to the supreme God. To accentuate this equivalence still more, the chief deity of the place receives the names of all the other gods. On the royal tombs of Biban-el-moluk, Ra is invoked under seventy-five different names, and the *Book of the Dead* has a whole chapter made up of nothing but the names of Osiris.[1] Or, again, the supreme soul receives a name formed by the union of all the appellations given respectively to the supreme gods of the different cycles: Sokar-Osiris, Ptah-Sokar-Osiris, are complex names which appear as early as in the ancient empire; and later on we meet with Horus-Chem, Chnum-Ra, Sebak-Ra, Amun-Ra, Amun-Ra-Tum-Harmachis.[2] And this was no mere juxtaposition of words or verbal syncretism. The Egyptians were really conscious that the gods thus drawn together were in truth identical one with another. It is, so to speak, the mythic formula of this fusion which is given us in the following words: "Osiris came to Mendes; there he met the soul of Ra; they embraced and became as one soul in two souls."[3]

We must note that in these identifications we are directly concerned with solar gods alone—that is to say, with the first persons of the triads; but just as the

[1] Le Page Renouf, *Hibbert Lectures, 1879*, p. 87.

[2] Cf. C. P. Tiele, *Anciennes religions de l'Égypte*, &c., Paris, 1882, p. 137 (*History of the Egyptian Religion*, London, 1882, p. 223).

[3] *Book of the Dead*, chap. xvii. lines 42, 43.

unity thus obtained especially represented the active principle of nature, symbolized by the solar rays, so, in like manner, the goddesses, reduced in their turn by an analogous process to a single type, easily passed into personifications of space, or of the matter upon which the divine activity worked to produce the world.[1] At Dendera, Hathor is assimilated not only to Isis, but to Neith of Sais, to Saosis of Heliopolis, to Bast of Bubastis, to Sothis of Elephantine, and others.[2] As to the gods whose nature or attributes or special local circumstances prevented them from melting into the great solar deity, they readily united with the third person of the triad, the son of the divine couple, the personification and the synthesis of the phenomenal world begotten in continuous generation.

The triune god of Egypt. All that was now needed was one more effort of abstraction, to put above and behind this triad the being in which it was resumed and into which, so to speak, it melted. That higher unity was sometimes found in the first person of the triad, regarded as reproducing itself by eternal generation; sometimes in a "spirit more spiritual than the gods; the holy soul which clothes itself with forms, but itself remains unknown."[3]

It is this triune god, who, to employ an expression of the Egyptian theologians, perpetually "creates his own members, which are the gods."[4] The latter are

[1] Paul Pierret, *Panthéon Égyptien*, p. 27.
[2] Le Page Renouf, *Hibbert Lectures, 1879*, pp. 87, 88.
[3] Cf. *Book of the Dead*, xv. 46.
[4] Maspero, *Histoire des peuples de l'Orient*, 4me ed., Paris, 1886, p. 279.

V. MONOTHEISM. 215

the universal aliment, "an immense loaf in the middle of which dwells the Only One," or "a divine society completing itself in a single heart."[1] Yet further, each one of these apparently secondary gods may become in its turn a centre of emanation, giving birth to other gods by the genesis of triads. But when all is said and done, they are never more than the names and aspects of the one only being. "Amon is an image," says a hymn copied by Brugsch from the walls of El Khargeh, "Atmu is an image, Chepera is an image, Rā is an image; he alone maketh himself in millions of ways."[2]

Semitic monotheism. An analogous movement of theological concentration took place amongst the western Semites. It was immensely facilitated by the habit, already formed, of designating the most important deities solely by their titles; for whatever difficulty might be found in welding together divine representatives or governors of the heaven, the sun, the thunderbolt, the wind, and such like phenomena, or even the illustrious dead, or mere abstractions of one kind or another, there could be little objection to identifying all the superhuman beings known as the Mighty, the Strong, the King, the Creator, the Eternal,—to say nothing of those Redoubtables, or *Elohim*, who, as M. Renan observes, act in harmony as a single being and even take a singular verb. The Phœnician states, or rather the principal Phœnician cities, formed their triads, not by uniting three of the most powerful deities of the local pantheon, as in Mesopotamia,

[1] Paul Pierret, *Panthéon Égyptien*, p. x.
[2] Le Page Renouf, *Hibbert Lectures, 1879*, p. 233.

but by combining with the worship of the divine king, that of his consort and of their child. As in Egypt, the first person of this triad was probably borrowed from the luminous personifications of the air or the sun and represented the creative power, the ruler *par excellence;* the second, perhaps originally a personification of the earth or moon, represented nature properly so called, under her two-fold fruitful and murderous aspect; the third seems to have been very much effaced, except where mythology interposed to give it distinctive features. For the rest, the great goddess herself, the "Mistress" (Baalith) or "Queen"(Milkath), was regarded less as the spouse than as the visible manifestation, "the face," and therefore the reflection of the supreme god. Sometimes, indeed, like Tanith of Carthage or Astarte of Cyprus, she succeeded in throwing her spouse into the background, but it was more often she herself who fell into the second rank, or even disappeared in the rays of her lord and master.

One cannot dispute the anthropomorphic character of the deity as represented in the oldest traditions of the Bible. Yahveh moulds man like a potter; he plants the garden of Eden and walks through it in the cool of the evening like a rich Mesopotamian. Adam hears his footsteps. He comes down from heaven to see the building of the Tower of Babel. He eats and drinks with Abraham, and the latter washes his feet. He struggles with Jacob and allows himself to be overcome. At the time of the Prophets he is no longer seen in person. Whoso looks on him must die. But he reveals himself in the manifestations of light and of the storm. Finally, he rises above these natural phenomena, and becomes a voice speaking to the conscience of the righteous.

Nowhere have I found this development of the Hebrew idea of divinity, or, to speak more accurately, this spiritualization of Yahveh, better followed out and expounded than in a memoir by M. A. Sabatier, Professor of the Faculty of Protestant Theology of Paris, on the "Hebrew Conception of the Spirit."[1] Here we see how the breath, the "ruakh" of the Eternal, at first simply identified with the wind which "makes the heaven serene" (Job xxvi. 13) and "parches the grass" (Is. xl. 7), becomes the synonym of force in the moral as well as in the metaphysical sense, and finally comes to represent the abstract idea of absolute force, "He who is."

God as distinct from matter. Here we have a first form of monotheism, in which the god is regarded as external to the universe, or at least as distinct from matter. We observe that this system, generally spoken of as Deism, has especially prevailed amongst peoples who, like the Semites, regard force as the essential attribute of the superhuman beings, and have risen to the conception of unity by developing their ideas of causality. On the contrary, peoples who, like the Indo-Europeans, seem to have been more struck by the identity of nature running through their divine personifications, have found the corner-stone of their monotheism in the idea of self-existence; and then, by a further extension, have transformed it into a pantheism in which the Creator and the creation melt into a higher unity. It is interesting to

[1] In the volume entitled *La faculté de théologie protestante de Paris à M. Edouard Reuss*, Paris, 1879, pp. 5 sqq.

follow this development wherever it has passed through all its successive phases, if only to establish the uniformity of the process in every case.

God creating the universe out of his own substance. The conception of a unique being resolving himself into fragments to create the universe is found in rudimentary form amongst peoples still in a state of barbarism. The Chinese traditions speak of a certain Panku who produced the wind by his breath, made day by opening his eyes, and thunder by lifting up his voice. His right eye became the sun, his left eye the moon, his blood gave birth to the rivers, his flesh to the soil, his locks to the stars, the hairs of his body to the trees, his bones to the metals, his marrow to the pearls and diamonds, and finally—by an analogy scarcely flattering to our race—the parasites upon him became men.[1] The study of the Edda reveals an analogous conception, that of the giant Ymir, whose body and blood respectively produced the earth and the ocean, whilst his head formed the vault of heaven and his brain the clouds.[2] The Vedas likewise tell us of a primordial being, Purusha, whose body, according to some stories, served the gods for the creation of the universe, but who, according to others, doubled himself into male and female to engender the cosmic egg.[3] Thus, again, the Chaldean traditions speak

---

[1] A. Réville, *La Religion Chinoise*, Paris, 1889, pp. 38, 39.

[2] *The Journey of Gylfe*, viii. In Snorre Sturleson's *Edda*.

[3] Monier Williams, *Indian Wisdom*, p. 24. In the Marianne Islands they believe in a primordial being, Pontan, who charged his sisters, when he died, to form the heaven and the earth out of his chest and shoulders, the sun and the moon out of his eyes, and the rainbow

of the monstrous Tiamat, the personification of Chaos, whom Bel cut into halves to make heaven and earth; though, according to another version, it was Bel who cut off his own head to create gods and men with his blood.[1]

Finally, the idea rose that the being who had thus severed himself into fragments still survived, or rather that his disintegration was but apparent and did not affect his substantial unity. This thought is found, alike in the Vedic song chanted in honour of Varuna, and in the Egyptian hymn graven on the walls of El Khargeh, in terms identical with those of the Orphic poet of Greece, who cries, "Zeus was the first. Zeus is the last. . . . Zeus is the centre. It is by Zeus that all things were made. Zeus is the male. Zeus is the eternal female. Zeus is the sun and the moon. For all these things lie in the great body of Zeus."[2] "Thou art youth and age," said the scribe of El Khargeh in his turn. "Thou art heaven, thou art earth; thou art fire, thou art water, thou art air, and whatever is in the midst of them."[3] "Purusha," the Vedic poet exclaims, "is in truth the universe. He is what is, what has been, and what shall be;"[4] and a hymn of the Atharva Veda keeps equally close to the same idea in this description of Varuna: "The two seas are the belly of Varuna, and even in this little pool of water he reposes."[5]

out of his eyebrows.—De Freycinet, *Voyage autour du monde*, vol. ii. Paris, 1829, p. 381.

[1] Lenormant, *Origines de l'histoire*, Paris, 1880, vol. i. p. 507 (*Beginnings of History*, London, p. 500).

[2] J. Darmesteter, *Essais orientaux*, p. 125.

[3] Le Page Renouf, *Hibbert Lectures, 1879*, p. 232.

[4] *Rig-Veda*, x. 90. 2.   [5] *Atharva Veda*, iv. 16. 3.

Are we to conclude that the religions whose theologies these old documents reveal, developed on purely materialistic lines, as has been affirmed? To do so would be to forget, at the very outset, that, at the period of which we are speaking, no one dreamt, as yet, of a body, even the body of the universe, without a soul to move and to guide it.

<small>God as the soul of the universe.</small> It is this soul of the world, "more spiritual than the gods," as the Egyptians had it, that becomes the true God. It remains to see under what form it is conceived. It would be difficult to give it the character of the double, although Plato, consistently enough, represents it as an archetype of the universe, pre-existing in the divine spirit. In general it would be regarded rather as a subtle element penetrating all things, like heat or ether.

"Spiritus intus alit, totamque infusa per artus
Mens agitat molem, et magno se corpore miscet."[1]

Thus the Stoics pictured it sometimes as a subtle fire animating all portions of the world, sometimes as ether, sometimes as life *par excellence*, even deriving the name of Zeus from the verb ζῆν. The school of Ionia sought the same principle sometimes in water with Thales, sometimes in air with Anaximander; while the Pythagoreans found a supreme intelligence (νοῦς) at the origin of things.

Thus conceived, the soul of the world may remain impersonal. But most of these systems had a religious as well as a philosophical side; and there their "first principle," confounding itself with Zeus, recovered the

[1] *Æn.* vi. 726, 727.

attributes of personality, reason, consciousness, pity, love. "O, Thou, whosoever thou art, difficult to know, Zeus, or necessity of nature, or spirit of man, Thee I invoke, who treading the secret path disposest mortal affairs in accordance with justice!"[1] Pythagoras, in his philosophical teaching, might indeed represent the universe as developing out of the linked progression of numbers, starting from unity; but this unity, the primordial monad, was no other than Zeus Soter, placed at the centre of the sphere; and the first derived numbers were the equivalents of the great gods of the Hellenic pantheon. The Stoics, on their side, though likening their "reason of things" to the ether pervading nature, none the less erected it into a real and living god, endowed with all moral qualities, whether they called it by the name of Zeus or not.

In India, even before the Vedic epoch, light was regarded as the essential and general attribute of the chief deities, as their very name *devas* indicates. It was but a step to make light the common soul of the divine beings and therefore the deity *par excellence*, of which the other gods merely represented the diverse names and aspects. "Oh, Agni," says a hymn, "thou art born Varuna, thou becomest Mitra when kindled; all the gods are in thee."[2] "They have styled him," says another hymn, "Indra, Mitra, Varuna, Agni, for the poets give many names to the one."[3]

Presently this identification was carried still further. Seeing that fire is met, under some form or another,

---

[1] Euripides, *Troades*, 885—888.
[2] *Rig-Veda*, v. 3. 1.   [3] *Rig-Veda*, i. 164. 46.

throughout nature, it was regarded as the element common to gods and men, to beings and to things, the principle that reveals itself in light, heat, movement, conscience; and consequently the universal material, or rather the universal soul. The idea of fire or of light itself finally appeared too concrete, too material, to give form to the idea of this subtle principle. "I am incomprehensible in form," says Krishna in the Bhagavad Gita, "more subtle than the subtlest atoms; .... I am the light in sun and moon, far, far beyond the darkness; I am the brilliancy in flame, the radiance in all that's radiant; .... the sound in ether, fragrance in the earth; the seed eternal of existing things, the life in all; .... I dwell as Wisdom in the heart of all; I am the Goodness of the good; I am the Beginning, Middle, End; eternal Time, the Birth, the Death of all."[1]

Something less concrete, or at least less material, than the fire or the light must be sought to serve as the form, or rather the symbol, of this spiritual principle; and it is found in the breath, the *prana* or *atman*, which also came to symbolize the human soul. The *atman*, that is to say, the being that each one felt within himself, thus became an emanation of the *Paratman*, the supreme Soul, the Unique without a second, who alone exists in himself. Agni yields the first place in religion to Prajapati, the Lord of creation; to Brahmanaspati, the Lord of prayer; to Viçvakarman, the universal artificer, and other abstract denominations which better lend themselves to a more spiritual conception of the deity.[2]

[1] Monier Williams, *Indian Wisdom*, pp. 144, 145.
[2] A. Barth, *Religions de l'Inde*, p. 21; Eng. trans., pp. 29, 30.

V. MONOTHEISM. 223

The unique Being, without a second. As yet, however, we have not got beyond the *anima mundi* which directs the universe, as life and intelligence animate and inspire individual beings; and this point of view still implies a certain opposition between God and the world.[1] But neither India nor Greece could stop half-way in the pantheistic reconstruction. Religious India, or, to speak more accurately, the Brahmanism which gave ever freer admission to the Vedantic idealism, ended by inferring the non-existence of the sensible world, which it regarded as a pure illusion, the work of the deceiving Maya; an internal thought of the absolute Being, dreaming in and through his successive creations. As to the nature of this Being it can only be defined, say the Upanishads, by means of negatives. Of anything which comes under the range of our senses and can be defined, we may say that God is not that. We cannot even affirm that he exists, because that is to limit him by ascribing to him the attribute of existence; at the very most we can

---

[1] The Egyptian hymns might declare that the supreme god was the unique being without second, "the immanent and abiding in all things" (Hymn of El Khargeh); but all the same he appears to have been limited by matter, and in that respect Gnosticism may be briefly described as the heir of the old Egyptian religion no less than of neo-Platonism. "Admitting the eternity of an essentially inert matter," says M. Grébaut (Hymn to Ammon Ra, p. vi), "this religion inferred, from the organization of this matter, the existence of a hidden being, the prop of universal order; the eternal principle of the truth, which was that order realized; intelligent, good, almighty; adored in the sun, the visible instrument which he uses in creating and maintaining life, and so imparting truth in spite of all evil principles or Typhonic powers."

only say that in Him existence and non-existence are combined.

In the same way amongst the Greeks, the neo-Pythagoreans and neo-Platonists, by dint of logically developing their respective principles, finally met in a pure Pantheism. Plato had taught that God created the world after an ideal type, which existed in his reason from all eternity, as the plan of a city exists, before its foundation, in the mind of an architect. The world was formed after an invisible model conceived by reason and intelligence. Seeing that all visible things were tossed about in a confused and disordered movement, the Creator drew them from the bosom of disorder and subjected them to order, "thinking the latter far preferable."[1]

This ideal plan, to which Plato ascribed an objective existence, included the archetypes of all things; and these archetypes realized themselves, so to speak, by penetrating and fashioning matter, into which they introduced a spark of real being. "Ideas are as it were the models of nature. Things become like them, and are their copies. The participation of things in ideas consists in their resembling them."[2] The God thus conceived is still an active being, who thinks, wills, and lives, although he does not directly intervene in the work of creation.

But the neo-Platonists of Alexandria relegated the deity more and more completely into a sphere wholly beyond conception, and, under pretext of removing his

[1] *Timæus*, § 10, 11. [2] *Parmenides*, § 13.

V. MONOTHEISM. 225

limitations, deprived him of the last attributes which would justify worship.[1] Proclus, like Plotinus, declared that it was still possible to unite oneself to the deity, withdrawing oneself from the restrictions of the phenomenal world, by dint of renunciation and ecstasy. But their latest successors declared that their God was as inaccessible as he was unknowable. It seems as though agnosticism were to be the logical conclusion and inevitable consequence of the whole ancient philosophy.

We may note that in China, too, where the official religion re-organized by Confucius hardly rose above the conception of a divine monarchy, imitated from the Chinese empire, the philosophical sect of Taoists seems to have risen at a single bound to the height of metaphysical Pantheism. The Tao, that is to say the principle or source of all things, is represented by Lao-tsze as evading all definition, and even all comprehension. "You look upon the Tao and you see it not, it has no colour; you listen and you hear it not, it has no voice; you would handle it and you touch it not, it has no body."[2] "The Tao which can be expressed is not the eternal Tao."[3] Might one not suppose one was lis-

[1] Philo says: "He is incomprehensible: not even the whole universe, much less the human mind, can contain the conception of him: we know *that* he is, we cannot know *what* he is: we may see the manifestations of him in his works, but it were monstrous folly to go behind his works and inquire into his essence. He is hence unnamed; for names are the symbols of created things, whereas his only attribute is to be." See Edwin Hatch, *Hibbert Lectures, 1888*, p. 245.

[2] *Tao-te-King*, chap. xiv. (translated by Stanislas Julien, *Le livre de la voie et de la vertu*, Paris, 1842).

[3] Ibid. chap. i.—The "Tao that can be named," which Lao-tsze calls " the mother which produces all beings," is, according to

Q

tening to the Upanishads, as they declare God "unknown to those who profess to know him, known only to those who profess not to know him"?[1]

Amongst the Persians, Ahura-Mazda, exalted as his position is, remains more or less limited by the temporary existence of Ahriman, and this opposition is too marked to allow of his absorbing his opponent into himself. In the end, however, the two came to be regarded as offspring or hypostases of "Time without limit," Zervanem Akaranem. The germ of this conception is already found in the Avesta, where "time without limit" is distinguished from the "time of long rule." In the *Minokhired*, time without limit is assimilated to destiny, by which all things take place. Finally, under the Sassanides, Zervanem Akaranem becomes the Supreme Unity.[2]

The ancient gods before the face of the Only God. But, in the monotheistic evolution which we have just witnessed, what becomes of the ancient gods of polytheism? Were they not destined to vanish with the conception of the only God, into which all the individual forces of nature had in some sense melted?

I would point out, in the first place, that if the idea of an only God can be reconciled with the real existence

M. Ch. de Harlez, the indeterminate Tao made active by the appearance of desire.

[1] "He is truly known to him who conceives him not; he is unknown to him who conceives him: he is incomprehensible to those who comprehend; he is comprehended by those who comprehend him not."— *Kena Upanishad*, i. 2. 3, after de Harlez; cf. Max Müller, *Sacred Books of the East*, vol. i. *The Upanishads*, p. 149.

[2] J. Darmesteter, *Ormazd and Ahriman*, Paris, 1877, pt. iii. chap. i. pp. 316 sqq.

of terrestrial beings, there is no reason why it should not harmonize equally well with the belief in intermediate beings, superior to human nature, but taking part in the affairs of this world. The monotheistic transformation of almost all the historical religions seems, in this matter, merely to have brought upon the ancient deities a fate analogous to that which the polytheistic transformation of nature-worship brought upon the secondary spirits, when it threw them into a subordinate rank as agents, servants, messengers, and ministers of the chief gods. Thus the establishment of monotheism has not generally constituted so sharp and radical a revolution as one might have supposed, especially where it has remained the privilege of the enlightened few. Even Buddhism, though it could dispense with any deity at all, did not attack the existence of the ancient Vedic gods; it was content to represent them as beings who had raised themselves by their merits above the level of humanity in the scale of transmigration—something like those "planetary brothers of man" whom a contemporary of our own (who certainly cannot be suspected of any tenderness for religious dreamings), the author of *The Irreligion of the Future*, M. Guyau, imagines may, somewhere in the universe, represent a higher product of the universal evolution.[1] Islam preserves the angels and the djinns of previous beliefs, to say nothing of the almost superhuman position which it assigns to its founder. Post-exilian Judaism is, no doubt, reputed the monotheistic religion *par excellence*. Nevertheless, it surrounds Yahveh with angels and

[1] *L'irreligion de l'avenir*, Paris, 1887, p. 446.

archangels, powers, dominations, and thrones, which replace, at a higher degree of abstraction, the Bené Elohim of a former time, and play a part analogous to that of the demons in the Greek philosophy of the latest period.

Hypostases, demiurges, mediators.
In the worships which I have just mentioned, it may be maintained that the retention of the ancient divinities was a concession to popular traditions; and that these divinities, though retained in the religious system, were only there as survivals.[1] But, at any rate, this will not apply to the monotheism that takes a pantheistic turn. Here, in fact, the existence of superhuman beings, intermediate between the absolute God and the visible world, becomes necessary to explain the passage from the infinite to the finite, from the noumenal to the phenomenal world. Not only was this passage incomprehensible in itself, but the erection of the deity into the Absolute must have had the effect of breaking all his direct ties with man, and thus putting an end to the very possibility of the relations which constitute worship. To re-establish them, there was nothing for it but to throw across the abyss a chain of superhuman powers bordering on the one side upon supreme perfection, and on the other upon the sensible world. Now the ancient gods, already arranged by polytheism in a hierarchy, were naturally marked out for this office of hypostases and of demiurges.

[1] According to strict Islamite doctrine Allah alone should be addressed in prayer or invocation, for except him nothing and no one "can help or hurt."—Ignace Goldziher, *Le culte des saints chez les Musulmans*, in the *Revue de l'Histoire des Religions*, vol. ii. p. 262.

Thus in latest period of the classical paganism the neo-Platonist doctrine of emanation established a whole chain of intermediary beings between God and man, growing in perfection as they approached the Supreme Being and as they freed themselves from every material bond; and again the demonology of Plutarch and Porphyry filled the world with demons arranged in a hierarchy, with the ancient gods of paganism at their head; and the combination of these two conceptions inspired a last effort to bring paganism into harmony with the philosophical and universalistic tendencies of the time.

It should be remarked that, almost everywhere, as the supreme God became more powerful and majestic, the popular conscience had spontaneously fixed upon some other divine personage nearer to its own sentiments, aspirations, or even passions, to fulfil the function of interceder, or rather mediator, between man and the Sovereign of the skies. This mission had already been exercised in a subordinate degree by all the superhuman beings, from the genii of the hearth to the souls of the deceased; and now it generally, but not necessarily, fell to a personification of the sun; perhaps because mythology had almost universally made him the mythical hero of quasi-human adventures, the ideal type of man exposed to the extreme vicissitudes of fortune, more accessible than the other deities to sentiments of sympathy and pity. Passing alternately between death and life, he had necessarily become the pledge, and to a certain extent the dispenser, of immortality. Finally, he was a divinity essentially visible—*deus certus*, as

Aurelian calls him—more regular in his ways than fire or the wind, more personal than the heaven, more active than the moon, more beneficent than the thunderbolt. Did he not fulfil his function of mediator by tracing the road that leads between heaven and earth? We need not be surprised, then, that as the chief gods of the great pantheons withdrew behind the veil of metaphysical speculation, we note a remarkable revival by which gods hitherto regarded as secondary mount to the first place in adoration and worship. It was so with Merodach in Mesopotamia, Vishnu in India, Helios and Mithra in the Roman empire. And if we have not a parallel phenomenon to note in Egypt, it is because there the absolute God was in some sense drawn directly from the solar personality. Osiris or Ammon became the Unique Being "more mysterious than the gods," without ceasing to be the deity who dies each day to be born again, who fights with the darkness, and who judges the dead.

Even in the religion of Israel we find that, in proportion as Yahveh actually becomes "he who is," he deputes to his angels all the interventions that appear incompatible with his growing majesty. It is the angel of Yahveh who reveals himself in the form of flame, who consumes the flesh of the sacrifice, who struggles with Jacob, who reveals himself to Moses, and so on. Later on, this rôle is taken by abstractions, such as the Word, the Voice, the Name, the Glory, the Wisdom, the Breath of Yahveh, considered objectively, and, in a way, detached from God himself. In the 8th chapter of Proverbs, Wisdom, that is to say the intelligence of God, who conceives the world, is already almost personified. She is represented as existing side by side with God, she is called his "foster-child," and she "rejoiced before him at all times."[1] "I alone," says the same Wisdom, as represented in a later work, "have fixed the limits of the heaven and hollowed the depths of the sea; I have established my dominion over every portion of the earth and over all the nations."[2] In the same way the Word—perhaps the only human power which can apparently create and not only fashion, since it can make the image of a thing arise solely by naming it— appears as early as in Isaiah in the character of messenger, or agent, despatched by the Eternal to execute his orders, a veritable angel, like Ossa (Fame), the messenger of Zeus.[3] When Yahveh was so far exalted above the universe as to be incomprehensible in his essence—an idea already formulated by the author of *Ecclesiasticus* (xliii. 27—33)—or, indeed, as soon as he was conceived as too pure to come into direct contact with matter, all active and creative power is lodged in his abstract intermediaries. Thus the Hellenized Jews of Alexandria, such as Aristobulus, and above all Philo, had no difficulty in concentrating these intermediaries into a kind of hypostasis, which, under the Greek name of *Logos*, bore a singular resemblance to the *anima mundi* of the Stoics, and the intelligible world of Platonism.

Amongst the Hindus, the Brahmans took care to retain the principal popular deities in their religious system, while placing at their head the three great gods of the post-Vedic epoch, Brahma, Vishnu, and

[1] *Proverbs* viii. 30. [2] *Ecclesiasticus* xxiv. 5, 6.
[3] *Iliad*, ii. 93, 94.

V. MONOTHEISM.

Çiva, themselves regarded as hypostases of a neuter and impersonal Brahma. Thus—inspired doubtless by the necessities of worship—side by side with the metaphysical idealism which regarded the universe as a product of universal illusion, they taught a kind of exoteric theology which allowed some objective reality to the world of men and of gods. The impersonal Brahma was thought to evolve the universe from his own substance, like a spider spinning its web out of its own entrails, and to re-absorb it in an endless series of evolutions and dissolutions.[1]

Religious syncretism. We must not forget that the first corollary of a truly pantheistic religion is not so much toleration of all forms of worship, as a tendency to embrace them all in a single syncretistic system. The one God is the same for all. What, then, does the name they give him matter? As for the secondary deities, are they not all alike equivalent and interchangeable hypostases of the Deity? He who adores them all still fails, in the sum of the phases they represent, to grasp the divine unity reflected in the infinity of beings and things. We have already seen how, in Egypt, the gods were regarded sometimes as the members, sometimes as the varying names, of the one Being; and how the conception of the one Being still left the existence of the gods unchallenged alike in popular worship and in theological speculation. Amongst the Hindus, the system of incarnations or *avatars* (literally, *descents*) provided a means of absorbing into Brahmanism the local deities that might otherwise have checked the worship of the

[1] Barth, *Religions of India*, p. 47.

Devas. Buddha himself thus became an incarnation of Vishnu.[1]

The classical paganism owed its last period of vigour to the growing conviction that the gods of all the peoples were equivalent, or rather that they were connected with the same deified forces and were a part of the same divine order. Every one has heard of the chapel in which Alexander Severus placed Jesus, Abraham, Orpheus, and Alexander the Great, side by side with Apollonius of Tyana. The same emperor, whose reign marks the culmination of religious toleration in Rome, took part indifferently in the worship of Jupiter, Mithra, Serapis, and Baal. He is even said to have contemplated the erection of a temple to Christ. And he certainly confirmed the Christians in the possession of a church in the Transtiberine district which had once been public property, and which was claimed by the public authorities.

M. Jean Réville, in his *Histoire de la Religion à Rome sous les Sévères*—which might equally well be entitled, "How Paganism met its End"—has shown with great clearness and judgment that this syncretistic tendency resulted at once in prolonging the existence and in facilitating the fall of the ancient beliefs; for it united all the worships of the time in a kind of vague, solar monotheism.[2] The gods of the old national pantheons

---

[1] Conversely, the Japanese Buddhists taught that the gods of Shintoism were manifestations of the Buddha.—*Religious Systems of the World*, p. 90.

[2] *La Religion à Rome sous les Sévères*, Paris, 1886, chap. x.

were too deeply compromised by particularism and by their own mythological past to lend themselves to the new part they were now called upon to play. On the other hand, the abstractions of the theosophical schools— Reason, Wisdom, even the Word—lacked the vivid and anthropomorphic characteristics needed to secure them the homage and sympathy of the masses. But when, in the bosom of Alexandrine theology, the hypostasis of the *Logos* became flesh in the person of Jesus, who was already the centre of a moral doctrine answering to the aspirations of the age, then, indeed, a religion was born destined to conquer all its rivals, and to preside for more than fifteen centuries over the destinies of Western civilization.

The Christian theodicy. The question has often been discussed, whether the rise of Christianity hastened the fall of the ancient world, and whether it must be held responsible for the long intellectual night of the Middle Ages. The truth is, that the ancient civilization was irrevocably doomed, and that Christianity itself was involved in the decline which followed the fall of ancient paganism. It is not my present purpose to trace the history of Christian theology during the centuries which followed. You know how it oscillated between a monotheism, in which the persons of the Trinity approximated to simple hypostases of the Deity, and a veritable Tritheism, which accentuated the distinction of the three persons to the prejudice of the divine unity. The reconciliation of these two extreme terms remained impossible : it was a mystery which the believer must admit without professing to explain it; such was the decree of the Church, raised in its capacity of living interpreter of the Deity above the very Scriptures themselves.

No doubt the conception of God, or rather Theology, gave rise to innumerable speculations in the Middle Ages. But these speculations were bound down to the bed of Procrustes provided by an orthodoxy that was often itself a mere mechanical compromise between contradictory opinions. Nominalists and realists, rationalists and mystics, were successively condemned as soon as they attempted to draw out the logical consequences of their respective principles. We have nothing but respect for the labours of such thinkers as Scotus Erigena, Abelard, St. Bernard, Roger Bacon, David of Dinant, Albertus Magnus, and Thomas Aquinas, who kept the light of philosophic culture burning during those dark days. But whatever services some of these scholars may have rendered in elaborating logical and philosophical method, and whatever influence some may still retain in orthodox circles, the labours of Scholasticism can hardly be regarded as having made any more substantial contributions to the advancement of the religious problem than are due to the intermittent and often irregular explosions of the heresies which were one after another drowned in blood.

The Reformation re-opened a gate to the spirit of free inquiry, and thereupon philosophical criticism, to which the Renaissance had given a new life and vigour, straightway applied to the dogmas of Christianity the methods it has long ago directed against the theodicy of Greek paganism.

God identified with the absolute unity by modern philosophy. The idea of God was thus reduced to the conception of Unity, freed from mythical functions, released from the limitations of anthropomorphism, stripped of every attribute common to human nature, till German idealism, treading in the steps of Spinoza, reduced it once more to the conception of sole and absolute Being. Even intelligence, justice, and love, have once more been challenged as attributes of the Deity, because they imply the notion of a personal and therefore a limited being. The pessimist philosophers allow at most a kind of unconscious will to the Deity; the Evolutionists reduce, or, if you will, expand it into "an Infinite and Eternal Energy, from which all things proceed."[1] In a word, we find ourselves returning from every side to the Inaccessible of the latest neo-Platonists.

In truth, it is not the existence of God that modern philosophy and science challenge. Or, if criticism has attempted any such task, it has only been as a philosophic exercise. Systems may, if they choose, forbid us to think about such questions, but whenever we do think about them—and will not that be always?—we shall find this idea of God embedded in our consciousness as the very foundation of all relative existence. What science really has proscribed is a belief in æons, avatars, mediators—in a word, "secondary gods;" and this it is which complicates with a new difficulty every attempt at religious reconstruction.

We have just seen how the ancient philosophy, by the expedient of hypostases and divine emanations, found

[1] Herbert Spencer, *Ecclesiastical Institutions*, p. 843.

means, not only of giving the deities formerly worshipped a place in a rational system, but even creating fresh deities when it suppressed the old ones. But now, if there is one axiom which has sunk deeper than another into our minds, it is that all phenomena are ruled by laws, and that outside the contingent world thus organized there is room for naught save the One Absolute Being from whom all things proceed.

Gods and demons have disappeared, to return no more. Or, if their equivalents exist anywhere in the universe, here on our planet at least we must perforce admit that they have no power of making themselves felt or known; and we are more and more tempted to make Cicero's words our own: "Think not that any such thing can happen as we often see in plays, that some god, coming down from heaven, should join the assemblies of men, hold intercourse on the earth, and converse with mortals."[1]

If any intermediaries between man and God, as now conceived, exist, they can only be our own faculties, such as Reason, or Conscience, or such abstractions as Moral Order, the Law of Progress, Humanity, and so forth. But these are entities with no personal and discrete existence; they can only take shape by becoming attributes of something or of some one. This is why Unitarians, and the Rationalistic communities of modern Christendom, in general, have come to reverence the Ideal in that man who seems in their eyes most nearly to approach it, even if not to realize it in all its plenitude. And so, too, the Positivists, in pro-

[1] *Oratio de haruspicum responsis*, cap. xxviii.

claiming the Religion of Humanity, have but organized the worship of those types which have contributed most to the development of human society. But here we must admit that the saints of the Comtist calendar, and the Jesus of Liberal Protestantism himself, are no longer in any sense hypostases of the Deity; for they are no longer superhuman beings, freed from the normal conditions of humanity, nor are they the necessary and permanent media of the Deity in his relations with the world.

We are perpetually thrown back, then, on the unknown, unknowable Being of the latest Alexandrines as the object of religion. Yet neither religion nor philosophy, nor even science, compels us to be content with this purely negative solution.

The eternal and infinite energy whence all things proceed.   We are aware what the Unknowable has become in the hands of Herbert Spencer. The conclusion to which his brilliant and daring scientific generalizations lead him is not only a belief in the positive existence of the Absolute, but a vindication of our right to attribute to that supreme reality the characters of unity, activity, immanence, omnipresence, and eternity, which make it "the infinite and eternal energy whence all things proceed."[1]

---

[1] Mr. Spencer has been reproached with this as a contradiction and an inconsistency. Perhaps the great representative of Evolutionism would have done better had he used the term Incomprehensible rather than Unknowable, to mark our inability to express, or even adequately to conceive, either the essence or the attributes of that almighty energy. But we may remark that he himself is careful to distinguish between two kinds of knowledge; the definite knowledge, the laws of which are formulated by logic, and the indefinite knowledge, which can only be formulated by the aid of symbols. If I understand

It is true that he refuses to assign to this energy the attributes of conscience, of goodness, and of personality, as we conceive them in the system of our relations with the finite world; but he explains that this is simply because of our inability to seize the true modes of the Infinite. "Is it not just possible," he asks of those who accuse him of want of religion, "that there is a mode of being as much transcending Intelligence and Will as these transcend mechanical motion? It is true that we are totally unable to conceive any such higher mode of being. But this is not a reason for questioning its existence; it is rather the reverse. Have we not seen how utterly incompetent our minds are to form even an approach to a conception of that which underlies all phenomena? Is it not proved that this incompetency is the incompetency of the conditioned to grasp the unconditioned? Does it not follow that the ultimate Cause cannot in any respect be conceived by us because it is in every respect greater than can be conceived?"[1]

The power, not ourselves, that makes for righteousness. Some of Spencer's disciples, the right wing as we may call them of Evolutionism, have gone still further, sometimes with the more or less formal sanction of the master.[2] From the

him rightly, it is because it is an object of this imperfect knowledge only that he qualifies the supreme reality as unknowable.—*First Principles*, chap. iv. § 26, p. 88.

[1] *First Principles*, chap. v. § 31, p. 109.

[2] See his letter to the Rev. Minot Savage, author of *The Religion of Evolution* (Boston, 1876), in which he congratulates him on having "exposed the religious and ethical bearings of the evolution doctrines." "I rejoice very much," adds Mr. Spencer, "to see that those doctrines

fact that all observable phenomena, that is to say the contingent manifestations of Energy, realize themselves in accordance with law, they have concluded that the reign of law is one of the modes .in which the Unknowable operates, and they have taken occasion herefrom to attribute to the supreme Power, if not a conscious and determined goal like the objects pursued by man, at any rate a tendency to secure the utterance of universal order in the moral as in the physical world. "While such a tendency," says Mr. John Fiske, "cannot be regarded as indicative of purpose in the limited anthropomorphic sense, it is still .... the objective aspect of that which, when regarded on its subjective side, we call Purpose."[1] In fact, not only does order exist in the universe, but this order is progressive, as we are taught successively by astronomy, geology, paleontology, and the history of civilization. This progress manifests itself first in the physical domain, where it takes the form of growing complexity and adaptation of organisms; next, in the spiritual domain, where it reveals itself in the rise and development of morality. Thus "the infinite and eternal energy whence

are coming to the front. It is high time that something should be done towards making the people see that there remains for them, not a mere negation of their previous ethical and religious beliefs, which, as you say, have a definite scientific and unshakable foundation. . . . . I have been long looking forward to the time when something of this kind might be done, and it seems to me you are the man to do it." This letter, published with Mr. Spencer's sanction, in *The Christian Register* of Boston, March 29, 1883, is all the more significant, inasmuch as Mr. Savage attributes to evolution a goal in some sort predetermined.

[1] John Fiske, *The Idea of God as affected by Modern Knowledge*, Boston, 1885, p. xxiv.

all things proceed" becomes a regulating power of which we have the right to say that it tends to good, even though its ultimate goal should for ever escape our vision.

Not that I am called upon to take sides as between the various explanations of the world current in our day, or even to enumerate the systems which a history of philosophy would have to deal with. If I have dwelt on the theology of Evolutionism, it is because that philosophy is so much in vogue that it forces us to pay special attention to it, and further because it is the one amongst all the great syntheses of our day which breaks most completely with the traditions and the methods of the past. But I should be the first to admit that it has no right to claim the monopoly of conformity with the demands of science. Side by side with those who attempt to complete Spencer's doctrine on the lines indicated by the spiritual and moral demands of our nature, it is but right to refer, however rapidly, to the attempts of those thinkers who remain faithful in their philosophic constructions to the method of internal observation. It would be mere dogmatic narrowness to deny the legitimacy of this method, provided always that its advocates, while themselves laying greater stress on ideas of immanence, side by side with those of development, are careful not to put themselves into opposition with any facts established by impartial observation of nature. Indeed, for that matter, we may go as far as to assert that German Idealism long anticipated the generalizations of the science of to-day.

The attitude just indicated is notably that of Robert Flint, Thomas Hill Green, F. W. Newman, James Martineau, and Matthew Arnold, in England; of Pfleiderer, Wundt, and the Neo-Hegelians, in Germany; of Paul Janet, Vacherot, Secrétan, and Fouillée, in France; of R. Waldo Emerson and Francis E. Abbott, in the United States,— whether they have chosen Will rather than Force to express, in terms of our own experience, the action of the power at the source of things; or whether they have regarded spirit and matter as two phases of one mysterious reality rising into self-consciousness in man; or whether they have sought in our moral aspirations the reflexion of a higher ideal, which reveals at once the objective existence and the essential nature of the Deity. It is impossible to predict the measure in which these speculations are destined respectively to influence the theology of the future, though the present tide of philosophy seems to flow more strongly than ever through the channels opened out by Kant and Hegel; but the essential point is, that the systems whose best-known representatives I have just enumerated, while differing widely on many questions as to which metaphysicians have always differed, nevertheless agree in representing the history of the world as an evolution the progressive development of which bears witness to the universal presence and unceasing action of an eternal Power "not ourselves that makes for righteousness."

Mr. Herbert Spencer's formula, thus completed by Matthew Arnold's, perhaps furnishes the point of reconciliation between the philosophy of evolution and the religious school of positivism, by allowing these two systems to supplement each other without bating a jot of their respective principles. In the words of the

American Positivist, W. Frey, "The intense feeling of gratitude and admiration which [the Positivists] feel towards humanity will become only deeper and stronger if humanity be regarded as mediator between man and the infinite, because then will come into play the strongest chord of religious sentiment, i.e. man's yearning for the Infinite."[1]

And, again, this conclusion enables us to combine the fact of human freedom with the demands of scientific determinism, if we can but admit the theory of *idea-forces*, so brilliantly expounded in France by M. A. Fouillée. According to his teaching, the idea of liberty, when once developed in the conscience, leads human activity to take its bearings afresh. "It is realized by being desired." Its very birth is itself the natural and logical result of evolution, the development of a germ present in all nature as the manifestation of the primordial Will. "First comes a war of forces, brute fatality, infinite confusion of beings striking one against another without recognition, in a sort of blind misconception; then progressive organization, which allows consciousness to emerge, and, with consciousness, will; then progressive union of beings gradually recognizing one another as brethren. The evil will will be transient, the offspring of mechanic necessity or intellectual ignorance. The good will, on the contrary, will be permanent, fundamental, normal, and will spring from the very roots of the being itself. To bring it into distinct existence in oneself will be to pass out of the transient

[1] Boston, *Index* for Aug. 8th, 1882.

and the individual for the benefit of the permanent and the universal, to become truly free, and therefore to love."[1]

It cannot be denied, then, that there exist in our times all the elements of a monotheistic faith reconcilable with the demands of the most exacting reason. All that modern science postulates is the unity of the productive power and the unchangeableness of the laws in accordance with which it manifests itself. And, as Dr. James Martineau has well observed, modern science, so conceived, "does not even disturb us with a new idea; for Evolution is only *growth;* it merely raises the question *how far* into the field of Nature that idea can properly be carried,—a question surely of no religious significance..... The Unity of the Causal Power—which is all that the spreading network of analogies can establish—cannot possibly be unwelcome to those who regard it all as the working of One Mind,"[2] or even, I would add, as the utterance of a mysterious force seeking an end.

[1] A. Fouillée, *La Liberté et le Déterminisme*, second edition, Paris, 1884, pp. 355, 356.

[2] Preface to John James Tayler's *Retrospect of the Religious Life of England*, second edition, London, 1876, p. 32.

Lecture VI.
THE FUTURE OF WORSHIP AS DEDUCED FROM ITS PAST.

Evolution of the incentives to worship. HITHERTO we have been concerned with the development of the idea of God in the consciousness of man as he slowly ascended towards the higher regions of intellectual and moral culture. It remains to examine the corresponding modifications which this development of doctrine has produced in the inward springs and outward manifestations of worship. Theology, interesting as its problems may be in themselves, derives its general significance from the measure in which it forms the character and influences the life of man. Of the three motives which have been the main factors of religion from the very first,— to wit, fear, admiration, and sympathy,—the first hardly survives except as that emotion of awe called forth by the thought of the Absolute, by the contrast between human weakness and the irresistible might of the universal evolution, and by the certain punishment which sooner or later overtakes the least attempt to violate the order of the universe, in the moral as in the physical domain. Fear, then, is transformed into respect for the moral law and reverence for its mysterious Author. And, by the same evolution, the second factor passes from the irreflective to the reasoning stage, as admiration for the divine work is deepened by the science that enables us to form a loftier and broader conception of the universal harmony. And, finally, both these elements tend to lose themselves in the third, which alone can leap the barriers between man and the Deity.

Transformation of the sentiment of love of God. The old adage, *Si vis amari, ama*, may here be applied. As soon as men believed themselves loved by the gods, the gods were straightway loved by them; and this feeling, that had hardly existed at the outset, became ever more generous and powerful as respect for the moral superiority of the deity reinforced it. Henceforth sin was shunned and virtue practised, not with a view to reward in this world or the next, but simply to please the object of love.

The belief in the rewards of a future life, whether it take the form of metempsychosis, of personal survival, or of resurrection, may fade and disappear; but love of God, if strong enough, may adequately replace it as a chief incentive to virtue and love; and I would even add that it is a nobler because a more disinterested motive.[1] The religion of the categorical imperative no doubt touches an equally certain and equally exalted spring of action; but in enjoining duty because it is duty, it remains a severe and abstract philosophy, like the Stoicism of former times, and can never be more than the privilege of a select few. Love is accessible to all, whether its object be the God of the Christians dying on the Cross to redeem humanity, or the sage of Kapila-

---

[1] Abelard notes that fear of hell has no moral value, and that the only true penitence is inspired, not by fear of punishment, but by love of God.—Pfleiderer, *Philosophy of Religion*, vol. iv. p. 259.

vastu renouncing the Nirvana to teach men the way of salvation; whether it concentrate itself on the unlimited power of which the whole universe is the harmonious manifestation, or whether it address itself to the *grand-être* Humanity of which Comte aspired to be the revealer and the apostle.

This has been understood by all the higher religions, including not only Christianity, but the mystic sects of Brahmanism and even of Islam. For all alike have striven to place love—or rather the desire to realize the completest possible unity with the Deity—above knowledge, above even obedience, as the highest principle of life.

Love of God, it is true, is in danger of culminating in a mysticism which engulfs man in sterile contemplations and selfish ecstasies. Thus amongst the Hindus the outpourings of love for God have always culminated in ascetic negation of action and even of thought. But as the love of God may vary in degree, so likewise it may show itself in more or less worthy forms. When the good of the universe is regarded as the essential purpose of the Deity, and when it is just this very conception that strikes the chords of sympathy in the human heart, then the desire to please the supremely loved being does not assert itself as an exclusive and jealous sentiment, but as an irresistible impulse to love what the loved one loves. Thus it becomes the love of man in God; and yet more, transcending the limits of humanity, it embraces all creatures in a common sympathy which may even pierce the unknown spaces with the torch of imagination, and seek in other worlds beings to love and one day to aid.

After declaring that the first commandment is to love God with all the heart, and all the soul, and all the mind, and all the strength, did not Jesus add that the second, which bids us love our neighbour as ourself, was like unto the first? (Matt. xxii. 36—40). "Love is practical in its nature," says a modern Indian writer; "if genuine, it must come out in action; love that is not active, is no love at all."[1] I need not insist on the splendid development of charitable and philanthropic works which sprang and still springs from the Wesleyan movement. It proves, better than any argument, that mysticism, when it falls on good ground, may assume an essentially fruitful and practical character, by conceiving the love of God as the source of all moral activity, and grafting the love of man upon it. The life of a Channing, a Theodore Parker, a Rammohun Roy, or a Keshub Chunder Sen, and the institutions founded and developed in England and America and on the European continent by the liberal Protestants of every shade, prove that the religious source of this devotion to humanity is not to be found in the belief in the supernatural, but in a sense of fraternity begotten by communion with God, and in a disinterested desire to share in the divine work of human regeneration.

This development of the religious sentiment has not taken place at a single stroke. We can trace its gradual growth in the history of the several religious institutions which combine in worship.

Disappearance of the lower elements of worship. I pointed out at the close of my second Lecture that the external or practical manifestations of religion may be classed, even

[1] *Brahmo Public Opinion*, Jan. 23rd, 1879.

amongst the most backward peoples, under the five following heads: prayer, sacrifice, magic, divination, and symbolism. Some of these are recalcitrant to all progress or even transformation. Such appear to be the processes of sorcery, which remain, amongst ourselves, exactly what they were in antiquity and still are amongst the savages. The whole religious development has gone on outside them. Everywhere rejected or despised by the modern churches, they have taken refuge amongst the lower classes; or if they have kept their place here and there in official liturgies, it is only on condition of ascribing the whole merit of their traditional efficacy to the free intervention of the Deity; and even these surviving concessions to weak souls are falling more and more into discredit, and their final extinction is easy to foresee.

Divination has completely disappeared from the bosom of the great contemporary religions. It is true enough that faith in the inflexibility of the divine decrees, or, in other words, in the immutability of the order established by the gods, gave a fresh impulse to divination in the ancient polytheisms, but it was also the beginning of the end; for when the art of predicting breaks away from the arbitrary intervention of the superhuman powers and attaches itself to the connected order of cause and effect, it escapes from the domain of religion and enters into that of science. No sooner had astrology given birth to astronomy, than its own progress was decisively arrested. The almanac of Nostradamus shows no advance on the processes of the astrological tablets of ancient Chaldea. Here, too, progress is impossible beyond a certain point, and astrological divination is definitely relegated to its place among popular superstitions. The Pythian and the Sybil henceforth are dumb, or rather their awful voices find no echo save in the degenerate tongue of the wizard and the fortune-teller.

But other institutions which date from the origins of religion maintain their place in our worship, because their nature was susceptible of modification in accordance with the changed aspect of the deity itself.

The evolution of prayer. We have seen that originally prayer was essentially petition. When religion is penetrated by the moral idea, no doubt material blessings are still sought, but at the same time the superhuman powers are implored for pardon of sins or even for power to resist temptation. The Bible itself has no more exalted utterances of repentance than some of the Chaldeo-Assyrian hymns which François Lenormant has well called "Penitential Psalms," or the staves of some of the Vedic chants addressed to the gods of justice or pity, Varuna, Agni, Aditi, and others.

Another stage of advance is marked when men ask for no specified favours from the gods, but throw themselves upon their insight and their goodness, in the belief that they know best what is good for their worshippers. Thus the cry of Jesus in the Garden of Gethsemane implied absolute self-abandonment to an almighty and all-loving Providence: "Father, not my will, but thine, be done" (Luke xxii. 42).

But can prayer survive the rejection, not only of belief in miracles, but of all belief in the intermittent and arbitrary intervention of the Deity? Surely it may remain as a subjective expression of the loftiest religious aspirations of man, transformed into the spontaneous utterance of that gratitude, admiration and love, which the normal unfolding of the divine works inspires. As petition, prayer may disappear; but as invocation, as homage, and, above all, as self-dedication to the task of moral co-operation with the Deity, it will remain as long as the religious sentiment itself abides.

The poetry which personifies everything has surely the right to ascribe the most elevated attributes of human nature to the supreme Reality. Profoundly religious minds have admitted that prayer can have no effect on the Deity, yet have not renounced it. Even should we become convinced that invocations are no more than monologues, and wake no echo outside our own consciousness, like the Comtist prayers addressed to the *grand-être*, Humanity, we might yet draw from this communion with our Ideal such strength as comes from any effusion that raises us above the relative and the transitory, and places our feet in the region of the Eternal and the Absolute. Nevertheless, it is only if we believe in the real existence of an omnipresent Power, even though we refuse to define its attributes, that prayer, or, if you prefer it, invocation, gives to the spiritual, moral, and even æsthetic faculties of the human soul their highest satisfaction. This truth is amply illustrated by some of the liturgies in use in Theistic or Free Christian Churches.

The evolution of sacrifice. Man begins by supposing the superhuman beings to eat and drink like men. The Caribees think they hear their *cemis* cracking their jaws when they are eating the provisions placed in special huts for them. So, too, the Negroes of Labode professed to hear the gurgling and smack as their fetish drank the bottle of rum they had put within his reach.

Such illusions may be maintained by the fact that sooner or later the food is decomposed or carried off by animals, and the drink evaporates or sinks into the ground. A Russian traveller amongst the Ostyaks now and again empties a horn of snuff which has been set before an idol, and in the morning the people say the god must have been hunting, he has snuffed so much.[1] This explains the prevalence of certain forms of sacrifice which facilitate the disappearance of the offerings, e.g. burying or immersing them for subterranean or aquatic deities, and burning them for celestial or atmospheric ones.

Fire is more especially charged with this mission, not only because it so soon reduces combustible objects to volatile forms, but further because it seems to bear them to heaven in the smoke. "O Agni," says the Rig-Veda, "the offering which thou encirclest on all sides, unhurt, that alone goes to the gods."[2] Thus fire, personified as the agent of sacrifice, assumes an ever more important place as the mightiest and most formidable deities are located in the sky. The Vedas call it the "Divine Priest appointed for sacrifice."[3] The Proto-Chaldeans named it the "Supreme Pontiff on the face of the Earth."[4] The Chinuks implore it to intercede with

---

[1] Tylor, *Primitive Culture*, vol. ii. p. 345 (3rd edition, p. 381).
[2] *Rig-Veda*, 1. 1. 4.   [3] *Ibid.* 1. 1. 1.
[4] Tiele, *Anciennes religions de l'Égypte et des peuples semitiques*, p. 176.

the Great Spirit to obtain abundant game, swift horses, and plenty of male children for them. Amongst the Egyptians, Ptah, the god of the Cosmic Fire, has a son Imhoteb, whose name means, "I come in the sacrifice" or "in peace," and who personified, as Tiele assures us, the fire of sacrifices regulated according to the sacred book.[1]

Spiritualizing of sacrifice. The custom of committing sacrifice to the fire gave rise, in its turn, to the belief that the gods only consumed the essence, transmitted to them in the form of smoke or odour. This is the idea of the Redskin who smokes his calumet in honour of the Great Spirit. "Fire and Earth," cry the Osages, "smoke with me and help me to overthrow my foes."[2]

The brothers Lander tell us of a village on the Niger where they had slaughtered an ox, and the natives asked them to roast it under a certain fetish, that the latter might have the benefit of the smell.[3] The same order of ideas re-appears in the offerings of burnt fat amongst so many peoples, from the Jews and Greeks down to the Zulus, and the burning of incense or perfumes which still prevails in most parts of the world. "The smell of burning fat," says Homer, "rose to heaven on the billows of smoke;"[4] and we know that holocausts long continued to be a "sweet savour to Yahveh."[5] And

---

[1] Tiele, *Anciennes Religions de l'Égypte et des peuples semitiques*, p. 64 (*History of the Egyptian Religion*, p. 91).

[2] Tylor, *Primitive Culture*, vol. ii. p. 347 (3rd edition, p. 383).

[3] Richard and John Lander, *Journal of an Expedition to explore the Course and Termination of the Niger*, London, 1832, vol. iii. pp. 104 sq., under date Oct. 29.

[4] *Iliad*, i. 317.   [5] Cf. Genesis viii. 21.

again, in proportion as the distinction between body and soul is carried down to inanimate things, the belief tends to arise that the superhuman beings confine themselves to consuming the spiritual part, or *double*, of the sacrifice. I have already cited the Negro's explanation that it was not the tree that ate the sacrifice, but the spirit of the tree that ate the spirit of the sacrifice. Some critics have thought that this is almost too subtle to be true, but we find the same thing more or less explicitly formulated in the most diverse parts of the world.

And now note these consequences. It matters little what may become of the sacrifice itself; it may be thrown away, left there to decay, or abandoned to animals, just as well as buried or burned. Nay, the worshippers may eat it themselves; and this latter alternative tends to prevail, in the first place because it saves waste, and in the next place as a means of entering into communion with the gods by sharing their repast, and as giving the sacrifice a higher character of solemnity as a social and religious festival. Unquestionably these are the ideas which lie at the root of those sacrificial banquets which are common to all organized religions.[1] Sometimes the

[1] It is interesting to note that an analogous superstition has survived in European countries, where the belief prevails that the repast of the survivors helps to redeem the soul of the departed. Indeed, in some parts of Flanders *pannekoeken* (fritters) are still made on All-Souls-day, to be eaten for the benefit of the departed. Every *pannekoeke* swallowed redeems a soul. MM. Henry Havard and Ginisty respectively report that at Bruges and at Dixmude men are hired to consume as many of these dainties as possible, since they are found to injure the digestions of the living as much as they benefit the souls of the dead.

material portion of the sacrifices is handed over to the priests, who are thus directly interested in their multiplication: "That which remains of the meal offering shall be for Aaron and his sons" (Lev. ii. 3); or, finally, it is given to the poor, as in certain temples in the India of to-day.[1]

Transformation of offerings into homage. The belief that the gods only eat the soul of the victim, combined with the growing conviction that their existence and felicity are independent of human generosity, diminishes the objective importance of sacrifice, and tends to make the idea of homage preponderate over that of actual gifts or services.

Hence flow two results, contradictory enough in appearance, the one manifesting itself as an aggravation, and the other as an attenuation, of sacrifice.

On the one hand, since the intention alone constitutes the virtue of sacrifice, its value will be proportioned to the privation the worshipper inflicts upon himself, and the worth of the thing sacrificed in his own eyes. The Greeks, with whom hospitality was a sacred institution under the special protection of Zeus, at one period sacrificed strangers to the Lycian Zeus, perhaps because a curious perversion of the argument just indicated led them to regard this as an eminently precious offering.[2]

We know what efficacity the Semites attached to the sacrifice of the first-born son. When the king of Moab was besieged in his capital by the united forces of Israel,

[1] A. Chevrillon, *Dans l'Inde*, in the *Revue des Deux Mondes* for March 1st, 1891, p. 100.

[2] Cf. F. A. Maury, *Religions de la Grèce antique*, vol. i. p. 184.

Judah and Edom, he sacrificed his eldest son on the ramparts, and this was enough to make the investing army raise the siege. In like manner, when Carthage was reduced to the last extremities, the best families were compelled to give up their first-born sons to be burnt in a huge hollow statue of Baal-Hamman. But the hideous sacrifice did not prevent the triumph of Rome. Hence, too, the idea, always favoured by certain religions, that the absolute surrender of person and property constitutes the sacrifice of highest worth in the eyes of the Deity, because it is the most complete. Hence, too, that form of asceticism which consists in self-imposed fasting and abstinence, regarded as an expiation, and carried to the point of systematic renunciation, solely to please the Deity, of everything not absolutely necessary for the bare maintenance of a life reduced to its simplest elements.

Attenuation of sacrifice. But, on the other hand, since homage is the essence of sacrifice, the intention ought to be enough; and no hesitation need be felt in offering a part for the whole, the inferior as a substitute for the superior, or the image instead of the reality. This threefold method of attenuation has had a specially beneficent effect in eliminating human sacrifice.

(a.) *The Part for the Whole.*

The idea of substituting the part for the whole gave rise to those religious mutilations by which the worshipper (and especially the priest, who was supposed to give himself entirely to the Deity) sacrificed a part of his body as a substitute for his whole being. Sometimes it is a finger, a tooth, a piece of flesh, or a lock of hair, sometimes a few drops of blood.

In the time of Claudius, the Druids, who had formerly practised human sacrifice on a large scale, contented themselves with pouring a little blood upon the altar.[1] The same thing takes place in India, where the Brahmans retain the sacrifice of human blood in certain solemnities, but only "a quarter as much as a lotus-leaf will hold."[2] In Greece, Pausanias tells us that the altar of Artemis at Sparta had to be sprinkled with the blood of human victims chosen by lot. Lycurgus substituted the practice of flogging boys before the altar till the blood came.[3] In Central America, where human sacrifice reached such monstrous proportions, Quetzalcoatl, the least sanguinary of the Mexican deities, was supposed to have substituted simple bleeding.[4] Finally, it is by no means certain that the Jewish circumcision was not a similar attenuation. In fact, we read in Exodus that when Moses on his way to Egypt had stopped at a hostelry, Yahveh met him and sought to slay him, but Zipporah hastened to circumcise her child, and thus saved her husband.[5]

[1] Pomponius Mela, *Chorographia*, iii. 2 (18).
[2] A. de Gubernatis, *Mythologie des plantes*, vol. ii. p. 209.
[3] *Pausanias*, iii. 16. 10.
[4] A. Réville, *Hibbert Lectures, 1884*, p. 64.
[5] Ex. iv. 24—26. That this was the original significance of circumcision seems to follow very clearly from the passage of Sanchuniathon which says that after a famine and a pestilence, Cronos first sacrificed his only son, and then circumcised himself and compelled his companions to do the like. See M. Lenormant, *Origines de l'histoire*, 1880, vol. i. p. 546 (*Beginnings of History*, p. 531).—When some important

In many cases only the hides or the head, the horns or the entrails, of the slaughtered animal are sacrificed. The extreme of attenuation in this matter is realized by the Parsees, who, instead of sacrificing an ox, confine themselves to burning a few of his hairs. In like manner, the Peruvians were satisfied with pulling a hair out of their eyebrows and blowing it towards the idol.[1]

(b.) *The Inferior for the Superior.*

Elsewhere the burden or cruelty of human sacrifice is lightened by committing criminals, captives, slaves, or animals, to the knife, as a substitute for the more precious victims. Thus Yahveh allowed Abraham to offer him a ram as a substitute for Isaac. In Greece, likewise, the slaughter of an animal was substituted in certain sacrifices for that of a human victim; but, in fidelity to the ancient usage of the ritual tradition, a man was first led up to the altar, and then suffered to escape.[2]

(c.) *The Image for the Reality.*

Wherever we find human figures offered to the deities —for instance, the statuettes thrown into the Tiber at a certain period of the year—we may be sure the practice is a survival from ancient human sacrifices. The same kind of attenuation has affected the sacrifice of animals, and in general every kind of offering which involved the

personage in Fiji is smitten with disease, they circumcise, not the invalid, but his son or some young man who volunteers to submit to the operation.

[1] A. Réville, *Hibbert Lectures, 1884*, p. 219.
[2] A. Maury, *Religions de la Grèce antique*, vol. ii. p. 105.

worshipper in considerable loss. Thus, amongst the Greeks, worshippers too poor to sacrifice animals confined themselves to offering paste or wooden effigies of them.[1] The same idea re-appears in the wax or metal "ex-votos," representing diseased members, suspended round the chapels of saints or madonnas who have a reputation for working miracles. Tavernier noted the same usage in India.[2]

This form of substitution is fostered by the popular belief that a portrait is equivalent to the original. The Egyptians went so far as to believe that the double of the food painted for the benefit of the deceased on the walls of the tombs, would reproduce itself indefinitely in the other world, as long as its representation continued here. It was this same confusion between the copy and the original, manifested in connection with another order of ideas, that gave birth to the practice of destroying or burying the image of a man as a means of compassing his death.

By another step forward, it may come to be supposed that the sacrifice itself can be replaced by a simple pantomime. The Semites were often satisfied with passing their victims through or between the flames, and the same usage is found amongst the Malagassy, the ancient Mexicans, the Malays, and the Burmese. We must be careful, however, to inquire whether this may not sometimes be a form of purification, like that of baptism by water, and nothing more; for amongst savages and in

[1] A. Maury, *Religions de la Grèce antique*, vol. ii. pp. 95, 96, 100, 101.
[2] See *Revue des traditions populaires*, 1889, vol. iv. p. 20.

the lower strata of civilized peoples the same practice often expresses widely different ideas. In the sixteenth century, for instance, there were certain parts of Scotland in which, as soon as a child was brought home from baptism, it was swung three or four times over a flame, with the words, "Let the flame consume thee now or never."[1]

If the intention is all that signifies, it is not unnatural for the deity to be satisfied with the bare beginning of the sacrifice. We all remember how Yahveh held Abraham's arm at the moment when the knife was already raised to strike Isaac, saying, "Lay not thy hand upon the child, . . . now I know that thou fearest God" (Gen. xxii. 12). It is interesting to observe that analogous traditions arose amongst the Greeks and Chinese. It was said that at Lacedemon the oracle had required the sacrifice of Helen to put an end to a plague, but at the moment when the sacrificer raised the steel, an Eagle suddenly snatched it from his hand.[2] In China the Emperor Tang offered himself as a voluntary victim to put an end to a drought; but as he was preparing for the consummation of the sacrifice, heaven sent abundant rain.[3] In all these cases, the consummation of the ceremony is averted only by an event independent of the human will; but such precedents would be interpreted as manifest signs that the deity no longer required human sacrifices.

[1] J. Brand, *Observations on Popular Antiquities*, London, 1841, vol. ii. p. 48.

[2] Maury, *Religions de la Grèce antique*, vol. ii. pp. 104 sq.

[3] A. Réville, *La Religion chinoise*, vol. i. p. 207.

Even the representation, or the performance of the preliminaries, might thus become superfluous formalities. The mental sacrifices of the Brahman who leads a solitary life in the heart of the forest, are more efficacious than the most sacred sacrificial rites of external worship.

<small>Moral transformation of sacrifice.</small> The penetration of religion by morals tends to modify the idea of sacrifice profoundly, if not completely to suppress all offerings to the Deity. "I desire mercy and not sacrifice," the prophet Hosea makes the Eternal say: "and the knowledge of God, more than burnt offerings."[1] In that ancient country, China,—where sacrifice is the basis of the whole cultus and is offered everywhere, where the very professors never open their courses without offering fruits and lentils to the deceased philosophers—Confucius wrote, twenty-three centuries ago, "The perfume comes not from the grain [of the sacrifice]. It is purity and virtue that make it."[2] In India, where the priestly schools teach that sacrifice makes man the equal, if not the superior, of the Gods, the sacred poem of the Mahabharata includes such maxims as this: "The oblation to Agni, the life in the forest, emaciation of the body, all these may be but in vain unless the mind be unspotted."[3]

It is not surprising, then, that the sacrifice of propitiation has all but disappeared from the universalist religions. Judaism, in its synagogues, realizing the ecclesiastical ideal of the ancient prophets, has dispensed

---

[1] Hosea vi. 6. Cf. Isaiah i. 10—17, and Matthew v. 23, 24.

[2] Girard de Rialle, *Mythologie comparée*, p. 214.

[3] *Mahabharata*, iii. (*Vana-parva*), 13416.

with it, at least in theory, ever since the destruction of the Temple. Buddhism, Christianity and Islam have officially rejected it. But popular usages have hitherto been too strong for the reforming spirit. The infiltration of Hindu superstition has opened Buddhism to oblations in honour of the Master who preached the uselessness of sacrifices. Islam has been forced to tolerate the continuance of bloody funeral sacrifices. Thus about forty years ago, at the funeral of Mehemet Ali, Viceroy of Egypt, eighty buffaloes were slain at the tomb.[1] It is to be noted that the Mussulmans interpret these sacrifices as expiatory, and believe that they blot out the venial sins of the dead; and it is in this same special acceptation that sacrifice has been maintained, or if you will re-introduced, into Christianity; for we find the Roman Church encouraging the custom of giving alms, creating pious foundations, and celebrating masses, as a set-off against sins. On the other hand, we note how the longing for purification, so widely spread in the last days of Paganism, the belief that sacrifice alone could blot out transgressions, and the conviction that the efficacity of the sacrifice must be proportional to the importance of the victim, in combination with the character impressed on the Messianic hopes by the post-exilian prophets, begot the belief that nothing short of the voluntary sacrifice of a God could affect the salvation of fallen humanity. Thus was formed the Christian dogma of the vicarious expiation on the Cross. And

---

[1] Ignace Goldziher, *Revue de l'histoire des religions*, vol. x. p. 351. The same thing took place more recently at the funeral of Ismail Pasha. See the *Journal des debats* for Jan. 20th, 1892.

when the celebration of the Lord's Supper—a symbol instituted by Jesus in reminiscence of the Jewish Passover—received a mystic interpretation, which may perhaps be traced back to the rites of the Greek Mysteries, the ancient institution of sacrifice was re-incorporated in the Catholic worship under the form of a sacrament.[1]

We know how the Reformation proscribed offerings for the redemption of sins together with the trade in indulgences; and how, in due course, liberal Protestantism has rejected the dogma of expiation through the blood of Christ, and retained the Lord's Supper only as a commemorative celebration. An analogous movement has arisen in progressive Judaism and in reformed Brahmanism, where repentance is declared to be the only means of redeeming trespasses, and good works in the largest sense the only way of pleasing the deity.[2] If amongst such communities incense still smokes here and there on the altar, or flowers decorate the temple on certain anniversaries, it is no longer in the vain hope of gratifying the senses of the Deity, but to find vent for that æsthetic feeling which is never more in place than when associated with the most exalted and inspiring emotions of the human heart. Within as without the religious communions, if sacrifice has disappeared, the spirit of sacrifice, henceforth anchored in human nature, has become identified with obedience to duty and devotion to every just cause. Abnegation has ceased to be asceticism, and has become emancipation from the tyranny

[1] Edwin Hatch, *Hibbert Lectures, 1888*, pp. 300 sq.

[2] Compare Goblet d'Alviella, *Contemporary Evolution of Religious Thought in England, America and India*, London, 1885, passim.

of the passions. Finally, the generosity which enlarges the resources of education and beneficence, is still a pious work, for it co-operates with that Power which makes us toil for progress in the spirit of enlightenment and love.

The evolution of symbolism. Subjective symbols, that is to say acts or objects which serve to embody our inward sentiments, still find daily application in our religious as in our social life. Those only have disappeared which were inconsistent with the dignity of man or with a serious view of life; and therefore those which now survive bid fair to endure as long as religion seeks to find external, and, above all, collective expression. Indeed, man avails himself of them, not only to make his inmost feelings palpable as it were to the Deity, but also to realize them to himself, and above all to communicate them to his fellows.

And so too with those figurative symbols which aim at representing a divinity or his attributes. A process of slowly developed selection has more and more thrown into the background such images as wound morality, humanity, or even good taste. And as for those which are open to no such objection, their maintenance depends less upon the nature of the symbols than upon the permanence of the sentiments to which they give expression. The divine omniscience may be represented by an eye surrounded by a glory, and Providence by a hand issuing from a cloud, as long as men continue to attribute to the Deity the knowledge and providential guidance of the affairs of this world. And even a theriomorphic symbol, like that of the serpent biting its own tail, need not be banished as long as we feel any need of giving a sensible form to our conception of the Infinite and of Eternity. So too with the symbols, or rather the idiograms drawn from the Scriptures, that serve to represent the name of the Deity, such as the sacred Tetragram of the Hebrews, the Alpha and Omega of Primitive Christianity, the AUM of the Hindus. And all this applies still more to the emblems which have come to typify the various forms of worship, such as the Cross of the Christians, the Crescent of Islam, the Wheel of the Buddhist, to say nothing of that combination of the Cross and the Crescent with the AUM of the Brahmans and the trident of the Çivaites, which some Indian Brahmoists have inscribed on the frontage of their temples to signify their syncretistic attitude towards the chief cults of their country.[1]

Imitative symbols. Imitative symbols have perhaps filled a more important place than any others, for while transforming worship into a veritable dramatic representation of the life of the Deity, they also satisfy that longing for union with the Deity by assimilation (ὁμοίωσις τῷ θεῷ) which is an essential factor in worship. I have given examples of these practices, which originally implied a naturalistic conception of the universe, surviving in the popular traditions and even in the religious rites of our own times. The scope of imitative symbols was still further enlarged when anthropomorphism reached the point of ascribing not only the sentiments, but the features of man to the deities. These

[1] Cf. P. C. Mozoomdar, *The Life and Teachings of Keshub Chunder Sen*, Calcutta, 1887, p. 501.

imitative symbols then developed into a mythology in action, a true scenic presentation, especially where art had risen high enough to be capable of combining æsthetic enjoyment with the satisfaction of religious sentiment. On the other hand, when the anthropomorphic character under which the gods were represented began to raise a blush, their adventures came to be regarded more and more as having an allegorical significance. Here again, however, the imitative symbolism was modified in two parallel directions, the one esoteric or mystic, and the other exoteric or popular.

The first of these movements gave rise to the mysteries of Greece, in which the neophytes were put into communication with the superhuman powers by means of ancient rites more or less discordant with the progress of thought and conscience, but exalted, and, so to speak, transfigured, by being made the vehicles of some lofty form of metaphysical or moral teaching.

The second movement secularized the legends of the gods more and more, until it culminated in the profane theatre. This took place not only in Greece, but in Persia, India, and even Polynesia, where the corporation of the *Areoi* put the mystic adventures of the gods upon the stage.[1] You know how our own theatre rose out of religious representations which bore the name of Mysteries in the Middle Ages, and which are still celebrated in certain parts of Germany, notably at Ober-Ammergau.

Finally, the imitative symbols, or rather the longing for communion by means of imitation which lies at

[1] Réville, *Religions des peuples non-civilisés*, vol. ii. p. 85.

the bottom of all forms of worship, shows a tendency to change its character under pressure of moral ideas, and to turn to another object than the material reproduction of divine acts.

We have seen that even such backward peoples as the Hottentots perform dances in honour of the moon, in which they imitate her movements. When the earth trembles, the Caribees begin dancing because, as they say, when our mother dances, surely we ought to dance too. Many peoples perform ceremonies at the Winter solstice, in which they symbolize the death and resurrection of the sun; others, again, such as the Tartars and the Andaman islanders, abstain from work between sunset and sunrise. In former times, there were places in Germany, Denmark, and Belgium, where no one might drive a carriage for twelve days after the winter solstice. The sun rests, as M. Gaidoz puts it; so his symbol, the wheel, must rest too. In some localities, as Schwartz and Kuhn tell us, the prohibition extended to other kinds of work, such as spinning or carrying dung to the fields. It was like a Sabbath of twelve days.[1]

Nowhere, perhaps, has the sentiment which leads men to imitate the celestial bodies been more naïvely expressed than in the prayer of an old Samoyed to the sun, mentioned by Castrén: "Oh Jilibeambaertje, I get up when you get up; I go to bed when you go to bed."[2] But it is the same thought, at a further stage of abstraction and generalization, which re-appears in the Chinese theory

[1] H. Gaidoz, *Le dieu gaulois du soleil et le symbolisme de la roue*, Paris, 1886, p. 32.

[2] *Vorlesungen über die Finnische Mythologie*, St. Petersburg, 1853, p. 16.

that man ought to conduct himself methodically, according to fixed rules, in order to imitate the ways whereby heaven determines the movement of the stars and the phenomena of the earth. "I believe," says Cicero in his turn, "that the gods have put immortal souls into human bodies that beings may exist .... who shall contemplate the order of the heavenly things, and imitate it in the regulated constancy of their lives."[1] Truly it is a far cry from the astronomical dances of the Hottentots to the sublime precept of Leviticus: "Be ye holy, for I the Eternal, your God, am holy;" or to the profound saying of Plato: "God is supremely just, and nothing resembles him more than whosoever of us becomes just to the uttermost degree."[2] But I am not debasing Greek philosophy or Israelitish faith, if I show that in this matter both alike are attached, by an uninterrupted chain of intellectual and religious links, to the first naïve stammerings of the human conscience as it seeks communion with its ideal.

Symbolism as an ally of religious progress and free inquiry. It sometimes happens that symbols pass into fetishes or into formulæ of conjuration. This is when the analogies which they express are taken for real relations. Thus ablution, which began by being a ceremony of cleanliness and decency, a suitable prelude to entering into relations with the great, or with the gods, subsequently became an easily comprehensible symbol of purification, and often ended by drawing to itself a supernatural virtue. And in like manner certain forms of sacrifice—easily explained on the notion that the gods feed upon the

[1] *De Senectute*, cap. xxi. § 77.   [2] *Theætetus*, § 85.

offerings—became pure symbols when these gods were supposed to be satisfied with the mere intention, and finally passed into veritable sacraments, with power to regenerate the faithful and even to assure them immortality. An example is furnished by the sacrifice of the bull in the mysteries of Mithra. But more often the opposite phenomenon is witnessed; that is to say, objects once regarded as the actual body of the Deity, or acts regarded as expressing a real relation with the gods, gradually acquire a purely symbolic character. Thus, fire, which was regarded as a divine being by the ancient Persians, and, for that matter, by all the Indo-Europeans, is now in the eyes of modern Parsees no more than a symbol of the supreme being, Ahura Mazda. The Chaldeans long deified the planets themselves; but afterwards they simply regarded them as symbols of the great gods, and indeed a star became the generic sign of divinity in the cuneiform writing. It is probable that, with the Greeks as with the Egyptians, many of the gods were at first represented under the forms of certain animals. The Egyptians were content with modifying their physiognomy by adding traits borrowed from man; but the Greeks completely anthropomorphized their ancient animal deities, while retaining the animal which originally represented them in the several religious centres, as the companion or the symbol of the god.

This aptitude of symbols for modifying their meaning without changing their shape, combined with the affection always felt for traditional forms, is one of the chief causes of their longevity athwart all religious revolutions. It would not be hard to establish a direct line of filiation between emblems still current in Eastern and Western religions and the most ancient motives of Assyrian iconography; for example, the aureole as a symbol of celestial glory. The thunderbolt of the Greeks, which is also employed to this very day in the ritual all over the Buddhistic East, under the well-known form of the *dordj*, may be traced in both forms alike to the double trident which appears in the hands of the storm-god in the sculptures of the Mesopotamian palaces. The Phœnix, before representing the resurrection on Christian sarcophagi, was a symbol of apotheosis on the imperial medals of pagan Rome; and in yet more ancient times, it had served the Egyptians as an emblem of the annual re-birth of the sun.

The spectacle is not unfamiliar of religions borrowing almost all their symbolic images from the forms of worship which they profess to combat or replace. When the Persians had established themselves in Mesopotamia, they adapted the Chaldean iconography to the figurative representation of their own beliefs, and it was from pagan art that the Christianity of the Catacombs drew the greater part of its allegorical subjects. In Buddhism, the rites successively engrafted upon the doctrine of the Buddha borrowed their material from the previous forms of worship in India, particularly those of the sun, though of course a new signification was given to them.[1]

We may note, in this connection, that symbolism—that is to say, the power of attaching a new meaning to any given image—on the one hand aids the transition from

[1] Cf. Goblet D'Alviella, *La Migration des symboles*, Paris, 1891, pp. 332 sqq.

the traditional conception to a higher one, and on the other hand facilitates the co-existence, under a common form of worship, of the widest diversity of beliefs. This advantage of symbolism is especially perceptible in such religions as Brahmanism, Buddhism, and even Judaism, and a certain number of Christian communities which have no central authority to define their dogmas and interpret their liturgies. In such cases, respect for external forms may actually aid the emancipation of men's minds; as M. Anatole Leroy-Beaulieu has shown in the instance of the Old Believers, in his striking study of religion in the empire of the Czars.[1] Indeed, when unity simply consists in respecting an external form, there is nothing to prevent one section of the faithful preserving the full sacramental value of a rite, whilst others accept it in a purely symbolic sense, and attribute any meaning that suits them to the symbol. Symbolism is the natural ally alike of mysticism and of free inquiry— that is to say, of the two great foes which the orthodox spirit has always had to fear within the Churches themselves.

The evolution of the priesthood. We have seen that when the distinction between the priest and the sorcerer had been established, the latter, in his capacity of exorcist, still exercised his functions, first at the side of the priest, and then below him, since the latter had the monopoly of the relations with the higher deities. Finally, the priest expelled the sorcerer from the official cultus altogether, while himself assuming one of his rival's chief functions, namely, exorcism.

[1] *L'Empire des Tzars*, vol. iii. p. 336.

It is easy to understand that in primitive societies, where the family is the property of its head, the latter prays and sacrifices to assure the prosperity of his belongings. Such, at least, is the religious condition in which we first find the patriarchal communities of the Indo-Europeans, the Hebrews, and the Chinese. The same system prevails to this day amongst the Malagassy, the Khonds, the Ostyaks, and even the Samoans. By a natural extension of this principle, it is the chief of the tribe, and subsequently of the nation, who acts for the community in approaching the gods, whether he invokes his own special deities, as with certain Negroes, or addresses the general gods of his people, as in Polynesia. This is the origin of the sacrificing kings, regarded as religious as well as civil and military chiefs, whom we find amongst the ancient Chinese, Chaldeans, Egyptians, Assyrians, Persians, and on a smaller scale among the Mangaïans, the New Zealanders, the Chinuks, and others. It was probably the same with the Greeks down to Homeric times; and we know that when the Romans abolished royalty, they still maintained a special functionary, bearing the name of *rex sacrorum*, with a view to the celebration of certain sacrifices.

Such an organization may result in a complete theocracy, if the religious interest secures the first place. This seems to have happened in ancient Peru, and to a certain extent in Assyria and Egypt; but the multiplication of the duties of government on the one hand, and the growing complexity of rites on the other, often induced the chief to delegate his sacerdotal functions. This delegation was at first temporary, as when Numa appointed the flamens as his substitutes during his absence. Amongst the Blantyres of Western Africa, "if the chief is from home, his wife will act; and if both are absent, his younger brother."[1]

This temporary delegation tends to become permanent, in virtue of the prestige which surrounds its recipients. The chiefs relieve themselves altogether of their religious functions, in favour of chaplains retained about their persons, or priests set over the chief sanctuaries. Thus the sacerdotal office, like that of the sorcerer, tends to become a special profession. Among the Hindus, the Brahmanic families seem to have been constituted, in the first instance, under petty local rajahs, who entrusted them with the conduct of divine service.[2] Amongst the Israelites, every head of a family was originally a *cohen*; but influential men gradually took private chaplains into their service to preside over their domestic sanctuaries, as we learn from the history of Micah (Judges xvii.).

Establishment and overthrow of theocracies. At first, these priests were no more than delegates or functionaries, as we see clearly enough in China, where the functions of public worship are assigned to the various administrative officers of the empire; and in classical antiquity, where the principal priests were sometimes directly elected by the people, just like other magistrates. Meanwhile, as the sacerdotal class grew in power and importance, it tended to close itself as an independent order, either by drawing in recruits from outside, as in the case of the Druidical colleges, or by making itself hereditary, like

---

[1] See H. Spencer, *Ecclesiastical Institutions*, p. 729.
[2] Cf. *Manu*, xii. 46.

the Brahmans and Levites. In Russia, we have seen the actual establishment of a sacerdotal tribe in the heart of Christianity within modern times. I refer to the white clergy, or parish priesthood, on whom marriage is obligatory, whom the force of circumstances has erected into a genuine hereditary caste, supplying the whole *personnel* of the Russian Church, from father to son.[1]

Naturally enough, when once the clergy have become independent, they tend to become supreme in the State. With this view, they centralize themselves and group themselves in a hierarchy, at the head of which stands the high-priest; as at Jerusalem after the restoration of the Temple, or at Thebes under the degenerate descendants of Rameses. And, again, the members of the priesthood propagate the belief that the faithful require their mediation in addressing the gods, that they alone are commissioned to distribute the divine favours, with authority to bind and to loose in the name of the Supreme Power, and therefore that they form a class of beings superior to the rest of humanity, and clothed with a portion of the divine authority. Finally, the whole direction of private and public affairs passes into their hands, and so a second form of theocracy is developed. Under this regime, God is supposed to govern through the agency of his ministers, whether the latter assume direct power, as in ancient Ethiopia, and quite recently in the States of the Church, or exercise it through the medium of lay delegates, as in the Japan of the Mikado, the Thibet of the Grand Lama, or the Paraguay of the Jesuits. And note that the clergy may exercise this universal rule

[1] Leroy Beaulieu, *L'Empire des Tzars*, vol. iii. pp. 260 sqq.

without even organizing themselves in a rigorous hierarchy; witness the Brahmans, who have no ecclesiastical centralization, but none the less have exercised, on the bare prestige of their hereditary functions, an authority without example in the ecclesiastical history of the world.

When once the theocracy has succeeded in acquiring the civil power, it only remains for it to take in hand the education of the successive generations, and it would then seem to be raised above all risk of overthrow save by a shock from outside. And yet it is evident that such a regime cannot be prolonged indefinitely. There will always be independent spirits who challenge some dogma, or at any rate canvass some point of discipline; and they will wake a more or less emphatic response in the nation, in proportion to the correspondence of their views with the intellectual and moral wants of the time. Little by little, this opposition to the pretensions of the spiritual authority on the field of dogma will grow into a vindication of the right of free inquiry, and this vindication in its turn will end—perhaps after long and bloody struggles—in bringing about the rupture of the union of Church and State.

Doubtless dogmatic intolerance survives civil intolerance. But one consequence of the separation of Church and State will be, that the faithful will tend to group themselves in ever more numerous and ever less stable ecclesiastical associations. And this again will lead, on the one hand, to a stronger affirmation of the rights of free inquiry, and, on the other hand, to a still further reduction of the authority of the priest. In principle he is now no more than a chosen officer of the community;

he loses his supernatural authority, and henceforth he confines himself to the functions of the religious and moral educator.

The pastorate under the conditions of modern society. Thus restricted, there is no reason why the pastoral office should not continue to exist indefinitely. As long as religious societies remain, they will need presidents, secretaries, lecturers, and administrators of every kind. Nay, it seems likely that the functions of the minister will increase in real importance, in proportion as he concentrates himself on his mission of moral educator, and as that mission assumes a more and more important place amongst the practical objects of religious association. We must note, however, that the minister has more in common with the prophet than with the priest; and the prophet may be genealogically traced to the diviner or seer, who in his turn descends from the primitive sorcerer. Thus the sorcerer avenges himself, in his descendant, upon the priest who once expelled him; but the really important point in this reversal of the tables is, that it heralds the triumph of private inspiration fructified by the moral sentiment, over the theory of sacerdotal mediation between the faithful and the Deity.

To sum up. The whole development of worship—that is to say, of acts of propitiation—may be characterized as follows:—at first, the deities demand the worship of the faithful with a selfish object, and the faithful render it with a similar purpose; gradually, duties towards our neighbours introduce themselves amongst the obligations of religion, side by side with duties towards the gods;

VI. THE FUTURE OF WORSHIP.

and finally, these two orders of ideas melt into one another, under the influence of the conception that "the service of humanity" is the best, if not the only, way of serving the Deity.

Is worship destined to disappear? Does it follow that all worship, as a special utterance of the relations of man to God, is destined to disappear? There are not wanting, even amongst Theists, generous spirits who allow a natural reaction against the abuses of religious formalism to hurry them into the belief in the inevitable, if not speedy, extinction of all religious practices. The founders of the Ethical movement have already made a practical attempt to establish their bond of communion solely on the identity of their humanitarian and progressive aspirations. One of the most authoritative exponents of this system in England, Dr. Stanton Coit, writes as follows: " We believe that by declaring devotion to the good of the world to be the bond, and the whole bond, of religious union, we shall ultimately induce men to remove all other qualifications for membership in the Churches; and that, immediately, men who are now outside of all religious fellowship, or who chafe under the dogmatic restraint of the Church, will form themselves into societies for the spread of goodness."[1] And he adds these enthusiastic words: " This idea of forming societies in devotion to good character and right conduct, we believe stands equal in dignity and power with Christ's conception of a Kingdom of God on earth, and that it comes to-day with all the freshness and vigour of a new social revelation, for

[1] *The Ethical Movement defined*, in *Religious Systems of the World*, pp. 538, 539.

which, however, the ages of Christian development have been preparing men's hearts and intellects."

Surely such associations can render signal service to the ideas of practical toleration and devotion to man. But considerable as their action on our feelings and our manners may become, I cannot believe that they will succeed in satisfying all the wants of which worship is the organ. It is not only—as has been maintained in a fit of aristocratic and masculine arrogance—women, children and the lower classes, who will feel the need of being elevated by religion beyond the narrow limits of a frivolous or material existence, nor is it only minds too much busied with the affairs of daily life to be able to attain to any higher culture, that experience this same demand. Without an appeal to the resources of poetry, music, painting, and of all the combinations of art which unite in worship to symbolize the æsthetic aspects of the ideal, even the most cultured of men must be sensible of a void, and must feel himself paralyzed in his attempt to express his aspirations towards the infinite and the absolute.

I doubt whether religious progress will take the form of a collective entry into newly created religious associations with a theology in harmony with the requirements of science, and a cultus reduced to its purely rational manifestations. When we think of the attraction of the old forms, we are more inclined to believe that religious progress will be achieved by the gradual emancipation of thought within the bosom of existing communions, or at least in such of them as lend themselves to a gradual modification of their beliefs.

VI. THE FUTURE OF WORSHIP.

There exist in most of the Churches three classes: those who accept the dogmas and the ceremonies in the spirit in which they have been handed down to them; those who accept them through force of habit, through a feeling of respect, through a vague desire to call down the Divine sanction on the most solemn acts of life, or simply through an idea of setting a good example to others; and, finally, those who have seen into the real meaning of religious questions, and who are pursued, even in ecclesiastical matters, by the longing for improvement. This last class has long been liberalizing religion, though it has too often been weeded out as fast as it grew, by trials for heresy, by the choking atmosphere of intolerance, or simply by the compulsory subscription to dogmatic articles. In many communions, liberty of thought now enjoys a tacit toleration; only let it become a formally recognized right, and there will be nothing to prevent the union of respect for ancient forms with the development of new ideas. Nay, more: the respect felt for these ancient symbols will be all the more sincere and unanimous when they have ceased to fetter free inquiry and have become historical monuments, venerable by their very antiquity, and worthy of all preservation for the sake of the link which they have established between the aspirations of the present, and the beliefs, the sentiments, the enthusiasms, perhaps the dangers and the sufferings, of the generations that are past. Here symbolism culminates in syncretism.

The future of the churches. Why should we not look forward to a state of things in which the principal religions of the actual world—Christianity, Buddhism, Brahmanism,

Judaism, Confucianism, and Islam—shall regard each other simply as different forms of worship in the bosom of a single Church, and shall apply to their religious differences the fine expression of a Russian bishop: "Our confessional partitions do not mount as high as heaven"?[1] Doubtless such an ideal of religious peace and union still seems far distant; but amongst enlightened minds of varied communions we trace the growing thought that all religions are good if they help us to live worthily, and even that they are all true in so far as they help us to realize the presence of a higher Power working, in accordance with law, for the good of the universe. The belief in the continuity of religious progress implies that no Church possesses the absolute truth, and that all have the right to seek it by the light of conscience and of reason. Graft this idea upon the conviction of our incapacity to represent the supreme Reality otherwise than by symbols, and you will be driven to the conclusion that all rites have a purely relative value, the only measure of which is the service they render to the progress of human culture.

In this connection, a remarkable sign of the times has recently appeared in London. I refer to the lectures organized by the South Place Ethical Society, in which men belonging to the most divergent sects were invited successively to expound the chief points of their respective religions. I am aware that their language must have been influenced by the surrounding medium; but making all allowances for that, is it not curious and suggestive that all of them—Jews, Parsees, and Positivists,

---

[1] Leroy Beaulieu, *L'Empire des Tzars*, vol. iii. p. 583.

as well as Baptists, Methodists, Independents, Anglicans, and Unitarians—agreed in proclaiming the existence of a great Church above all denominations, a communion of all who do their duty and work for the advancement of the human race. " The life and work of Baptists," said the Rev. John Clifford, President of the Baptist Union, " is a valuable part of British Christianity, only so far as it has become one of the successive steps in which the human spirit has been forced onward by the immanent logic of the religious life in its organic development. Service to humanity, in its higher ranges of life and work, is the supreme test of the worth of Churches."[1]

I am convinced that this point of view will gain more and more adherents, especially in the bosom of the Protestant Churches.[2] As for the sects that are determined

[1] *Religious Systems of the World*, p. 428.

[2] As these sheets are passing through the press, I have received a circular from a Committee formed to organize a Central Congress of Religions at Chicago in 1893 during the Exhibition, side by side with the sectarian gatherings which are sure to be arranged. " Now that the nations are being brought into closer and friendlier relations," it runs, " the time is apparently ripe for new manifestations and developments of religious fraternity. . . . . Convinced that of a truth God is no respecter of persons, but that in every nation he that feareth Him and worketh righteousness is accepted of Him, we affectionately invite the representatives of all faiths to aid us in presenting to the world, at the Exhibition of 1893, *the religious harmonies and unities of humanity*, and also in showing forth the moral and spiritual agencies which are at the root of human progress." The remarkable thing about this circular is, that it is signed by sixteen ministers representing all the confessions of the United States, from a Catholic Archbishop (Mgr. P. A. Feehan) and an Episcopalian Bishop (the Rt. Rev. W. E. McLaren) to a Unitarian of the advanced Western School (the Rev. Jenkin Lloyd Jones) and a Jewish Rabbi (the Rev. E. S. Hirsch),—the President being a Presbyterian (the Rev. J. H. Barrows).

to cling to the letter of their traditional formulæ, they will see their ranks thinned more and more by the defection of all who wish to advance with the age. And will these latter, in their turn, end by uniting on the basis of their larger conception of the Deity and his action on the universe, or will they simply go to swell the ranks of the indifferent, who have lost all interest in religious questions, and in many cases failed to replace them by any other interests of an exalted or wide-reaching type? This question is all the more worth investigation, because it presents itself once more in connection with the masses of the people, who are every day more completely estranged from the religious movement in the great cities and the industrial centres of Europe. This is a factor which we cannot neglect when investigating the prospects of religion itself—not merely this or that form of worship—in the society of the near future.

Religion and the people. Our working classes are not indifferent to religion. They are positively hostile to it. For they reproach it with having done nothing to better their condition, with having entered into an alliance with the rich and strong, and finally with having drawn off to the problematic solutions of a future life the attention which ought to be directed to the reform of the life that now is. This hostility has been specially accentuated since Socialism rose to offer the masses a new ideal in which material amelioration of their lot is combined with the satisfaction of the sentiments of harmony and justice. Verily, the Churches have enough to do to clear themselves of the reproach thus levelled against them. The boast that Religion is the synonym of Socialism, if Socialism means replacing the interest of the individual by the interest of society as the goal of all our action, stands in dire need of such illustration as it may receive from the part which all Christian communities are now rousing themselves to take in social movements.

And, on the other side, I do not hesitate to add that Socialism will become religious or will cease to be. I mean, that to achieve enduring results it will have to borrow from Religion its best elements of altruism and abnegation, together with the idea of a superhuman Power making for the material and moral progress of humanity.

Pure science can but establish the presence of a force tending to develop life upon the earth. It is dumb when we ask if this progressive life is destined to culminate in an increase of the welfare of individuals. Nay, its great law of the struggle for existence seems rather to discourage the hope of general well-being and universal harmony which is the key-stone of the Socialist ideal.

Doubtless one may conceive a society of the higher peoples in the bosom of the human race withdrawing themselves from the general conflict, or rather uniting to wage that conflict with the rest of nature, and—by means of a wise direction of social forces, combined with the systematic limitation of the number of births— banishing from their midst the scourges of war and penury. But, in the first place, to realize this Utopia, which is not without its grandeur, what lever have the State-Socialists to reckon on? Surely not the harmony of individual interests, for they proclaim the impotence of individualism and call on us to renounce it. Is it the sense of duty? But, to say nothing of their depriving that sentiment of its religious basis, they have generally adopted materialistic explanations of the universe, which logically tend to undermine the foundations of moral obligation and therefore the very conception of duty, by destroying the idea of human liberty and responsibility.

The need of a more comprehensive motive than individual interest. I do not deny that it is reason which reveals, and which alone can reveal, the different kinds of duty resulting from men's necessary relations with each other; but even should science succeed in showing that the true good of the individual invariably coincides with the requirements of the general good, it will still have to find the means of enforcing respect for this principle upon those who continue to think otherwise, or who deliberately prefer immediate satisfaction, or who are seduced by the overmastering force of human passions.

The need of appealing to some stronger control than that of mere instincts or longings is so evident, that the founder of the Positivist school had recourse to the love of humanity to suppress the revolt of individual interest; but this amounts to an indirect return to the religious idea, which in Comte's system takes Humanity instead of Deity for its object. And, as Mr. Herbert Spencer has well remarked, "to suppose that this relatively evanescent form of existence ought to occupy our minds so exclusively as to leave no space for a consciousness of that Ultimate Existence of which it is but one form out of multitudes—an Ultimate Existence which was manifested in infinitely varied ways before humanity arose, and will be manifested in infinitely varied other ways when humanity has ceased to be, seems very strange—to me, indeed, amazing."[1]

The love of humanity can doubtless inspire noble and fruitful devotion; but does it not lose its rational basis when it rests solely upon certain specific resemblances of human beings one to another? And does it not wantonly fling away its most powerful means of action, when it assigns the reign of justice and of general happiness as the goal of human effort, but at the same time refuses to enwrap this noble purpose in the larger desire to co-operate with the Power that rules the universe? Thus Comtism has succeeded in gathering a few select groups, and earning the sympathy of all generous minds; but its religious influence, in the sense which it attaches to the term, does not exist as far as the masses are concerned.

Growth of pessimism. Again, it is a mere illusion to suppose that the general spread of a certain degree of comfort, or even the suppression of all social inequalities would be enough to satisfy the legitimate aspirations of humanity. However fully you secure to man the necessaries and even the enjoyments of life, his cup will always be embittered, if only by the disease that lies in wait for him at every turn, by the death that prematurely snatches from him those he loves, by the old age which throws an ever-darkening shadow over his path, not to speak of the eternal longing which

---

[1] In the controversy with Mr. F. Harrison, re-published as *The Nature and Reality of Religion*, New York, 1885, p. 95; cf. *Study of Sociology*, p. 312.

ever develops his wants in advance of his means of satisfying them, and constitutes at once the grandeur and the misery of human nature. And suppose we treated this infinite susceptibility to further desires as a disease, and succeeded in killing the germs of it in our hearts,—would not this contracting of our personality result in diminished powers of reaction against the fatalities of nature, in loss of the chief joys of life, and ultimately in a full career of pessimistic reaction?

If pessimism dominates Eastern society, it is not because the lot of man is intolerable there—for it is only in comparison with our own that it appears to be so; it is because centuries of political despotism and moral relaxation have robbed the Orientals of elasticity of will. If the same disease has begun to attack our Western society in the full swing of wealth and knowledge, it is in large measure because the significance of the individual has been disputed and belittled by the prevalence of a philosophy that denies to man the very possibility of aiming at freedom.

What are we to expect, then, if this purely mechanical conception of the universe should serve as a type for the whole organization of social life after the communist or collectivist ideals? In that case, pessimism will no longer confine its attacks to the delicate and super-refined spirits whom want of any higher interest has disgusted with life; but it will invade the masses. The spirit of competition and personal initiative, that scapegoat on whose head all our social and economic sins are laid, will be found to have carried with it into the desert all the stimulating motives which give variety and worth to existence.

And remember that we are not speaking of an exalted and generous pessimism like that of the Stoics, which could at least take refuge in the impenetrable fortress of the human soul, nor yet of a tender and expansive pessimism like that of the Buddha, which after leading through enlightenment to renunciation leads back through love to action, but of a selfish and apathetic pessimism, on which no light of hope will break and which no rays of self-abnegation will warm. And this will continue until some Boddhisattva shall come again to teach men that nought save all-embracing love can enable us to escape the fetters of personality, and that the true path of self-annihilation is the path of self-devotion; or perhaps until a Jesus shall come, once more to reveal to suffering humanity the forgotten truth that there is a Father in heaven who cares for the moral amelioration of the world, and that the best way of serving Him is the way of brotherly love. Then will the new dawn be followed by a new day.

Danger of a reaction. Turning our attention to another quarter, we may ask whether we are so sure of the future as to be free of all apprehension of a return of supernaturalism, perhaps under the forms most opposed to the present drift of men's minds. It is impossible to deny that a mystic reaction has already set in throughout the West. Who knows where it will stop, should it find sustenance in a desperate rally of conservative interests, or in the decisive bankruptcy of revolutionary theories? It is easy to foresee that the classes in possession, taken as a whole, will always prefer superstition to spoliation; and as for the masses, who reckon on their full access to power for removing all inequalities from the earth, is there not room to fear that on the inevitable day which brings home to them the impotence of the State to realize their ideals, they will fling themselves into the arms of the first religion that can offer them the mirage of some new millennium? Such a movement might well become irresistible should it happen to coincide with one of those periods of stagnation or even of retarded progress which occur from time to time in the development or co-ordination of scientific discovery.

Yet more. There is solidarity between all the branches of freedom. Every attempt to enslave man on the economic field must sooner or later re-act upon the realms of thought. In this connection we cannot too gravely consider the warning addressed to the evolutionary spirit by the great formulator of evolutionism himself, when, in spite of his optimistic tendencies, he thus concludes his synthesis of the religious development: "If, instead of further progress under that system of voluntary co-operation which constitutes industrialism properly so called, there should be carried far the system of production and distribution under State-control, constituting a new form of compulsory co-operation, and ending in a new type of coercive government, the changes above indicated, determined as they are by individuality of character, will probably be arrested and opposite changes initiated."[1]

Brighter prospects for the future of religion. Doubtless you will think I have painted a dark picture; but when one tries to fathom the future, one must take account of the

[1] Herbert Spencer, *Ecclesiastical Institutions*, § 654 (p. 824).

extremest possibilities; and, even in the face of all that can be urged, those who believe with me that the freedom of man is destined to pass unscathed through the present crisis, will still have a right to expect that the religious evolution will, after all, pursue its way on the great lines that I have sketched in these Lectures, gradually purifying the main factors of religion, and making for the establishment of a universal cultus at once rational and fruitful.

It has been asked whether the "eternal and infinite Energy" of evolutionism can succeed any better than the inaccessible God of Neo-platonism or the impersonal Brahma of the Vedantic schools, in inspiring man with emotions and aspirations that can crystallize round the religious sentiment and express themselves in worship.[1] Note that this *Energy*—so called for want of a better name, and not to be confounded with *Force*, as revealed to us in our own conception of physical effort[2]—presents itself to our minds, not only as the supreme Reality but also as a Power superior to all known forces, and at the same time essentially mysterious in its being. Now the idea of power, combined with that of mystery, is the essential basis and invariable characteristic of the Object of the religious sentiment. But I have also shown that another factor must enter into worship, namely, the possibility of coming into relations with this mysterious

[1] Compare the trenchant but often unfair criticism which Mr. Frederick Harrison has brought to bear upon the religion of the Unknowable in his controversy with Mr. Herbert Spencer in *The Nature and Reality of Religion: a Controversy between Frederick Harrison and Herbert Spencer*, New York, 1885, p. 49.

[2] Herbert Spencer, *First Principles*, §§ 18 and 50.

Power. Now in the face of an Energy, anonymous, deaf, blind, dumb, inexorable as the ancient Fate, man may well experience a kind of sacred horror—nay, a fascination under which his brain whirls—without such feelings in any degree influencing his conduct in the face of the unknown Power which inspires it. At the most, one could but exclaim with Littré: "Infinity, alike material and intellectual .... is revealed to us under its two-fold aspect of reality and inaccessibility. It is an ocean which beats upon our shores, for which we have neither barque nor sail, but the clear vision of which is as salutary as it is awe-inspiring."[1]

Even Mr. Spencer's remark that the supreme Reality may be endowed with modes of existence as superior to intelligence and will as the latter are to mechanical movement, cannot save the divine manifestations from sterility, as far as the actions of man are concerned, if he, man, feels incapable of representing them under any form drawn from his own concepts.

But it is no longer so when, without attempting further to define this incomprehensible Power, we assign to it the function of securing the order of the universe. The great problem on the solution of which the direction of the religious movement of the future depends, is not why the Absolute realizes itself under the limitations of time and space. This question appeals to our metaphysical curiosity alone, and its insolubility presents no obstacle to the development of the religious sentiment. What in truth affects, and even rends, our labouring thought,

[1] *Auguste Comte et la philosophie positive*, third edition, Paris, 1877, p. 505.

is the question, perfectly formulated by Mr. Graham, "whether Chance or Purpose governs the world."[1] On the answer to this question it depends whether there is such a thing as duty, and even whether life is worth living.

Conclusion. The conception of God in the future. One of our greatest natural philosophers declared, speaking, on a memorable occasion, of material atheism : "I have noticed during years of self-observation that it is not in hours of clearness and vigour that this doctrine commends itself to my mind; that in the presence of stronger and healthier thought it ever dissolves and disappears, as offering no solution of the mystery in which we dwell, and of which we form a part."[2]

Atheism, properly so called, has always been to me what you, in England, call *unthinkable;* for my mind is incapable of conceiving of the transient and the finite without an underlying Absolute, the direct source of all phenomena and their laws. In moments of philosophical depression—which I have not escaped any more than the majority of my generation—what I have asked myself has not been whether there is a God in whom we live and move and have our being; it has been whether that mysterious Power has any purpose, and specifically any beneficent purpose, in the universe. But I too have felt these doubts disappear as my thought became "stronger and healthier," and as I have contemplated the whole

---

[1] *The Creed of Science, Religious, Moral, and Social,* second edition, London, 1884, p. 49.

[2] J. Tyndall, *Address delivered before the British Association assembled at Belfast, with Additions,* London, 1874, p. viii.

moral and religious evolution of humanity, continuing and crowning the organic evolution of the universe, or at least that part of it which comes within the field of our observation. At bottom, pessimism can only establish itself in the minds of those who think that pleasure is the goal of life, or—which comes to the same—that life has no goal at all. It disappears when one thinks that the highest aim of man consists in taking a share in the work by which God himself is perfecting the universe.

This brings us back to the religious theory which we have seen to reach its fullest utterance amongst the Jews and the Persians, but which has really never been absent from any religion which identified the moral with the divine order. God *is*, but his work is *being done*. And here on earth it is done above all by humanity, which alone is conscious of it, and conscious therefore of an alliance with the divine Power in the struggle for good. Who shall deny that this community of aspiration and effort may give birth in man—even though he have no assurance of literal reciprocity—to the feelings of gratitude and affection which the Comtists even claim for their collective humanity? Who shall deny that it may give rise to that unalterable faith in the final result of the alliance between man and the Divinity which inspired the ancient prophets when, in the midst of perils and disasters, they preached, and in preaching prepared for, the great day of Yahveh, the triumph of justice and brotherhood in the world?

Such an eschatology, however, necessarily involves freedom of the imagination to expatiate in the future, in this world or another. If, as Mr. Spencer says, every evolution after culminating in a perfect equilibrium, must be followed by a corresponding dissolution; or, in other terms, if the ameliorations progressively and laboriously acquired by humanity must on some fatal day melt in a cataclysm in which humanity itself will perish together with all known beings; if, in a word, the history of the universe is, as the Eleatic and Stoic philosophers and the Brahmans have alike believed, no more than a perpetual re-beginning,—then man will ask himself whether, in truth, it is worth while to devote oneself to mere ephemeral conquests, and whether the Power that makes for righteousness is not working like a squirrel in a cage-wheel, capable of amusing an idle spectator, but incapable of rousing those feelings on which religion lives. For a man to believe in the ideal and devote himself to it, the future must be assured, either in the expectation of another world in which the injustice of the terrestrial life may be righted, or in the indefinite progress of humanity towards a perfection which, if never absolutely realized, may be indefinitely approached. Happily, astronomers and physicists agree in declaring that the destruction of our planetary system is a hypothesis based on premature assertions; that our risks of dissolution, even supposing them to be established, may always be indefinitely adjourned by forces acting in a contrary sense; and, finally, that there is nothing to exclude the future possibility of communication between the worlds.[1]

---

[1] M. Guyau, *L'irréligion de l'avenir*, pp. 441 sq.—"Perhaps some day, when full self-consciousness has been reached, it will produce a corresponding power adequate to arrest the march of dissolution at

It is true that science can neither answer our questions as to personal immortality,[1] nor demonstrate mathematically that the world advances towards a goal. At the very most, it can but raise a presumption, and conclude, with John Stuart Mill, that "there is a large balance of probability in favour of creation by intelligence."[2] To transform that probability into certainty will perhaps always need an act of faith, but at any rate it will be an act of rational faith, that is to say, of faith which cannot be contradicted by reason and which is postulated by the demands of moral obligation graven on our consciences, just as the belief in the universality of law and even in the conservation of energy are acts of faith postulated by the demands of the logical consistency graven on our minds. For us, as for the *rishis* of India, the scribes of Thebes, and the philosophers of Greece, this is the supreme conclusion by which religion completes science, and in this sense we may repeat with that great American

the point it may then have reached. Beings capable of distinguishing, in the infinite complication of cosmic movements, those which favour their evolution from those which tend to destroy it, would perhaps be capable of resisting the latter, and thus securing the definitive triumph of the more desired combinations."

[1] "At first sight it might appear that the doctrine [of evolution], as applied to the subjective world, by removing the broad distinction between the human and the animal mind, would discourage the hope of a future life for man's soul. Yet it may be found, after all, that it leaves the question very much where it was. It may perhaps be said that it favours the old disposition to attribute immortality to those lower forms of mind with which the human mind is found to be continuous."—James Sully, in his article on "Evolution," prepared, with Prof. Huxley's assistance, for the *Encyclopædia Britannica*, ninth edition, vol. viii. p. 772 *b*.

[2] *Three Essays on Religion*, London, 1834, p. 174.

thinker, rationalist and mystic in one, Ralph Waldo
Emerson, "The whole course of things goes to teach us
faith! We need only obey."[1]

Doubtless the world may still witness many philosophical revolutions and reactions. If we may read the future in the past, religions may yet follow and replace each other; forms of worship may rise as different from ours as the synagogue was from the temple, or the churches of the early Christians from the pagan sanctuaries. Attributes which many of us regard as essential to the Deity may be cancelled by the theological system which shall gain the ascendant. We or our children may have to relinquish many a cherished conception of the action of God and the destiny of man. Nay, "God" may die, as his known and unknown predecessors—the Baalim and the Teotl, Assur and Ammon, Odin and Jupiter, have died; as his contemporaries of to-day, the Brahm of Hindustan, the Allah of Islam, Ormuzd "the Lord Omniscient," Thian "the Celestial Emperor," and even Yahveh "the Holy One of Israel," shall one day die; but what cannot die is the conception, enshrined in these names, of a mysterious and superhuman Power, realizing himself in all the laws of the known universe, revealing himself to man in the voice of conscience and the spectacle of the world.

Here we have the truth implicitly contained in that three-fold illusion out of which, as we have seen, religion sprang—the erroneous extension of the idea of personality, the confusion between concomitance and

[1] *Spiritual Laws*, in his *Works*, two vols., London, 1882, vol. i. p. 59.

causality, and the failure to distinguish between dreams and reality. Here we have the truth which will remain when it has freed the conception of the Deity from all the confusions which originally covered it, and the parasitical accretions which have since laid hold of it, when it has stripped off, as so many borrowed plumes, anthropomorphic attributes and moral limitations, and has set forth the existence of deity as Unity and the action of deity as Harmony. Here, then, we stand at last before the impenetrable veil which will ever separate the Deity, in its grandeur and its majesty, from our eyes, but which does not cut off either the manifestations of its power or the revelations of its law, or, may be, even the mysterious radiation of an attractive force answering to our terms of sympathy and love.

www.ingramcontent.com/pod-product-compliance
Lightning Source LLC
Chambersburg PA
CBHW022053230426
43672CB00008B/1153